FOURTH EDITION

Reading POWER 2

Extensive Reading • Vocabulary Building • Comprehension Skills • Reading Faster

Linda Jeffries

Beatrice S. Mikulecky

PEARSON
Longman

Reading Power 2, Fourth Edition

Copyright © 2009 by Pearson Education, Inc.
All rights reserved.

Pearson Education, 10 Bank Street, White Plains, NY 10606

Staff credits: The people who made up the *Reading Power 2, Fourth Edition* team, representing editorial, production, design, and manufacturing, are Pietro Alongi, Danielle Belfiore, John Brezinsky, Dave Dickey, Oliva Fernandez, Massimo Rubini, Barbara Sabella, Jaimie Scanlon, Jennifer Stem, Paula Van Ells, and Pat Wosczyk.

Text composition: Rainbow Graphics
Text font: 12/14 Caslon
Illustrations and tech art: Bergandy Beam and Rainbow Graphics
Credits: See page 296.

Library of Congress Cataloging-in-Publication Data
Mikulecky, Beatrice S.
  Reading power 2: extensive reading, vocabulary building, comprehension skills, reading faster/ Beatrice S. Mikulecky, Linda Jeffries.—4th ed.
    p. cm.
  Summary: Its innovative design allows intermediate-level students to use four key sections concurrently to become better readers in school, college, or business.
  ISBN 978-0-13-814388-6
  1. English language—Textbooks for foreign speakers. 2. Reading comprehension—Problems, exercises, etc. 3. Thought and thinking—Problems, exercises, etc. 4. Vocabulary—Problems, exercises, etc. I. Jeffries, Linda. II. Title. III. Title: Reading power two.
  PE1128.M566 2009
  428.6′4–dc22

                                                                    2009017283

ISBN-10: 0-13-814388-9
ISBN-13: 978-0-13-814388-6

PEARSONLONGMAN ON THE **WEB**
Pearsonlongman.com offers online resources for teachers and students. Access our Companion Websites, our online catalog, and our local offices around the world.

Visit us at **pearsonlongman.com**.

Printed in the United States of America
7 8 9 10—V016—13

Contents

Acknowledgments

I would like to thank teachers around the world for their feedback regarding *Reading Power 2*. The following colleagues and reviewers have been particularly helpful: Anna Masetti, University of Modena; Esther Robbins, Prince George's Community College, Largo, MD; Kate Johnson, Union County College, Elizabeth, NJ; Lesley Morgan, West Virginia University, Morgantown, WV; Meghan Ackley, University of Texas, Austin, TX; Paula Richards, Northern Essex Community College, Haverhill, MA; Marjorie Stamberg, Hunter College, New York, NY.

I am also very much indebted to the development editor, Jaimie Scanlon, who helped me enormously with her sharp eye for detail and her clear vision of the book as a whole, as well as with her patience and sense of humor.

Thanks,
Linda

About the Authors

Linda Jeffries holds a master's degree in TESOL from Boston University. She has taught reading, writing and ESL/EFL at Boston College, Boston University, the Harvard University Summer ESL Program, the University of Opole, Poland, and the University of Bologna, Italy. She lives in Italy, near Bologna, and teaches academic reading and writing at the University of Modena.

Bea Mikulecky holds a master's degree in TESOL and a doctorate in Applied Psycholinguistics from Boston University. In addition to teaching reading, writing, and ESL, she has worked as a teacher trainer in the Harvard University Summer ESL Program, in the Simmons College MATESL Program, and in Moscow, Russia. She is the author of *A Short Course in Teaching Reading Skills*.

Introduction to *Reading Power 2*

To the Teacher

Reading Power 2 is unlike most other reading textbooks. First, the book is organized in a different way. It has four separate parts that correspond to four important aspects of proficient reading, and therefore it is like four books in one. **Teachers should assign work on all four parts of the book every week.**

The four parts of *Reading Power 2* are:

- Part 1: Extensive Reading
- Part 2: Vocabulary Building
- Part 3: Comprehension Skills
- Part 4: Reading Faster

Second, the focus of *Reading Power 2* is different. While most books focus on content, this book directs students' attention to their own reading processes. The aim is for students to develop a strategic approach to reading at this early stage, so that they learn to view reading in English as a problem–solving activity rather than a translation exercise. This will enable them to acquire good reading habits and skills and to build confidence in their abilities. In this way, they will gain access more quickly to English-language material for study, work, or pleasure.

For a successful outcome, teachers should follow the indications for work in pairs or small groups. Talking about their work will help students formulate ideas and consolidate vocabulary learning.

Reading Power 2 is intended for students who are at the advanced-beginner or low-intermediate level in English. It is assumed that students who use this book will be literate and have an English vocabulary of about 600 words.

In this fourth edition of *Reading Power 2*, the approach remains the same as in the earlier editions, though in response to recent research as well as feedback from teachers, there is more emphasis on vocabulary acquisition and learning strategies. All the units have been updated and more guidance has been added for students in learning the skills. The major changes in this edition include:

Part 1: Extensive Reading—a new nonfiction passage and more guidance in vocabulary learning

Part 2: Vocabulary Building—guidance in vocabulary learning methods including dictionary work, strategies for guessing meaning from context, work on word parts (prefixes, suffixes, and word families), sentence structure, collocation, and lexical phrases

Part 3: Comprehension Skills—a new "Focus on Vocabulary" section in each unit with a reading passage containing ten target words and exercises to teach these words

Part 4: Reading Faster—new readings and revised comprehension questions

A separate Teacher's Guide contains the answer key, a rationale for the approach taken in *Reading Power 2*, specific suggestions for using it in the classroom, and a sample syllabus.

To the Student

Reading is an important part of most language courses. Improving your reading skills can also help you improve your general skills in English.

It can help you
    . . . learn to think in English.
    . . . build your English vocabulary.
    . . . write better in English.
    . . . prepare for study in English.

Reading Power 2 can help you learn to read well in English. In this book, you will work on reading in four ways in the four parts of the book:

Part 1: Extensive Reading—reading a book that you choose and reading a lot

Part 2: Vocabulary Building—learning new words

Part 3: Comprehension Skills—learning to understand what you read

Part 4: Reading Faster—learning to read faster and understand more in English

Work on **all four parts** of the book every week. This way you can become a good reader in English.

Extensive Reading

Introduction

What does reading mean to you?

A. Complete this questionnaire about reading in your life.

Reading Questionnaire

1. What is your name? _____

2. Where are you from? _____

3. What is your first language? _____

4. Do you like reading? _____

5. Do your parents like reading? _____

6. Do your friends like reading? _____

7. What do you enjoy reading in your language? Check (✓) your answers.
   ____ books   ____ magazines   ____ webpages/articles
   ____ newspapers ____ other (_____)

8. Do you have a favorite book or writer? _____

   Book title: _____

   Writer's name: _____

9. Do you read in English? _____

   If so, what do you read in English? _____

   _____

B. Work with two other students. Talk about your answers. Do you like to read the same things?

The best readers are people who **love to read** and who **read a lot**. In Part 1, you will learn about and practice extensive reading.

What Is Extensive Reading?

- Reading **a lot**—many books in a semester
- Choosing books that *you* want to read
- Reading as fast or as slow as you want
- Not having any tests on your reading

Why Is Extensive Reading Important?

If you read a lot in English, you can become a better reader, and you can improve your English in many ways.

Extensive reading will help you

... read faster and understand better.
... learn new words.
... write better.
... learn about the world.

When you read a lot in English, you get a lot of practice with the language. You learn to recognize words more quickly and understand sentences better. You may even begin to *think* in English. But this only happens if you read *a lot*!

New Vocabulary in Your Reading

When you read stories or books, you will find new words. Sometimes you may not know the exact meaning of a word, but you can guess the general meaning. This may be enough to follow the story.

Follow these guidelines for dealing with new vocabulary in your reading:

- Don't stop to look up many new words in the dictionary. If you stop often for new words, you will read slowly and forget the story.
- Try to use the other words and sentences in the story to help you guess the general meaning of words you don't know.

In the following exercises, you will read some passages with missing words. This is like reading a passage with words you don't know.

EXERCISE 1

A. *This passage is from the beginning of a story. Some words are missing. Read the passage, but don't try to guess the missing words. Then answer the questions.*

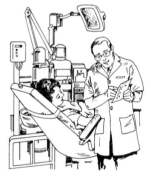

Susan Conley and Sam Diamond live in Rosebud, a small town in New Jersey. It looks like many other xxxxxx in the United States. On Main Street, there is a post office and a police xxxxxx. The drugstore and the library are down the xxxxxx. There's also a shopping center with a supermarket, a video store, and a fast xxxxxx restaurant.

Dr. Sam Diamond is a dentist. His xxxxxx is in the middle of Rosebud, near the post office. Everybody in town knows and likes Dr. Diamond. He's a good dentist and a xxxxxx person. He likes telling funny stories to his xxxxxx. They forget about their teeth when they listen to him.

Susan Conley is Sam Diamond's wife. She's a scientist with a Ph.D. in Biology. She works with a xxxxxx of scientists in a laboratory in New York City. They're xxxxxx the human brain and looking for ways to xxxxxx people with Alzheimer's and other serious brain diseases.

Susan usually takes the xxxxxx from Rosebud to New York. Sometimes she stays at home and works on her xxxxxx. She's happy when she can work at home, but she also likes working in the lab with interesting people.

    a. Where do Susan and Sam live? _____

    b. What is Sam's job? _____

    c. Why do people like Sam Diamond? _____

    d. What is Susan's job? _____

    e. Where does she work? _____

B. *Talk about your answers with another student. Are they the same?*

EXERCISE 2

A. *The story continues in this passage. Read the passage, but don't try to guess the missing words. Then answer the questions.*

Susan and Sam are different in many ways. Susan is tall and thin. Sam is short and xxxxxx. Susan has blonde hair and blue eyes. Sam has dark hair and xxxxxx eyes. Susan is a quiet person, who can xxxxxx for hours alone in the laboratory. Sam loves to talk and meet xxxxxx.

Susan and Sam's children are now grown up and live far away. Their daughter, Jane, is an airline pilot. She lives in California and xxxxxx all around the United States. Their son, Ted, is a journalist. He lives and works in Washington, D.C. He is xxxxxx to a young Brazilian painter named Maria. Jane and Ted come to visit Rosebud as often as they can.

In their xxxxxx time, Susan and Sam like to work in their xxxxxx. Susan takes care of the rose bushes and the many other flowers. Sam takes care of the vegetable garden. He's very proud of his tomatoes and his xxxxxx.

Susan and Sam also care a lot about the town of Rosebud, and they try to make it a better xxxxxx to live. Susan often goes to meetings about xxxxxx in the town. Sam helps with the town vegetable garden. People in the town can work in the garden and take xxxxxx some of the vegetables.

    a. Do Susan and Sam look alike? _____

    b. How many children do they have? _____

    c. Where do their children live? _____

    d. What do Susan and Sam like to do in their free time? _____

    e. How do they help the town of Rosebud? _____

B. *Talk about your answers with another student. Are they the same?*

A. Read the passage again. This time, try to guess the missing words. Write your guesses in the blanks.

Susan Conley and Sam Diamond live in Rosebud, a small town in New Jersey. It looks like many other _____ 1 _____ in the United States. On Main Street, there is a post office and a police _____ 2 _____. The drugstore and the library are down the _____ 3 _____. There's also a shopping center with a supermarket, a video store, and a fast _____ 4 _____ restaurant.

Dr. Sam Diamond is a dentist. His _____ 5 _____ is in the middle of Rosebud, near the post office. Everybody in town knows and likes Dr. Diamond. He's a good dentist and a _____ 6 _____ person. He likes telling funny stories to his _____ 7 _____. They forget about their teeth when they listen to him.

Susan Conley is Sam Diamond's wife. She's a scientist with a Ph.D. in Biology. She works with a _____ 8 _____ of scientists in a laboratory in New York City. They're _____ 9 _____ the human brain and looking for ways to _____ 10 _____ people with Alzheimer's and other serious brain diseases.

Susan usually takes the _____ 11 _____ from Rosebud to New York. Sometimes she stays at home and works on her _____ 12 _____. She's happy when she can work at home, but she also likes working in the lab with interesting people.

B. Talk about your answers with another student. Are they the same?

EXERCISE 4

A. ***Read the passage again. This time, try to guess the missing words. Write your guesses in the blanks.***

Susan and Sam are different in many ways. Susan is tall and thin. Sam is short and _____. Susan has blonde hair and blue eyes. Sam has dark hair and
____1____
_____ eyes. Susan is a quiet person, who can _____ for hours
____2____   ____3____
alone in the laboratory. Sam loves to talk and meet _____.
                                                    ____4____

Susan and Sam's children are now grown up and live far away. Their daughter, Jane, is an airline pilot. She lives in California and _____ all around the
                                                                ____5____
United States. Their son, Ted, is a journalist. He lives and works in Washington, D.C. He is _____ to a young Brazilian painter named Maria. Jane and
            ____6____
Ted come to visit Rosebud as often as they can.

In their _____ time, Susan and Sam like to work in their
        ____7____
_____. Susan takes care of the rose bushes and the many other flowers.
____8____
Sam takes care of the vegetable garden. He's very proud of his tomatoes and his
_____.
____9____

Susan and Sam also care a lot about the town of Rosebud, and they try to make it a better _____ to live. Susan often goes to meetings about
                ____10____
_____ in the town. Sam helps with the town vegetable garden. People in
____11____
the town can work in the garden and take _____ some of the vegetables.
                                          ____12____

B. ***Talk about your answers with another student. Are they the same?***

Remember

You can tell a lot about a word from the other words and sentences around it. You can often guess the meaning. You will practice this more in Part 2.

Fiction and Nonfiction

In this unit, you will learn about two types of reading material: fiction and nonfiction. You will practice some steps for reading and understanding fiction and nonfiction.

What Is Fiction?

Fictional stories or books are about people and events that are not real. The author makes up the people, the events, and sometimes the place. Fiction often includes a "message"—an idea or opinion about life in general.

There are different kinds of fiction:
- realistic stories about people and places today, or about people and places in the past
- fantastic stories about unreal worlds, or about our world in the future

EXERCISE 1

This story was written in 1933 by the famous American author Ernest Hemingway. The definition for some words are given at the bottom of each page. These will help you follow the story better. You do not need to learn these words.

A. *Preview.*

- Look at the picture and read the title. What do you think this story is about?
- Do you know anything about the author, Ernest Hemingway?

B. *Read the story to the end. Don't stop to look up new words.*

A Day's Wait

He came into the room to shut the windows while we were still in bed, and I saw he looked ill. He was shivering,[1] his face was white, and he walked slowly as though it ached[2] to move.

"What's the matter, Schatz?"[3]

5 "I've got a headache."

"You better go back to bed."

"No. I'm all right."

"You go to bed. I'll see you when I'm dressed."

But when I came downstairs he was dressed, sitting by the fire, looking a very

10 sick and miserable boy of nine years. When I put my hand on his forehead I knew he had a fever.

"You go up to bed," I said. "You're sick."

"I'm all right," he said.

When the doctor came, he took the boy's temperature.

15 "What is it?" I asked him.

"One hundred and two."

Downstairs, the doctor left three different medicines in different colored capsules with instructions for giving them. One was to bring down the fever, another a purgative,[4] the third to overcome an acid[5] condition. The germs[6] of

20 influenza[7] can only exist in an acid condition, he explained. He seemed to know all about influenza and said there was nothing to worry about if the fever did not go above one hundred and four degrees. This was a light epidemic[8] of flu and there was no danger if you avoided pneumonia.[9]

Back in the room I wrote the boy's temperature down and made a note of the

25 time to give the various capsules.

"Do you want me to read to you?"

"All right. If you want to," said the boy. His face was very white, and there were dark areas under his eyes. He lay still in the bed and seemed very detached[10] from what was going on.

30 I read aloud from Howard Pyle's *Book of Pirates*, but I could see he was not following what I was reading.

"How do you feel, Schatz?" I asked him.

"Just the same, so far," he said.

I sat at the foot of the bed and read to myself while I waited for it to be time

35 to give him another capsule. It would have been natural for him to go to sleep, but when I looked up he was looking at the foot of the bed, looking very strangely.

"Why don't you try to go to sleep? I'll wake you up for the medicine."

"I'd rather stay awake."

(continued)

---

[1] **shivering** shaking because you are cold or afraid
[2] **ache** hurt
[3] **Schatz** a nickname (*Treasure* in German)
[4] **purgative** a kind of medicine
[5] **acid** chemical, sour (e.g., lemon)

[6] **germs** bacteria, small things that make you sick
[7] **influenza** a common disease like a bad cold
[8] **epidemic** a disease that affects many people
[9] **pneumonia** a serious illness in your lungs
[10] **detached** distant

After a while he said to me, "You don't have to stay in here with me, Papa, if it
bothers you."

"It doesn't bother me."

"No, I mean you don't have to stay if it's going to bother you."

I thought perhaps he was a little lightheaded and after giving him the
prescribed[11] capsules at eleven o'clock I went out for a while.

It was a bright, cold day, the ground covered with a sleet[12] that had frozen so
that it seemed as if all the bare trees, the bushes, the cut brush, and all the grass
and the bare ground had been varnished with ice. I took the young Irish Setter[13]
for a little walk up the road and along a frozen creek,[14] but it was difficult to stand
or walk on the glassy surface, and the red dog slipped and slithered, and I fell
twice, hard, once dropping my gun and having it slide away over the ice.

We flushed a covey of quail[15] under a high clay bank with overhanging brush,
and I killed two as they went out of sight over the top of the bank. Some of
the covey lit[16] in trees, but most of them scattered into brush[17] piles, and it was
necessary to jump on the ice-coated mounds of brush several times before they
would flush. Coming out while you were poised[18] unsteadily on the icy, springy
brush, they made difficult shooting, and I killed two, missed five, and started back
pleased to have found a covey close to the house and happy there were so many
left to find another day.

At the house, they said the boy had refused to let anyone come into the room.

"You can't come in," he said. "You mustn't get what I have."

I went up to him and found him in exactly the position I had left him,
white-faced, but with the tops of his cheeks flushed[19] by the fever, staring still, as
he stared, at the foot of the bed.

I took his temperature.

"What is it?"

"Something like a hundred," I said. It was one hundred
and two and four tenths.

"It was a hundred and two," he said.

"Who said so?"

"The doctor."

"Your temperature is all right," I said. "It's nothing to
worry about."

"I don't worry," he said, "but I can't keep from thinking."

"Don't think," I said. "Just take it easy."

"I'm taking it easy," he said and looking straight ahead. He was evidently[20]
holding tight onto himself about something.

---

[11] **prescribed** ordered by the doctor

[12] **sleet** frozen rain

[13] **Irish Setter** a kind of hunting dog

[14] **creek** a small river

[15] **flushed a covey of quail** made birds fly up

[16] **lit** landed

[17] **brush** small trees

[18] **poised** standing in a careful position

[19] **flushed** red

[20] **evidently** clearly

"Take this with water."

"Do you think it will do any good?"

"Of course it will."

I sat down and opened the pirate book and commenced to read, but I could see he was not following, so I stopped.

"About what time do you think I'm going to die?" he asked.

"What?"

"About how long will it be before I die?"

"You aren't going to die. What's the matter with you?"

"Oh, yes, I am. I heard him say a hundred and two."

"People don't die with a fever of one hundred and two. That's a silly way to talk."

"I know they do. At school in France the boys told me you can't live with forty-four degrees. I've got a hundred and two."

He had been waiting to die all day, ever since nine o'clock in the morning.

"You poor Schatz," I said. "Poor old Schatz. It's like miles and kilometers. You aren't going to die. That's a different thermometer. On that thermometer thirty-seven is normal. On this kind it's ninety-eight."

"Are you sure?"

"Absolutely," I said. "It's like miles and kilometers. You know, like how many kilometers we make when we do seventy miles in the car?"

"Oh," he said.

But his gaze at the foot of the bed relaxed slowly. The hold over himself relaxed too, finally, and the next day it was very slack,[21] and he cried easily at little things that were of no importance.

---

[21] **slack** loose

C. *Read the story again. Underline any new words you need to know to understand the story. Show the words to your teacher. If your teacher agrees, look them up and write the meanings in the margins.*

D. *Discuss these questions with another student:*

- Where does the story take place? Who are the people in it, and what happens to them?
- Did you like the story? Why or why not?
- What do you think about the doctor's cure for the flu? What do you do when you have the flu?
- Hemingway often wrote about hunting. Why do you think he wrote about hunting in this story? What do you think about hunting?
- Why was the boy confused? Have you ever had a similar misunderstanding?

E. *With another pair of students, retell the story from beginning to end. Try to use your own words. (You can look back at the story.)*

F. *Choose five words you want to learn from the story. Write them in your vocabulary notebook with the parts of speech, the definitions, and the sentences where you found them. (See Part 2, Unit 1.)*

What Is Nonfiction?

Nonfiction is about real people, places, or things, for example, history, science, psychology, travel, nature, a person's biography, or other real-life subjects. In nonfiction books, the writer gives facts and information that he or she says are true.

EXERCISE 2

Read and discuss the following nonfiction story.

A. *Preview.*

- Read the title. What do you think this passage is about?
- What do you know about the Middle Ages in Europe? What do you know about the plague?[1]

B. *Read the passage to the end. Don't stop to look up new words.*

[1] **plague** disease that causes death and spreads quickly to a large number of people

The Black Death

The Black Death was the name people gave to a terrible disease called the *bubonic plague.* It lasted for two years in Europe, from 1347 to 1349. In those two years, twenty-five million people died. That was one third of all Europeans, or one out of every three people. Whole families disappeared. Farms and villages were left empty. Cities came to a stop. Churches, universities, banks, and shops closed. How did this happen?

Life in Europe in the Middle Ages was very different from life today. In 1300, there were no cars or trains. People walked, rode horses, or traveled in boats. There were no machines to help farmers or to make clothes. There were few factories. People made most of the things they needed by hand: clothing, shoes, food, tools. There were no printed books or newspapers. And of course, there was no telephone, Internet, or television. The news traveled from one person to another by word-of-mouth. And it was usually bad news. Violence was a part of everyday life. There were wars that went on for years and years. Robberies and murders were common. People often died young from accidents or illness.

In those days, most Europeans lived in small villages. But the cities were growing. In the early 1300s, the weather was colder and wetter than usual. Because of this bad weather, farmers often couldn't grow enough food for their families. Many country people didn't have enough to eat, so they went to the cities.

The cities became more crowded and unhealthy. In fact, they weren't very pleasant places. The rich people had big, beautiful houses. But everyone else lived in dark, crowded little houses. No one, rich or poor, had running water or toilets. All the waste[2] was thrown into the streets or rivers.

This was one reason why the plague spread so easily. This disease was caused by bacteria.[3] The waste from sick people's homes was full of these bacteria. Soon the streets and rivers and drinking water became very unhealthy. Many people got sick from drinking the dirty water. Others got sick from the waste in the streets— and because of the rats. There were many rats, and they ran freely through the streets, in and out of houses. People then didn't understand that rats were part of the reason for the plague. The bacteria that cause the disease were carried on fleas[4] that lived on rats.

The plague started in China in the early 1300s. Today diseases move quickly from one part of the world to another. In the Middle Ages, diseases—like people—traveled more slowly. It took about twenty years for the plague to move west from China. At that time, rich Europeans liked to buy silks and spices from Asia. Traders could make a lot of money from these things, so they took long trips to get them. Sometimes they went over land, sometimes by sea. That was how the rats that carried the disease probably traveled—by ship.

(continued)

---

[2]**waste** anything not used, things thrown away by humans
[3]**bacteria** small living things that can cause disease
[4]**flea** a small jumping insect that bites animals or people to drink their blood

By 1347, the plague had reached the countries around the Black Sea in eastern Europe. In October of that year, an Italian ship stopped at a Black Sea town and picked up the disease. By the time the ship arrived at Messina in Sicily (Italy), many sailors were dead. A few days later, people in Messina were sick, too. They sent the ship away, but it was too late. The plague had arrived in Italy.

For two years after that—village by village, town by town—the disease spread north through Europe. By the end of the year 1349, it had spread as far as Scotland and Norway. Only one part of Europe (central Poland and Lithuania) stayed free of the disease. No one knows why.

What happened when the plague arrived in a town? People got sick and died—fast. Italian writer Giovanni Boccaccio wrote about the plague in Florence, Italy. "How many men and women had breakfast with their families, and the same night, had dinner with their ancestors[5] in the next world!" Not everyone died the same day, but most people died within three days. And it was a horrible death. The first signs were black lumps[6] around the neck and other places. That's why it was called the Black Death. Then, there was high fever and blood—and that was the end.

No one understood what was happening or why. Many people thought it was a punishment sent by God. Some doctors in Paris thought it was caused by the planets and the stars. Other doctors believed it was caused by a bad smell. (Cities with the plague smelled horrible.) They told people to keep flowers and use perfume. Some people thought they could keep away the disease with loud noises, so they rang church bells and fired guns. None of these cures[7] helped, of course. There was no cure in those days. There was no way to help a sick person.

People were terrified. Some stayed in their homes and didn't let anyone in. But the fleas and rats went in and out, and so did the disease. Other people ran away from the cities and into the country. The countryside was probably healthier than the city, but these people often brought the disease with them, and they helped to spread it.

In some towns in Germany and France, people also got angry. They wanted to find someone to blame for the plague, so they blamed the Jews. They said the Jews had put poison in the water. Angry groups of people went to the Jewish neighborhoods. They set fire to houses and killed whole families. In Strasbourg in 1349, 200 Jews were burned to death. In those years, many Jews moved east, to Poland and Lithuania.

The disease died down in 1349, but it didn't disappear completely. It came back many times in Europe, though it never again spread so far so fast. The last big outbreak[8] was the Great Plague of London in 1665, when about 100,000 people died. After that there were smaller outbreaks in Marseilles, Vienna, Moscow, and other cities, until the early 18th century.

---

[5] **ancestor** a member of a family who lived in past times
[6] **lump** an area on someone's skin or body that becomes larger and hard
[7] **cure** a medicine or treatment that can stop a disease
[8] **outbreak** the sudden start of something

80   In other parts of the world, however, the plague continued to be a problem. Between 1855 and 1929, outbreaks of the plague killed over 12 million people in India and China. Even now, the plague is still present in some countries, for example, Madagascar, Tanzania, Brazil, Peru, Myanmar, and Vietnam. Every year around the world, several thousand people get the plague, and several hundreds of
85 them die.

    Could a new outbreak of the Black Death kill millions of people today? Probably not. Now we understand how the disease is carried and we can stop it from spreading. We can also cure it with modern medicines. However, another disease could still be a problem. Even today, new diseases can suddenly appear.
90 Then scientists and doctors have to work fast to understand it and find a cure.

C. ***Read the passage again. Underline any new words you need to know to understand the story. Show the words to your teacher. If your teacher agrees, look them up and write the meanings in the margins.***

D. ***Discuss these questions with another student:***

- Why did the plague kill so many people? How did it spread?
- How did people in the Middle Ages try to stay healthy? How do you try to stay healthy?
- Do you think there could be another plague today?
- Do you know about any diseases that spread and killed many people? What was the disease? When and where did it spread?

E. ***With another pair of students, retell the story from beginning to end. Try to use your own words. (You can look back at the story.)***

F. ***Choose five words you want to learn from the story. Write them in your vocabulary notebook with the parts of speech, the definitions, and the sentences where you found them. (See Part 2, Unit 1.)***

Choosing the Right Book

It's very important to choose the right book for extensive reading. First of all, you should choose a book that interests you. Your teacher and friends may have good ideas, but it should be a book that you want to read.

It's also important to choose a book at the right level. If the book is too easy or too difficult, you won't enjoy it, so you won't read it. You need to find a book that you *will* read.

Preview a book to find out if it is right for you.

➤ Read the title, back cover, and first page. What is the book about? Is it interesting?

➤ Check the level: Look again at the first page. How many words are new to you?
No new words → This book may be **too easy**.
1–5 new words → This book is **the right level**.
6 or more new words → This book may be **too difficult**.

EXAMPLE

A. **Look at the example on page 17. Then answer these questions.**

1. What is the title? *Anne of Green Gables*

2. Look at the front cover and back cover copy. Then read the first page.
What is this book about? _____
Is it interesting to you? _____

3. Look at the first page again.
How many words are new to you? _____
Is this book the right level for you? _____

B. **Talk about your answers with another student. Are they the same?**

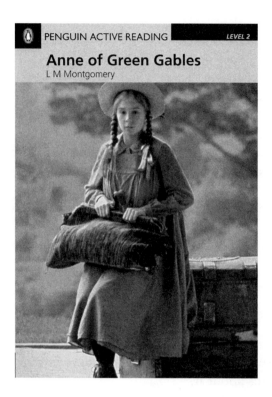

PENGUIN ACTIVE READING   LEVEL 2

Anne of Green Gables
L M Montgomery

(from the back cover)

"You don't want me!" cried Anne. "You don't want me because I'm not a boy! Oh, what shall I do?"

Marilla and Matthew Cuthbert want a boy from the orphanage to help them on their farm. But a thin little girl is waiting for Matthew at Bright River Station. Anne, a funny and sometimes difficult child, changes everybody's life and wins everybody's love.

CHAPTER 1

Anne Arrives in Avonlea

"You don't want me!" cried the child suddenly.
"You don't want me because I'm not a boy!"

One fine spring afternoon in Avonlea, Mrs. Rachel Lynde sat by her kitchen window. She often sat there because she could see the Avonlea road very well from there.

A man with a horse and **buggy** came up the road. It was Mrs. Lynde's neighbor, Matthew Cuthbert.

"Where's Matthew going?" thought Mrs. Lynde in **surprise**. "It's half past three in the afternoon and he has a lot of work on his farm. Where's he going and why is he going there?"

Matthew Cuthbert lived with his sister, Marilla, in Green Gables, a large old house near Mrs. Lynde's home. Later, Mrs. Lynde walked to Green Gables.

buggy /ˈbʌgi/ (n) In past times, people sat in a *buggy* and a horse pulled it.
surprise /səˈpraɪz, səˈpraɪz/ (n) When a friend plans a *surprise* for you, you don't know about it. When you learn about it, you are very *surprised*.

1

Anne of Green Gables

Marilla Cuthbert was busy in the kitchen. She was a tall, thin woman with gray hair. Marilla wasn't young or pretty, and she didn't smile very much. But she had a kind **heart**. She wasn't surprised by Mrs. Lynde's visit.

"Hello, Marilla," said Mrs. Lynde. "I saw Matthew on the road. Where's he going?"

"To Bright River Station," answered Marilla. "We're getting a little boy from an **orphanage** in Nova Scotia. He's coming on the train this afternoon."

Mrs. Lynde couldn't speak. Then she said, "An **orphan** boy! Why do you want an orphan boy?"

"Matthew is sixty years old," answered Marilla. "His heart isn't very strong. He wants a boy to help him on the farm.

"We heard about Mrs. Spencer at White Sands. She's getting a little girl from the orphanage. Matthew and I want a little boy. Mrs. Spencer went to the orphanage today. She's bringing a boy back on the train and she's going to leave him at the station. Matthew will meet him there."

heart /hɑrt/ (n) When your *heart* stops, you are going to die. People say that your feelings come from your *heart*.
orphan /ˈɔrfən/ (n) An *orphan* has no parents because they are dead. An *orphanage* is a home for a lot of *orphans*.

2

Getting the Most from Your Reading

After you choose a book for extensive reading, follow these guidelines.

Guidelines for Extensive Reading

- Read for at least 30 minutes every day. Find a regular time in your day for reading. When you stop reading each time, write the date in pencil in the margin. Try to finish your book quickly. Your teacher will check on your progress.

- Don't stop to look up new words unless they are necessary to understand the story.

- Look up useful words after you finish reading the chapter or book. Write the words in your vocabulary notebook with the parts of speech, the definitions, and the sentences where you found them. (See Part 2, Unit 1.)

- When you finish a book:
  - ➤ Tell your teacher.
  - ➤ Write the name of the book on your Reading List on pages 21–22.
  - ➤ If you liked the book, tell your classmates about it.

Talking about Your Books

Book Conferences

A book conference is a conversation with your teacher. It is not a test. Tell your teacher when you finish a book. Then your teacher will ask you questions about it. You don't need to study for a book conference. You just need to read the book!

Here are some questions your teacher may ask:
- What is the title?
- Who is the author (writer)?
- Where does the story take place?
- Who are the characters (people in the story), or what is it about?
- What happens in the story?
- Did you like the book? Explain your opinion.

Reading Circles

A reading circle is a small group of students. The group meets often to talk about the books they are reading.

Rules for reading circles:
- ➤ The group should have four to five students. It should meet about once a week.

- ➢ At each meeting, students talk about their books. Each student takes a turn talking about his or her book (not more than four minutes).
  Suggested talking points:
  - where you are in the book (beginning, middle, end)
  - the level (easy, not so easy, difficult)
  - the setting (where it takes place)
  - the characters (fiction) or the subject (nonfiction)
  - what happens (fiction) or what it tells about (nonfiction)
  - your opinion about the book

- ➢ Students who are not talking must listen and then ask questions. One student should also watch the time and say when four minutes are finished.

Book Talks

In a book talk, you talk to the class about your book. You should only talk for a few minutes (not more than five minutes).

How to get ready for a book talk:
- ➢ On a small piece of paper, write the information below. Don't write whole sentences. Write only a few notes (words or phrases) for each answer.
  - the title and author
  - the level of difficulty
  - the characters (fiction) or subject (nonfiction)
  - the setting (where it takes place)
  - what happens (fiction) or what it tells about (nonfiction)
  - your opinion about the book

- ➢ Use your notes to talk about the book.

- ➢ Practice your talk by yourself or with a friend or classmate. Try not to read from your notes. Look at them only when you need to. Look up as much as possible. Speak slowly and clearly. Try not to stop or say "um" or "ah" too often. Practice saying the sentences until you can say them fluently.

- ➢ Time your talk before you give it in class. If it takes less than four minutes, think of more things to say. If it takes more than five minutes, cut out some parts.

Writing about Your Books

Book Reports

When you finish a book, fill in a book report form. Ask your teacher for a form, or copy these questions onto a separate piece of paper. Your book report may help your teacher decide which books to get for the class or library.

BOOK REPORT

Title: _____

Author: _____ Fiction _____ Nonfiction _____

Pages: _____ Level of difficulty (1 = very easy, 10 = very difficult): _____

Characters (fiction) or subject (nonfiction): _____
_____

Setting (where): _____

Story (fiction) or what it tells about (nonfiction):
_____
_____
_____

Your general opinion: _____
_____

The best parts, characters, or other things you liked about the book:
_____
_____

The worst parts, characters, or other things you disliked about the book:
_____
_____

Rate this book: _____

★★★★ = a great book!   ★ = not very interesting
★★★ = a good book   ✕ = a terrible book
★★ = some good parts

Book Files

When you finish a book, ask your teacher for a book file card. Then make a card for your class book files. You and your classmates can use the files to find books you like.

On the card, write information about your book. Follow the example below. Remember to rate your book.

★ ★ ★ ★ = a great book!
★ ★ ★ = a good book
★ ★ = some good parts
★ = not very interesting
✕ = a terrible book

EXAMPLE
. . . .

TITLE: *Anne of Green Gables*

AUTHOR: *L. M. Montgomery*

NUMBER OF PAGES: *60*   **FICTION OR NONFICTION:** *Fiction*

WHAT IS THE BOOK ABOUT? *An orphan girl is adopted by a*

farm family.

RATE THE BOOK: ☆ ☆ ☆

Reading List

Make a list of your extensive reading books here. For each book you read, write the title, author, and the date you finished.

1. Title: _____

Author: _____ Date finished: _____

2. Title: _____

Author: _____ Date finished: _____

3. Title: _____

Author: _____ Date finished: _____

4. Title: _____

Author: _____ Date finished: _____

5. Title: _____

Author: _____ Date finished: _____

6. Title: _____

Author: _____ Date finished: _____

7. Title: _____

Author: _____ Date finished: _____

8. Title: _____

Author: _____ Date finished: _____

9. Title: _____

Author: _____ Date finished: _____

10. Title: _____

Author: _____ Date finished: _____

11. Title: _____

Author: _____ Date finished: _____

12. Title: _____

Author: _____ Date finished: _____

13. Title: _____

Author: _____ Date finished: _____

14. Title: _____

Author: _____ Date finished: _____

15. Title: _____

Author: _____ Date finished: _____

Suggested Books

This book list may help you find a good book. But you don't have to read a book from this list. Any book is good for extensive reading—if it is interesting to you and it is the right level.

The books in **List A** were written for students of English. These books are called "readers." They are written at different levels of difficulty. Check with your teacher about the best level for you (probably Level 2). Ask your teacher where to find readers. There may be some in the school or classroom library. You may also find readers in bookstores or public libraries.

The Books in **List B** are popular with English speakers. Most of these books were written for young people. These books are easier to read than books for adults, but they are not childish. Adults can enjoy reading them, too. You will find them in either the young adult or the children's section of your library or bookstore.

Book List

List A: Readers

The books on this list are all published by Penguin Longman. Other companies also have readers for English learners. These books are all Level 2. You should start with this level. Then, if you find they are easy, you can try books from Level 3.

The books with a headphones symbol (🎧) also have an audio CD. Listening and reading at the same time is very good practice. If you listen and read the first time, you can try just reading or just listening another time.

Readers: Fiction

🎧 *Anne of Green Gables.* Montgomery, L.M. A young girl from an orphanage wins the love of her new parents.

Babe—The Sheep-Pig. King-Smith, Dick. Farmer Hogget is a sheep farmer. When he wins a pig, he doesn't want it, and his wife wants to eat it, but Babe has other ideas.

Black Beauty. Sewall, Anna. A classic horse story about Black Beauty who leaves the farm where he grew up and discovers the cruelty of humans.

🎧 *Christmas Carol, A.* Dickens, Charles. The famous tale about how cold, hard Scrooge learns that life is not all about money.

Dante's Peak. Gram, Dewey. A scientist who studies volcanoes goes to a small town where a volcano is about to explode.

Fly Away Home. Hermes, Patricia. Amy finds some goose eggs, but no mother, and so the baby geese think she is their mother. Can she teach them to fly south in the winter?

Freckles. Matthews, Andrew. Susie hates her freckles. Her best friend Donna doesn't have any. Then a new boy comes to school, and both Susie and Donna are interested.

Ghost of Genny Castle, The. Escott, John. Claire is staying near an old castle with a secret—accidents happen there: Animals and people die.

🎧 *Gulliver's Travels.* Swift, Jonathan. In this classic tale, Gulliver has adventures in a fantastic country of very small people.

🎧 *Jaws.* Benchley, Peter. At a quiet seaside town, a woman is killed in the water at night. The town policeman thinks it's a killer shark.

Jurassic Park III. Ciencin, Scott. Young Eric Kirby is in Jurassic Park with live, dangerous dinosaurs, and Dr. Alan Grant must save him.

🎧 *Kidnapped.* Stevenson, Robert Louis. An adventure story about an orphan boy who is put on a ship to America by his evil uncle.

Lady in the Lake, The. Chandler, Raymond. When the body of a woman is found in a lake, Detective Philip Marlowe must discover who killed her.

Last of the Mohicans, The. Cooper, James Fenimore. A classic tale about Indians, British soldiers, and settlers in early America.

Lost in New York. Escott, John. On Nicky's first visit to New York, he finds himself in trouble, and soon the police are looking for him.

Men in Black. Gardner, J.J. In a strange future world, Kay and Jay are the Men in Black who must watch the aliens on Earth.

🎧 *Moby Dick.* Melville, Herman. In this famous story, a young sailor tells about Captain Ahab and his search for the great white whale.

Moonfleet. Falkner, J. Meade. Fifteen-year-old John accidentally finds out some dangerous secrets, and his life changes.

Mr. Bean in Town. Atkinson, Rowan; Clifford, Andrew; Curtis, Richard; Driscoll, Robin. More funny adventures for this man who can never do anything right.

Mummy Returns, The. Whitman, John. The people of Egypt are afraid of the Scorpion King, and someone must kill him.

Mysterious Island, The. Verne, Jules. Three men, a boy, and a dog are in a balloon that comes down over the Pacific.

Of Mice and Men. Steinbeck, John. A young boy, George, has to decide what to do when his friend Lennie gets into trouble.

Persuasion. Austen, Jane. When Anne meets Captain Wentworth again after many years, she still loves him, but she doesn't know if he feels anything for her.

🎧 *Pirates of the Caribbean: The Curse of the Black Pearl.* Trimble, Irene. On a Caribbean island, pirates arrive and show interest in young Elizabeth. Where are they from, and what do they want?

Prince and the Pauper, The. Twain, Mark. Two boys born on the same day—one is a prince and one is very poor. Then they change places in a game.

Project Omega. O'Reilly, Elaine. Julia wants to find her father, who has disappeared, but someone is trying to kill her.

🎧 *Robinson Crusoe.* Defoe, Daniel. The classic tale of a man who is shipwrecked on an island.

Scarlet Letter, The. Hawthorne, Nathaniel. Young Hester Prynne has a baby in 17th-century Boston, but she won't say who the father is.

Simply Suspense. Aumonier, Stacy; Burrage, Alfred; Stockton, Frank. Three exciting short stories about dangerous people and places.

Stranger than Fiction Urban Myths. Healey, Phil; Glanvill, Rick. A man falls from a very tall building, but he doesn't die. Why not? Read about this and other strange stories.

🎧 *Three Musketeers, The.* Dumas, Alexandre. D'Artagnan and his friends go to fight for the king and their country against the dangerous Cardinal.

Three Short Stories of Sherlock Holmes. Doyle, Arthur Conan. Three of the classic Sherlock Holmes detective stories.

Walkabout. Marshall, James V. The story of an Aboriginal boy and two American children in the Australian desert.

Wave, The. Rhue, Morton. Mr. Ross wants to teach his history class about the Nazis, so he starts an activity called "The Wave." At first, the students love it, but then it becomes dangerous.

Whistle and the Dead Men's Eyes, The. James, M.R. Two men are on vacation. Strange things happen in the hotel. People see things that aren't there, and there are noises in empty rooms.

White Fang. London, Jack. Half dog, half wolf, White Fang, is taken from the mountains to the world of men, where he learns to fight and kill.

Readers: Nonfiction

Amazon Rainforest, The. Smith, Bernard. This forest is important for the world's weather and wildlife, but it is disappearing fast.

🎧 *Apollo 13.* Anastasio, Dina. The story of the excitement, difficulties, and glory of the first moonwalk in 1970.

Audrey Hepburn. Rice, Chris. Everyone loved this beautiful and successful actress, but her life was not always happy.

🎧 *Extreme Sports.* Dean, Michael. There are many new, exciting, and dangerous sports—what are they, and who does them?

Gandhi. Rolleson, Jane. Mahatma Gandhi worked for civil rights and led India to independence. In his time and today, many people follow his ideas.

🎧 *Nelson Mandela.* Degnan-Veness, Colleen. This is the story of a freedom fighter and one of the world's great leaders.

🎧 *Water for Life.* Smith, Bernard. We drink it, wash with it, cook with it. In some countries, people waste it; in other countries, they can't get enough.

List B: Books for Native Speakers

Easier Fiction

🎧 *Birchbark House.* Erdrich, Louise. The story of an Ojibwa (Native American Indian) girl in 1847 who lives through disease and difficulties. (256 pages)

🎧 *Children of the River.* Crew, Linda. A girl from Cambodia wants to fit in at her American high school, but she also doesn't want to go against her family. (213 pages)

Chocolate War, The. Cormier, Robert. A classic story of a high school student who becomes the hero of the school when he fights a secret society. (191 pages)

🎧 *Confessions of Charlotte Doyle, The.* Avi. Charlotte is accused of murder in this 19th-century tale of action on the high seas. (240 pages)

Esperanza Rising. Ryan, Pam Munoz. Esperanza's life on a farm in Mexico is happy but suddenly she is forced to escape to the United States. (261 pages)

🎧 *Fallen Angels.* Myers, Walter Dean. A realistic and intense novel about a young, African-American soldier in the Vietnam War in 1967. (309 pages)

Gentlehands. Kerr, M.E. A policeman's son falls in love with a rich girl and they discover an ex-Nazi in her family. (326 pages)

🎧 *Giver, The.* Lowry, Lois. Jonas lives in a future society where there is no pain, crime, or unhappiness. But as Jonas learns, people pay a terrible price for all this. (192 pages)

Hatchet. Paulson, Gary. Brian is on the way to visit his father when his airplane crashes and Brian finds himself alone in the Canadian wilderness. (195 pages)

Hattie Big Sky. Larsen, Kirby. In 1918, orphaned Hattie goes to Montana to make a life for herself and has to face the terrible prairie winter. (320 pages)

🎧 *Holes.* Sachar, Louis. A dramatic story in which Stanley is punished for a crime he didn't do and is sent to a detention camp for boys. (233 pages)

Homeless Bird. Whelan, Gloria. Married and widowed at the age of 13, Koly is caught between modern India and ancient Hindu culture. (192 pages)

How Tia Lola Came to Stay. Alvarez, Julia. At first Miguel and his sister are embarassed by their aunt from the Dominican Republic, but then she helps them. (112 pages)

🎧 *Island of the Blue Dolphins, The.* O'Dell, Scott. This beautiful book tells the story of a Native American girl left alone for years on an island. (192 pages)

Julie of the Wolves. George, Jean Craig. Julie, an Eskimo girl, is married against her will at 13 and runs away into the wilderness to live with the wolves. (176 pages)

🎧 *Last Shot: A Final Four Mystery.* Feinstein, John. Stevie and Susan discover that someone wants to fix the college basketball championships. (256 pages)

🎧 *Lion, the Witch, and the Wardrobe, The.* Lewis, C.S. The classic series about four children who travel through a wardrobe to another world. (206 pages)

No Turning Back. Naidoo, Beverly. A boy in South Africa runs away to the city and lives on the streets. (189 pages)

Pigman, The. Zindel, Paul. Funny and serious, moving and perceptive, this is a classic story about two young people's search for meaning in life. (192 pages)

🎧 *Princess Diaries, The.* Cabot, Meg. A high-school student in New York City, Mia, finds out that her father is really a European prince. (304 pages)

🎧 *Radiance Descending.* Fox, Paula. Having a younger brother with Down's Syndrome is not easy for Paul. (112 pages)

Roll of Thunder, Hear My Cry. Taylor, Mildred. An African-American family tries to keep their land and their dignity in 1930s Georgia. (288 pages)

SOS Titanic. Bunting, Eve. A young Irishman on the *Titanic* tries to rescue his friends as the ship sinks into the cold sea. (246 pages)

🎧 *Stormbreaker: An Alex Rider Adventure.* Horowitz, Anthony. In this spy thriller series, Alex finds out that his dead uncle was a spy. (192 pages)

Summer of My German Soldier, The. Greene, Bette. During World War II, an American Jewish girl falls in love with a German prisoner of war. (199 pages)

🎧 *Witch of Blackbird Pond, The.* Speare, Elizabeth George. In 1687, the Puritans in Connecticut think Kit is a witch when she moves there from the Caribbean. (256 pages)

🎧 *Wrinkle in Time, A.* L'Engle, Madeleine. Meg's father mysteriously disappears after experimenting with time travel. A classic. (217 pages)

Easier Nonfiction

Boy. Dahl, Roald. This is a story of the funny and shocking childhood and school experiences of this famous English writer. (176 pages)

Chimpanzees I Love: Saving Their World and Ours, The. Goodall, Jane. The world famous expert tells of her experiences with chimpanzees. (268 pages)

Escape: The Story of the Great Houdini. Fleischman, Sid. The rags-to-riches story of a poor Jewish boy who became a great magician and escape artist. (210 pages)

Go Ask Alice. Anonymous. The real diary of a fifteen-year-old girl who became addicted to drugs. (188 pages)

Helen Keller: From Tragedy to Triumph. Wilkie, Katherine E. Blind and deaf since she was a girl, Helen learned to communicate and became famous. (192 pages)

Immigrant Kids. Freedman, Russell. For immigrant children, America has meant freedom, but it has also meant hard work and horrible conditions. (80 pages)

It Happened to Nancy: By an Anonymous Teenager, A True Story From Her Diary. Sparks, Beatrice. The true story of a teenager who thought she had found love, but instead found AIDS. (238 pages)

J.R.R. Tolkien: The Man Who Created the Lord of the Rings. Coren, Michael. The fascinating and entertaining life of Tolkien. (125 pages)

Leonardo's Horse. Fritz, Jean. The life and times of Leonardo da Vinci, and the story of a sculpture that he never made. (127 pages)

Pelé. Buckley, James. This is the story of the childhood and worldwide success of this famous Brazilian soccer player. (128 pages)

Promises to Keep: How Jackie Robinson Changed America. Robinson, Sharon. The author shares her memories of her father—the first African American to become a famous baseball player. (64 pages)

Red Scarf Girl. Jiang, Ji-Li. This Chinese writer tells about her difficult childhood in China during the Cultural Revolution. (285 pages)

Rosa Parks: My Story. Parks, Rosa; Haskins, Jim. Rosa Parks tells of her life and her role in the civil rights movement in 1950s America. (188 pages)

🎧 *Sacagawea.* Bruchac, Joseph. This is the story of the young American Indian woman who helped Lewis and Clark find a way to the Pacific Ocean. (259 pages)

Team Moon: How 400,000 People Landed Apollo 11 on the Moon. Thimmesh, Catherine. A behind the scenes account of the people who made it possible to put a man on the moon. (80 pages)

Upstairs Room, The. Johanna Reiss. Two Jewish sisters were hidden by a Dutch family for two years during World War II. (196 pages)

More Difficult Fiction

🎧 *Alfred Kropp.* Yancy, Rick. Young Alfred finds himself in a world of action and adventure in this thrilling and entertaining series. (368 pages)

Code Orange. Cooney, Caroline. When a New York teenager discovers a 100-year old sample of smallpox, he and his friends are in danger. (208 pages)

🎧 *Code Talking.* Bruchac, Joseph. A novel about the Navaho Indians who joined the Marines during World War II and how they sent messages in their language to help America win the war. (240 pages)

🎧 *Countess below Stairs, A.* Ibbotson, Eva. After the Russian Revolution, a beautiful young countess has to leave Russia and work as a servant in England. (400 pages)

Double Helix. Werlin, Nancy. A suspenseful novel about love and the genetic-engineering experiments of Dr. Wyatt. (252 pages)

🎧 *Harry Potter and the Sorcerer's Stone (Original U.K. title: Harry Potter and the Philosopher's Stone).* Rowling, J.K. In these famous adventures, Harry discovers that he's a wizard. (312 pages)

Hitchhiker's Guide to the Galaxy, A. Adams, Douglas. This book is science fiction, fantasy, and lots of fun—a best-seller for many years. (224 pages)

House on Mango Street, The. Cisneros, Sandra. Young Esperanza learns to make a happy life in a poor Hispanic neighborhood in Chicago. (110 pages)

I Know What You Did Last Summer. Duncan, Lois. A horror story full of suspense about a group of young people and their secret. (198 pages)

🎧 *Kira-kira.* Kadohata, Cynthia. A Japanese-American family moves to Georgia in the 1950s, and young Katie has to deal with discrimination and death. (272 pages)

🎧 *Lavinia.* LeGuin, Ursula. This famous writer of science fiction has recreated the world before ancient Rome in a dramatic tale of passion and war. (299 pages)

Lord of the Flies. Golding, William. A classic. A group of English schoolboys find themselves alone on an island after their plane crashes into the sea. (208 pages)

Man from the Other Side, The. Orlev, Uri. In 1943 in Warsaw, Poland, a young man with anti-Jewish feelings discovers that his dead father was Jewish. (192 pages)

🎧 *Monster (Amistad).* Myers, Walter Dean. In this tense story, 16-year-old Steve tells about his trial for murder and his life until then. (288 pages)

Outsiders, The. Hinton, S.E. An intensely realistic and dark tale about youth gangs, written when the author was 16 years old. A classic. (208 pages)

Perks of Being a Wallflower, The. Chbosky, Stephen. Brilliant, but terribly shy, Charlie tells of his day-to-day life and dramas. (224 pages)

🎧 *Redheaded Princess, The.* Rinaldi, Anne. The dramatic story of the beautiful young princess who became Queen Elizabeth I. (224 pages)

🎧 *Silent to the Bone.* Konigsburg, E.L. Connor wants to find out what really happened to his best friend's sister, and why his friend will no longer talk. (272 pages)

Single Shard, A. Parks, Linda Sue. An orphan boy grows up and overcomes great difficulties in 12th-century Korea. (192 pages)

🎧 *Sisterhood of the Traveling Pants, The.* Brashares, Ann. Four teenage friends find a pair of magical jeans that they share over a summer. (336 pages)

Speak. Anderson, Laurie Halse. Why is Melinda no longer speaking to anyone? It's not because of the usual problems at home or at school. (208 pages)

Tamar: A Novel of Espionage, Passion, and Betrayal. Peet, Mal. A story of suspense and passion in Nazi-occupied Holland during World War II. (432 pages)

Uglies, The. Westerfield, Scott. This first book in a trilogy tells of a future world where everyone becomes beautiful at the age of 16. (432 pages)

🎧 *Whirligig.* Fleischman, Paul. Teenage Brent has to learn to live with the terrible consequences of his actions. (144 pages)

🎧 *Witness.* Hesse, Karen. When the Ku Klux Klan arrives in a small town in Vermont, the people in the town react in many different ways. (288 pages)

More Difficult Nonfiction

Alive: The Story of the Andes Survivors. Read, Pier Paul. The dramatic story of 16 people who survived a plane crash in the Andes. (398 pages)

Diary of a Young Girl, The. Franck, Anne. This well-known book tells the true story of a Jewish girl hiding from the Nazis in World War II Holland. (368 pages)

🎧 *Legend of Bass Reeves, The.* Paulsen, Gary. The true story of an escaped slave who lived with Indians and then became a successful rancher. (160 pages)

Letters to a Young Brother: Manifest Your Destiny. Harper, Hill. A young black American writer tells his own story and answers letters from other young men. (192 pages)

Marley: A Dog Like No Other. Grogan, John. As a family dog, Marley is 90 pounds of trouble, fun, and love. (208 pages)

🎧 *Night.* Wiesel, Elie. Taken from his Hungarian village as a boy, the author survived the Nazi death camps. This book asks fundamental questions about life and faith. A masterpiece. (120 pages)

One Kingdom: Our Lives with Animals. Noyes, Deborah. The author looks at the ways animals and humans have connected throughout history. (144 pages)

Only the Names Remain: The Cherokees and the Trail of Tears. Bealen, Alex W. The sad history of the Cherokees from the 16th century to their removal from Georgia in 1837. (80 pages)

Perilous Journey of the Donner Party, The. Calabro, Marian. In 1846, 90 people travelling to California were trapped for the winter—only a few survived. (192 pages)

Phineas Gage: A Gruesome But True Story about Brain Science. Fleischman, John. After an iron rod went through his brain in 1848, Phineas Gage lived for 11 years. (96 pages)

Poet Slave of Cuba: A Biography of Juan Francisco Manzano, The. Engle, Margarita; Qualls, Sean. This biography tells of the suffering and the talent of a 19th-century Cuban poet. (192 pages)

Shipwreck at the Bottom of the World: The Extraordinary True Story of Shackleton and the Endurance. Armstrong, Jennifer. In 1914, the ship *Endurance* was trapped in the Antarctic ice. This is the story of the remarkable survival and rescue. (144 pages)

Something Out of Nothing: Marie Curie and Radium. McClafferty, Carla Killough. Curie's life and work as a scientist and as an independent woman. (144 pages)

Zlata's Diary: A Child's Life in Wartime Sarajevo. Filipovish, Zlata. Ten-year-old Zlata tells about the bombings and hardship of life in Sarajevo. (208 pages)

Vocabulary Building

Guidelines for Learning Vocabulary

To become a better reader, you need to learn more vocabulary.

This part of *Reading Power 2* is about learning vocabulary. You will find out more about words and about how they are used. You will also learn about ways to study them and build a larger vocabulary.

But remember—you can learn vocabulary better if you read a lot. When you read a lot, you see words many times and you remember them better. This makes it easier to read, so you can read more. If you read more, you will learn even more words.

Vocabulary is very important in reading. To understand what you are reading, you need to know many words. In this unit, you will practice using the dictionary to learn new words. Then you will learn about and practice some new ways to study vocabulary.

Follow these guidelines for learning vocabulary:

- **Make good use of the dictionary.**
  Learn the pronunciation, spelling, and part of speech of new words.
  Learn the different meanings and how to use the words.

- **Study vocabulary often.**
  Use a vocabulary notebook and study cards to help you learn and review new words.

> ***Note:*** Ask your teacher which language to use when you write the meanings of words (in the exercises, in your notebook, and on your study cards). Should you write them in English or in your language?

Make Good Use of the Dictionary

Choosing a Good Dictionary

You will need a dictionary for some of the exercises in this unit (and for other vocabulary work). You may want to use a bilingual dictionary to find the words in your language.

If possible, you should also use an English learner's dictionary. For example, the *Longman Study Dictionary* or the *Longman Dictionary of American English* are good for this level.

Learner's dictionaries are easier to use than other English language dictionaries. The definitions are written in simple language. They also have a lot of information about each word. They tell you:

- the pronunciation
- the spelling and part of speech
- the different meanings of the word
- how to use the word

Pronunciation

You can read better and faster if you know how words sound. You can also remember the words better if you can say them. That's why it's important to learn how to pronounce new words.

Most dictionaries tell you how to pronounce words. They use special pronunciation symbols (letters). Look in your dictionary for the key to these symbols. (It's often on the inside back cover.)

EXERCISE 1

A. *Work with another student. Find the pronunciation key in your dictionary. Take turns saying the example words for each symbol.*

B. *Read the words and the pronunciation symbols. Say the words to your partner.*

1. a. blood /blʌd/   b. much /mʌtʃ/   c. won /wʌn/

2. a. give /gɪv/   b. five /faɪv/   c. thief /θif/

3. a. sign /saɪn/   b. thing /θɪŋ/   c. garage /gəradʒ/

C. *Say the words again for your teacher.*

A. *Work with another student. Follow these directions for each group of words:*

- Take turns reading the words aloud.
- Look up each word in the dictionary. Check the pronunciation symbols. Did you say the words correctly? Check with your teacher if you aren't sure.
- Practice saying the words correctly.

1. a. brown   b. goal   c. body   d. hour
2. a. weather   b. peace   c. area   d. bread
3. a. crime   b. fix   c. bright   d. field
4. a. again   b. explain   c. daily   d. hair
5. a. laugh   b. taught   c. farm   d. wall
6. a. ground   b. touch   c. young   d. through
7. a. hold   b. nothing   c. fork   d. cross
8. a. high   b. ago   c. thing   d. age

B. *Say the words again for your teacher.*

C. *Talk about these questions with another student:*

- What can you say about spelling and pronunciation in English?
- What can you say about spelling and pronunciation in your language?

Remember

When you look up a new word, check the pronunciation.
- A letter (or group of letters) may be pronounced in many different ways.
  Examples: book /ʊ/, cool /u/, blood /ʌ/
- Different letters (or groups of letters) may have the same pronunciation.
  Examples: field, leave, feet /i/

Spelling

It's important to know how to spell words in English. If you know the spelling of a word, you know what it looks like. Then you see and understand it quickly when you are reading.

When you learn new words, you should also learn the spelling.

EXERCISE 3

A. Cover Exercise 2 with a piece of paper. Your teacher will read the words in the first column (column a). Listen and write the words.

1. _____
2. _____
3. _____
4. _____

5. _____
6. _____
7. _____
8. _____

B. Now look back at the words in Exercise 2. Did you spell them correctly? Correct them if necessary.

EXERCISE 4

A. Work in pairs.
Student A: Look at Exercise 2. Copy the "b" words (goal, etc.) under List 1.
Student B: Look at Exercise 2. Copy the "c" words (body, etc.) under List 1.

List 1	List 2
1. _____	1. _____
2. _____	2. _____
3. _____	3. _____
4. _____	4. _____
5. _____	5. _____
6. _____	6. _____
7. _____	7. _____
8. _____	8. _____

B. Read the words on List 1 to your partner. Under List 2, write the words your partner reads to you.

C. Now look back at the words in Exercise 2. Did you spell them correctly? Correct them if necessary.

Parts of Speech

The dictionary tells you the part of speech for every word. This helps you understand the word and how to use it correctly. See the examples in the box below.

Noun (n):	a person, place, thing, quality, action, or idea
Examples:	**George** stayed in a nice **hotel** in **Tokyo**.
	Swimming is my favorite **sport** in the **summer**.
Verb (v):	a word (or words) that show an action, experience, or state
Examples:	I **was** hungry, so I **ate** all the food.
	Sam **is going** to Mexico next month.
Pronoun (pron):	a word that is used instead of a noun or noun phrase
Examples:	**Her** mother will drive **them** home.
	Roger watched the movie with **us**, but **he** didn't enjoy **it**.
	She's the woman **who** won a million dollars.
	We visited a church **that** was built a thousand years ago.
Adjective (adj):	a word that describes a noun
Examples:	Tickets to the concert are **free**.
	The **small** room was very **comfortable**.
Adverb (adv):	a word that tells you more about a verb, an adjective, or another adverb
Examples:	I read that book a year **ago**. It's **very** good.
	He walked **slowly** into the room.
Preposition (prep):	a word that is put in front of a noun to show where, when, or how
Examples:	There was a letter **from** my mother **in** my mailbox.
	In three hours, we drove **across** the state.
Conjunction (conj):	a word that connects parts of sentences or phrases
Examples:	In Rome, we walked a lot **and** saw many things.
	I went to bed **because** I was tired.

EXERCISE 5

A. Find these words on the dictionary page. Write the parts of speech. (A word may have more than one part of speech.)

Word	Part of Speech
1. overlook	_____
2. overly	_____
3. overlap	_____
4. overpass	_____
5. overnight	_____
6. overhear	_____
7. overhead	_____
8. overload	_____

B. Talk about your answers with another student. Are they the same?

overhead¹ /ˌoʊvɚˈhɛd/ *adj., adv.* above your head: *A plane flew overhead.* | *We put our bags in the overhead compartments.*

overhead² /ˈoʊvɚˌhɛd/ *n.* ECONOMICS money that you spend for rent, etc. to keep a business operating: *He's trying to lower our overhead.*

overhear /oʊvɚˈhɪr/ *v.* (past tense and past participle *overheard*) to hear by accident what other people are saying when they do not know that you are listening: *I overheard some people saying that the food was bad.*

overlap /ˌoʊvɚˈlæp/ *v.* (**overlapped, overlapping**) **1** if two or more things overlap, part of one thing covers part of another thing: *a pattern of overlapping circles* **2** if two subjects, activities ideas, etc. overlap, they share some but not all of the same parts or qualities: *Our jobs overlap in certain areas.* | *The study of history overlaps with the study of politics.* **- overlap** /ˈoʊvɚlæp / *n.*

overload /ˌoʊvɚˈloʊd/ *v.* **1** to load something with too many things or people: *Don't **overload** the washing machine **with** clothes.* **2** to give someone too much work to do **3** to damage an electrical system by causing too much electricity to flow through it **- overload** / ˈoʊvɚˌloʊd / *n.*

overlook /ˌoʊvɚˈlʊk/ *v.* **1** to not notice something, or to not realize how important it is: *It's easy to overlook mistakes when reading your own writing.* **2** to forgive someone's mistake, bad, behavior, etc: *I can't overlook his drinking any longer.* **3** to have a view of something from above: *Our room overlooked the beach.*

overly /ˈoʊvɚˌli/ *adv.* too much or very: *It is a problem but we are **not overly** concerned about it.*

overnight¹ /ˌoʊvɚˈnaɪt/ *adv.* **1** for or during the night: *She's **staying overnight** at a friend's house.* **2** (informal) suddenly: *You can't expect to lose weight overnight.*

overnight² /ˈoʊvɚˌnaɪt/ *adj.* [only before noun] continuing all night: *an overnight flight to Japan*

overpass /ˈoʊvɚˌpæs/ *n.* a structure like a bridge, that allows one road to go over another road

Different Meanings

Many words have more than one definition.

Look at the examples of the word *taste* on the dictionary page.

When the different definitions are different parts of speech, there are separate headings.

When the different definitions are the same part of speech, the definitions are numbered. The first definition is the most common.

To find the best definition for the word as it is used in a sentence follow these steps:

➤ Read the sentence. What part of speech is the word? Find the heading for that part of speech.

➤ If there is more than one definition under that part of speech, read the example sentences. Which definition makes the most sense in the sentence where you found the word?

taste¹ /teɪst/ *n.* **1** the feeling that is produced when your tongue touches a particular food or drink, for example how sweet it is: *I don't like the taste of garlic.* | *a bitter/sour/sweet, etc. taste* | *He no longer has any sense of taste or smell.* **2** the kind of things that someone likes: *We have similar tastes in clothes.* | *She never lost **her taste for** travel.* **3** your judgement when you choose clothes, decorations, etc.: *She has really good **taste in** music.* **4** a small amount of a food or drink, eaten to find out what it is like: *Here, **have a taste** and tell me what you think.* **5 be in good/bad/poor taste** to be appropriate or inappropriate for a particular occasion: *The joke was in very bad taste.* **6 a taste of sth** a short experience of something: *The trip gave us a taste of life on board a ship.*

taste² *v.* **1** to have a particular type of taste: *The chicken tastes really good.* | *This milk tastes a little sour.* ▸Don't say "is tasting."◂ | *What does the soup taste like?* (=how would you describe its taste)? **2** to put a small amount of food or drink in your mouth in order to find out what it is like: *Taste this and see if it needs more salt.* **3** to recognize the taste of a food or drink: *My cold's so bad I can't taste a thing.* ▸Don't say "I am not tasting."◂

EXAMPLE

Read each sentence and find the underlined word on the dictionary page above. Write the part of speech and the definition of the word in the sentence.

1. Alda <u>tasted</u> the Spanish cheese and the French cheese. She liked the French cheese better.

   Part of speech: *verb*

   Definition: *to put a small amount of food or drink in your mouth in order to find out what it is like*

2. Arlene never lost her <u>taste</u> for nice clothes.

   Part of speech: *noun*

   Definition: *the kind of things that someone likes*

EXERCISE 6

A. Read each sentence and find the underlined word on the dictionary page. Write the part of speech and the definition of the word in the sentence.

1. My teacher never lost <u>control</u> in class.
   Part of speech: _____
   Definition: _____
   _____

2. The rider could not <u>control</u> his horse.
   Part of speech: _____
   Definition: _____
   _____

3. On the old radios, there were few <u>controls</u>.
   Part of speech: _____
   Definition: _____
   _____

4. By midnight, the army <u>controlled</u> the streets.
   Part of speech: _____
   Definition: _____
   _____

5. The university was under the <u>control</u> of the students.
   Part of speech: _____
   Definition: _____
   _____

6. Javier was upset, but he was able to <u>control</u> himself.
   Part of speech: _____
   Definition: _____
   _____

---

control¹ /kənˈtroʊl/ *n.* **1** the power or ability to make someone or something do what you want: *They don't* **have** *any* **control over** *their son.* | *Newborn babies have little* **control of/over** *their movements.* | *The car went* **out of control** *and hit a tree.* | *The situation is now* **under control.** | *These events are* **beyond our control.** (= not possible for us to control). **2** the power to rule or govern a place, organization, or company: *Rioters* **took control of** *the prison.* | *The airport is now* **under the control of** *the UN troops.* | *The government is no longer* **in control of** *the country.* **3** an action, method, or law that limits the amount or growth of something: *an agreement on arms control* | *Fire fighters* **brought** *the fire* **under control** (= stopped it from getting worse). **4** the ability to remain calm even when you are angry or excited: *I just* **lost control** *and punched him!* **5** something that you use to make a television, machine, vehicle, etc. work: *the volume control* | *the controls of the airplane*

control² *v.* (**controlled, controlling**) **1** to make someone or something do what you want or work in a particular way: *If you can't control your dog, you should put it on a leash.* **2** to limit the amount of growth of something: *a chemical used to control weeds* **3** to rule or govern a place, organization, or company, or to have more power than someone else: *Rebels control all the roads into the capital.* **4** to make yourself behave calmly, even if you feel angry, excited, or upset: *I was furious, but I managed to control myself.*

B. Talk about your answers with another student. Are they the same?

Guidelines for Learning Vocabulary **37**

A. *Read each sentence and find the underlined word on the dictionary page. Write the part of speech and the definition of the word in the sentence.*

1. In English sentences, the <u>subject</u> usually comes before the verb.
   Part of speech: _____
   Definition: _____
   _____

2. The <u>subjects</u> of the experiment were all women with heart problems.
   Part of speech: _____
   Definition: _____
   _____

3. He liked all of his school <u>subjects</u> except chemistry.
   Part of speech: _____
   Definition: _____
   _____

4. The <u>subject</u> of the picture was the painter's mother.
   Part of speech: _____
   Definition: _____
   _____

5. The numbers in this report are <u>subject</u> to change.
   Part of speech: _____
   Definition: _____
   _____

6. When I asked Sam about his English test, he quickly changed the <u>subject</u>.
   Part of speech: _____
   Definition: _____
   _____

subject¹ /ˈsʌbdʒɪkt/ *n* **1** the thing you are talking about or considering in a conversation, discussion, book, movie etc: *Bashkiroff is the* **subject of** *the book, "For Sasha, With Love."* | *While we're* **on the subject of** *money, do you have $10 you owe me?* | *Stop trying to* **change the subject**. (= talk about something else) | *A member of the audience* **raised the subject** *of the president's age.* (=started talking about it) **2** something that you study at a school or university: *"What's your favorite subject?"* **"Science"** → UNIVERSITY **3** ENG. LANG. ARTS in grammar, a noun, noun phrase or pronoun that usually comes before the verb in a sentence, and represents the person or thing that does the action of the verb. In the sentence "Jean loves her cats," "Jean" is the subject. **4 subject matter** the subject that is being discussed in a book, shown in a movie or play, etc. **5** SCIENCE a person or animal that is used in a test or EXPERIMENT: *All the subjects were men between the ages of 18 and 25.* **6** ENG. LANG. ARTS the thing or person that is shown in a painting or photograph: *Degas frequently used dancers as his subjects.* **7** POLITICS someone who was born in a country that has a king or queen or someone who has the legal right to live there: *He's a British subject.*

subject² *adj.* **be subjected to sth a)** to be likely to be affected by something: *All prices are subject to change.* **b)** to be dependent on something: the deal is subject to approval by the bank. **c)** if you are subject to a law, you must obey it: *Congress is subject to the same laws as everyone else.*

B. *Talk about your answers with another student. Are they the same?*

How to Use the Word

The example phrases and sentences in dictionaries can tell you what words are often used together.

EXAMPLE
....

> **Look at the dictionary page in Exercise 7 on page 38. Read the example phrases and sentences. Then complete these sentences with the correct words.**
>
> Verbs or phrasal verbs (verbs + prepositions) that are used with the noun *subject*:
>
> a. Please don't <u>*change*</u> the subject every time I ask you about the money.
>
> b. Someone at the meeting <u>*raised*</u> that subject. But the president didn't let us talk about it.
>
> c. While we <u>*are on*</u> the subject of money, let's talk about our telephone bill.

EXERCISE 8

> **A. Look at the dictionary page on page 36. Read the example phrases and sentences. Then complete these sentences with the correct words. (In some sentences, more than one answer is possible.)**

1. Prepositions that are used with the noun *taste*:
   a. My mother doesn't like the taste _____ garlic.
   b. Mike's month in Moscow gave him a taste _____ life in Russia. But at the end of the month, he was glad to return home.
   c. My aunt never lost her taste _____ travel. She went to Mexico just a few months before she died.
   d. Many people lose their sense _____ taste when they get old.
   e. Joelle has good taste _____ clothes. She always looks nice.

2. Adjectives that can be used with the noun *taste*:
   a. This juice has a very _____ taste. What is it made of?
   b. Myra didn't like the iced tea they served at lunch. It had a very _____ taste.

c. The medicine had a _____ taste, so my mother put some sugar in it.

d. My friend Stacy and I have very _____ tastes in music. We both like the old Beatles songs.

e. She clearly has _____ taste in art. Her apartment is full of beautiful paintings.

f. The manager's words were in very _____ taste. Some people were very hurt by what he said.

B. *Talk about your answers with another student. Are they the same?*

EXERCISE 9

A. *Look at the dictionary page in Exercise 6 on page 37. Read the example phrases and sentences. Then complete these sentences with the correct words.*

1. Prepositions that are used with the noun *control:*

   a. They don't have control _____ their son.

   b. The car went _____ control and crashed into a tree.

   c. The situation is now quiet and _____ control.

   d. The government is no longer _____ control of the country.

   e. The airport is _____ the control of UN troops.

   f. The government said that events were _____ their control. There was nothing they could do.

2. Nouns or pronouns that are used after the verb *control:*

   a. He couldn't control the _____.

   b. They use a chemical to control the _____.

   c. The government soldiers now control _____.

   d. I managed to control _____.

B. *Talk about your answers with another student. Are they the same?*

Study Vocabulary Often

To learn words well, you need to see them and think about them many times. A vocabulary notebook and word study cards can help you remember new words and build your vocabulary.

Vocabulary Notebooks

Get a small notebook and use it only for vocabulary. Write new words in it every day or every week.

> ➤ Organize your notebook. Don't just write words as you find them. You need to put them in order, so you can find them later. For example, you can use alphabetical order, order by topic, or order by date.

> ➤ Write words you want to learn in your notebook:
>   • Write the word on the left page. Beside the word, write the part of speech.
>   • Below the word, write the sentence or sentences where you found it.
>   • Write the dictionary definition on the right page.

> ➤ Check the pronunciation of new words. Say the words and meanings aloud when you study them. This will help you remember them.

EXAMPLE

subject (noun)	something that you study at school or university
He liked all his subjects except chemistry.	

Using the Notebook for Review

To learn words well, you need to review them *often*. You should review them:
  • the same day you write them in your notebook
  • a day later
  • a week later
  • at the end of the month
  • at the end of the semester

When you review words in your notebook, follow these steps:

1. Cover the words and try to remember the definitions. Then cover the definitions and try to remember the words.
2. Make a mark beside words you don't remember. Review those words again.
3. Ask another student to test you:
    • Give the other student your notebook.
    • Tell him or her to ask you about words or definitions.
    • Write the answers. Did you remember them and write them correctly?

EXERCISE 10

A. *In your vocabulary notebook, write five new words you want to learn (from exercises in this unit, from other readings, or from class work).*

B. *Write the part of speech of each word and the sentence(s) where you found it.*

C. *Look up each word in the dictionary and write the definition.*

D. *Say the words and definitions to yourself. Then ask another student to test you.*

Study Cards

Make study cards and carry them with you. Review them often. Add new words that you want to learn. Take out cards when you have learned the words on them very well. You will need small cards (3 x 5 inches or 7 x 12 cm).

To review words with your study cards, follow these steps:

1. On one side of the card, write a word.
   Write the part of speech beside it.
   Below the word, write the sentence(s) where you found it.

EXAMPLE

subject (noun)

He liked all his subjects except chemistry.

2. On the other side of the card, write the definition of the word.

something that you study at school or university

3. Test yourself or ask another student to test you.

Using Study Cards for Review

Use the study cards in addition to your vocabulary notebook. Different students have different ways to use them. Find a way that is good for you. Here are some ideas:

➢ Use the cards for the words you have trouble remembering. At the end of each week, choose new words from your vocabulary notebook to write on your cards.

➢ Carry your cards with you all the time. Review them while you are waiting for class, while you are on the bus, before dinner, etc.

➢ When you make new cards, keep them all together in one pocket of a jacket or bag. When you know a word well, move that card to a different pocket. When all the cards are moved, review them again. If you know them all well again, make new cards.

EXERCISE 11

A. *On five study cards, write five words you want to learn. (You can use the same words as in Exercise 10 or different ones.)*

B. *Write the sentence(s) where you found the words.*

C. *Look up the words in the dictionary and write the definitions.*

D. *Review your cards. Then ask another student to test you.*

Learning New Words from Your Reading

You will find many new words when you are reading. You can't learn all of them—there are too many! You need to decide which words to learn.

Choosing Words to Learn

The rules for choosing words are simple:

➢ Learn the words that are used most often.
  These are listed in the Appendix (the 1,000 Most Frequent Words in English) on page 293. If you know these words, you will understand better when you read.

➢ Learn the words that will be useful for you:
  • words you need to know in order to understand a passage
  • words you have seen before and think you will meet again
  • words that are connected to your school subjects, your interests, or your job

EXAMPLES
. . . .

• In a newspaper article about a soccer game, you find the word *defeat* several times. It's on the list of the 1,000 Most Frequent Words. Look it up and learn it.

• In the same article, you find the word *injury*. It tells about something that happened to a soccer player. It's not on the list of the 1,000 Most Frequent Words. But you often read articles about soccer, and you've seen this word before. Look it up and learn it.

• In a passage about business in a textbook, you find the word *income*. It's not on the list, but there is a whole page about this topic. Look it up and learn it.

• In a magazine article about a film, you find the word *inadequate*. It's not on the list, and you only see it once. You can understand that it means something bad about the film. You don't need to look it up.

Guidelines for Choosing Words from Your Reading

Follow these guidelines to choose words to learn:

1. Read the passage to the end. Don't stop to look up new words.

2. Read the passage again and underline the new words.

3. Look for the new words in the Appendix on page 293. If you find a word on the list, circle it in the passage.

4. If you don't find a word on the list, think about the word. Is it useful? Ask yourself: *Have I seen or heard this word before? Is it related to my schoolwork, interests, or job? Do I need to know it to understand the passage?* If so, circle the word in the passage.

5. Look up all the circled words in the dictionary. Then write them in your vocabulary notebook. Write the parts of speech, the sentences where you found them, and the definitions.

EXAMPLE

A. *Read the passage to the end. Don't stop to look up new words.*

Reducing Stress

Everyday life can be full of <u>stress</u>. There are many possible causes: work or family problems, exams at school, <u>traffic</u>, or noise. This stress can have many bad <u>effects</u> on your <u>body</u> and <u>mind</u>. It can make you unhappy and even ill.

What can you do to <u>reduce</u> stress? <u>Psychologists</u> say that the most important
5   thing is not to get angry or <u>upset</u> about something. Instead you should try to <u>laugh</u>. If you can make a <u>joke</u> and laugh, you'll feel better. In fact, doctors say that laughter is good for your <u>mental</u> <u>health</u>. It makes your body stronger, too, so you are less <u>likely</u> to get sick.

Another way to <u>reduce</u> stress is to do something you <u>enjoy</u>. It doesn't matter
10   what activity you choose. Some people relax by watching a movie, others by playing basketball or cooking a nice dinner. According to doctors, even a very small amount of enjoyment can help. If you like chocolate, for example, you should eat a small piece when you feel stressed.

B. *Read the passage again. Do you know the underlined words?*

C. *On the lines below, write the underlined words you don't know. Look for the words on page 293. Circle the words below that are on the list.*

_____

_____

D. *Think about the underlined words you didn't find on the list. Are they useful for you? (See guideline number 4 on page 45.) Circle the words you want to learn. Then show them to your teacher.*

E. *Look up all the circled words from part C. Write the words in your vocabulary notebook with the parts of speech, the sentences where you found them, and the definitions.*

Remember

When you write a word in your vocabulary notebook, you should also write:
- the part of speech
- the sentence where you found the word
- the definition for the word in that sentence

EXERCISE 1

A. *Read the passage to the end.*

Pets for Better Health

If an animal can be a pet, someone has it in the United States. Today 61 percent of American families own pets. The most common animals are cats and dogs, of course. But people keep all kinds of other animals, from birds to mice, goats, rabbits, turtles, and even snakes.

5 Why do so many people have pets? According to psychologists, the main reason is loneliness. In the United States today, people are often very alone. Many people live by themselves, with no family nearby. They often change jobs and move to new neighborhoods, which means they don't develop close relationships with their coworkers or their neighbors. But people need company, and they need
10 someone to love. A pet can fill that need.

In fact, pets are good for people's mental health. Pet owners often develop close relationships with their animals. According to one study, 99 percent of dog and cat owners talk to their pets. For many people, their pet is like a member of the family. They keep pictures of their pets with them. They have parties on their
15 pets' birthdays.

Doctors say that pets are also good for people's physical health. Pet owners have lower heart rates and blood pressure. Studies show that they live better and longer than people who live alone.

B. *Read the passage again and underline the new words.*

C. *Look for the new words on page 293. Circle the words that are on the list.*

D. *Think about the underlined words you didn't find on the list. Are they useful? (See guideline number 4 on page 45.) Circle the words you want to learn. Then show them to your teacher.*

E. *Look up all the circled words in the dictionary. Write them in your vocabulary notebook.*

EXERCISE 2

A. *Read the passage to the end.*

The Common Cold

Around the world, mothers tell their children, "Dress warmly or you'll catch a cold." This is a common belief. But is it true? Can cold weather cause a cold?

The answer is basically no. Colds are caused by viruses. A cold always comes—directly or indirectly—from another person with the virus. However,
5 there is a connection with the weather. In fact, you are more likely to catch a cold in the winter. One reason is that windows are closed, which makes it easier for the cold virus to spread from one person to another. Another reason is that the body prefers to stay warm. If you get cold—particularly your feet—your body can't fight viruses as well, and you are more likely to get sick.

10 There is no sure way to prevent a cold, but you can reduce the number of colds you catch. The most important thing is to wash your hands often. Wash them before you eat. Wash them every time you come home from school or from work. And when your hands aren't clean, don't touch your mouth, nose, or eyes.

If you do catch a cold, you should be careful not to spread it. Try not to sneeze
15 or cough onto other people, into the air, or into your hands. If your hands have the virus on them, you will leave it on everything you touch. Instead, you should sneeze or cough into a tissue that you throw away.

B. *Read the passage again and underline the new words.*

C. *Look for the new words on page 293. Circle the words that are on the list.*

D. *Think about the underlined words you didn't find on the list. Are they useful? Circle the words you want to learn. Then show them to your teacher.*

E. *Look up the circled words in the dictionary. Write them in your vocabulary notebook.*

A. *Read the passage to the end.*

Flight Risks

In many ways, traveling is much easier and faster than it was in the past. But traveling fast doesn't always mean traveling in comfort. For many people, long plane flights are unpleasant. For some people, flying can even be dangerous. Why? Because passengers in planes have to sit still.

5 In fact, doctors say that sitting still for a long time is not good for you. When you sit still for many hours, your blood doesn't flow well, especially in your legs. When the blood stops flowing well, you may get a blood clot in your leg. This can be painful. It can also have more serious effects on your health. If the blood clot breaks up, the small clots can then travel to other parts of the body. If they get

10 into the lungs, the heart, or the brain, there is risk of death.

Fortunately there are simple ways to prevent that. First, before you go on a long flight, you should talk to your doctor. If you have a high risk of blood clots, you should wear special stockings on your legs. Second, you should try to keep your blood flowing well during a long flight. You can get up now and then

15 and walk down the aisle. You can also do exercises at your seat. Many airline companies now show videos that explain how to do these exercises. They are just simple movements of the arms, legs, and head, but they help the blood flow better.

B. *Read the passage again and underline the new words.*

C. *Look for the new words on page 293. Circle the words that are on the list.*

D. *Think about the underlined words you didn't find on the list. Are they useful? Circle the words you want to learn. Then show them to your teacher.*

E. *Look up the circled words in the dictionary. Write them in your vocabulary notebook.*

A. *Read the passage to the end.*

Europeans Stand Tall

Who are the tallest people on Earth? For most of the 20th century, American men and women could look down on everyone else. But in the 1970s, people in northern Europe began to grow taller. They reached the same height as

Americans and then grew taller. Now the Dutch are the tallest in the world,
5   followed by the Norwegians and the Danes. Why is this? Why did Americans
stop growing? There are two possible reasons.

According to scientists, one reason is related to diet. In the 1980s, Americans
began to eat a lot of meat and a lot of junk food. This is still true today. Many
Americans, especially young people, don't eat a healthy diet. Their bodies don't
10   get the vitamins and minerals that they need. On the other hand, they get a lot
of unhealthy sugar and fat. Not surprisingly, many Americans are overweight and
have health problems. Compared with Americans, Europeans generally have a
healthier diet. They eat less meat and less junk food, and they eat more fruit and
vegetables.

15   The other reason why Europeans are taller is because they get better health
care. In the United States, the health care system is private, and it's very expensive.
Because of this, many people who need medical care don't get it. Pregnant women
and children often don't get good care. In Europe, the health care system is
public. Doctors' visits are free and there are many free health services for families,
20   especially for pregnant women and children. This has generally helped Europeans
to stay healthier—and grow taller.

B. *Read the passage again and underline the new words.*

C. *Look for the new words on page 293. Circle the words that are on the list.*

D. *Think about the underlined words you didn't find on the list. Are they useful?
Circle the words you want to learn. Then show them to your teacher.*

E. *Look up the circled words in the dictionary. Write them in your vocabulary
notebook.*

EXERCISE 5

A. *Look in your vocabulary notebook. Choose ten words from this unit. Write
them on study cards. Follow the directions in Part 2, Unit 1, on page 41.*

B. *Review the words and test yourself with your cards.*

C. *Now give your cards to another student. Ask him or her to test you.*

Remember

When you are reading, follow the guidelines for learning new words. Use your
vocabulary notebook and study cards.

Guessing Meaning from Context

Learning about Context

What Is Context?

It is the sentence or sentences around a word.

From the context, you can learn a lot about a word.
- You can learn the part of speech.
- You can often understand the general meaning.

PRACTICE
·············

Read the sentences below. Write the part of speech of the missing word** (noun, verb, adjective, adverb, or preposition). **Then complete the sentence with a word from the box.

neighbor	shoe	near	remember	pretty	watch

Last week was Henry's birthday. He was twenty-one years old. His mother made him a chocolate cake, and his girlfriend bought him a new _____.

Part of speech of missing word: _____

Explanation
- Only a noun can follow the words *bought him a new*.
- The nouns in the box are *neighbor, shoe,* and *watch*.
- You need to choose a word that means something you might buy for a birthday present. You can't buy a neighbor, and you can't buy only one shoe. The best answer is *watch*.

A. *Read the sentences below. Write the parts of speech of the missing words. Then complete the sentences with words from the box.*

| read | small | money | grandmother | with | learned |

1. Oprah Winfrey is a successful actress and TV producer, and the first African-American billionaire in the United States. She was born in Kosciusko, Mississippi, a _____ town in America's south.

   Part of speech of missing word: _____

2. Her parents separated when she was a small child. For her first five years, she lived with her _____.

   Part of speech of missing word: _____

3. The family was very poor. Her grandmother never had much _____. But there were always some books in the house.

   Part of speech of missing word: _____

4. At a very young age, Oprah _____ to read. She often read aloud to her grandmother.

   Part of speech of missing word: _____

5. Her love of books stayed with her all her life. She believes that her ability to _____ well was a big help in her career.

   Part of speech of missing word: _____

6. When she was six years old, Oprah was sent to live _____ her mother in Milwaukee, Wisconsin.

   Part of speech of missing word: _____

B. *Talk about your answers with another student. Are they the same?*

A. *Read the passage to the end. Think about the part of speech of each missing word. Then complete the passage with words from the box.*

best	easy	got	out	report	sent
different	freedom	lot	ran	rules	young

Oprah's Childhood

Oprah's mother was very poor and uneducated, and Oprah was unhappy with her. At the age of thirteen, Oprah _____ away from home. The police
found her and _____ her to a special home for _____ people.
Then they _____ in touch with her father, Vernon Winfrey, and she
went to live with him in Nashville, Tennessee.

Life with her father was not _____ for Oprah. He was very
_____ from her mother. In his house, Oprah didn't have much
_____. Her father made her follow many _____. For example,
she wasn't allowed to go _____ in the evening. Instead, she had to do
schoolwork. She also had to read a _____. Every week, she had to read
a book for her father and write a _____ about it. He wanted her to do
her _____. And she did. She was an honors student and also the most
popular girl in her class.

B. *Talk about your answers with another student. Are they the same?*

A. *Read the passage to the end. Think about the part of speech of each missing word. Then write one word for each blank. (There is more than one possible answer.)*

Oprah's Success

At age 18, Oprah started her first job at a radio station. She also received a full scholarship to Tennessee State University. The next year, she went to _____ 1 _____ for a Nashville TV station. She _____ 2 _____ their youngest news anchor (TV news announcer). After she graduated from college, she

5   _____ 3 _____ a job at a big TV station. The _____ 4 _____ year, she began her own show, the *Oprah Winfrey Show.* It was a great success right away.

She also acted in television _____ 5 _____ and in several movies. In 1984, she started a production _____ 6 _____ and called it HARPO (HARPO = OPRAH backwards).

10   More than twenty years later, Oprah's show and her company continue to be _____ 7 _____. She also produces a very popular magazine for women. Oprah is now _____ 8 _____ and famous, but she remembers that she used to be _____ 9 _____. Every year she gives a _____ 10 _____ amount of money to people who help others. She also remembers how important _____ 11 _____ were

15   for her. In 2000, she started the Oprah Book Club, in order to get people to read more. In _____ 12 _____, millions of people read the books she talks about.

B. *Talk about your answers with another student. Are they the same?*

Guessing the Meaning of Words

The context around a word can help you guess the meaning. You may only be able to guess the general meaning, but that may be enough to understand the passage.

In the context, you may find:
- information about the word
- a word that has a similar meaning
- a word that has the opposite meaning (for example: long/short, new/old)

> **Note:** In these exercises, you will find the following parts of speech:
> *noun, verb, adjective,* or *adverb.*

PRACTICE

Read the sentences. Write the part of speech and the general meaning of each underlined word. Use the context to help you.

1. Last winter there was a big storm with lots of snow. A big old tree came down on the stone wall. Now there is a <u>gap</u> in the wall. The neighbor's dog comes into our garden all the time.

    Part of speech: _____

    General meaning: _____

    Explanation
    - It's a noun.
    - It's something that happens when a tree falls on a stone wall.
    - When there's a gap in a wall, animals can cross it more easily.

2. Mrs. Sweeney was ready to <u>retire</u> from her job. She was sixty-five years old. She was tired of working, and she wanted to have more time for herself at home.

    Part of speech: _____

    General meaning: _____

    Explanation
    - It's a verb.
    - You use it with the word *job.*
    - The meaning is similar to *have more time for herself at home.*
    - It means the opposite of *working.*

A. Read the sentences. Write the part of speech and the general meaning of each underlined word. Use the context to help you.

1. My mother is an <u>absentminded</u> person. She is always thinking about something else, so she often doesn't pay attention to things. One day, she went to work with two different shoes on!

   Part of speech: _____

   General meaning: _____

2. When the war started in Vietnam, many people left the country. Hundreds of thousands of them were <u>refugees</u> in Thailand. They had to live in big camps, and life was very hard for them.

   Part of speech: _____

   General meaning: _____

3. In American restaurants, you should leave a <u>tip</u> for the waiter. It's not included in the price of the meal. Most people leave between 15 and 20 percent of their total bill.

   Part of speech: _____

   General meaning: _____

4. We brought our boat into the <u>harbor</u> before the storm. It was a small harbor, crowded with other boats. But here the boat was safe from the strong winds.

   Part of speech: _____

   General meaning: _____

5. George likes to <u>boast</u> about his tennis. He says he can beat any of us! Next week I'm going to play him. I'll find out if he's really so good.

   Part of speech: _____

   General meaning: _____

B. Talk about your answers with another student. Are they the same?

C. Look up the words in a dictionary. Are your answers close to the dictionary definitions? Correct your answers if necessary. Then check your answers with your teacher.

A. *Read the sentences. Write the part of speech and the general meaning of each underlined word. Use the context to help you.*

1. You can get to Mercer Island by small boat taxis or by <u>ferry</u>. The ferry can also carry cars. In good weather, it takes about half an hour.

   Part of speech: _____

   General meaning: _____

2. Jimmy's medicine had a <u>nasty</u> taste. He took it the first time, but he didn't want to take it again. His mother had to put some sugar in it.

   Part of speech: _____

   General meaning: _____

3. George was standing by the door. He was very tired, so he started to <u>lean</u> against it. Suddenly, the door opened, and George almost fell down.

   Part of speech: _____

   General meaning: _____

4. Running is one of the cheapest sports. You can run anywhere, and you don't have to buy expensive <u>equipment</u>. All you need is a good pair of shoes.

   Part of speech: _____

   General meaning: _____

5. During the soccer game, Ruben ran into another player, and they both fell. The other player got up quickly, but Ruben stayed on the ground. He <u>was groaning</u> and holding his knee.

   Part of speech: _____

   General meaning: _____

B. *Talk about your answers with another student. Are they the same?*

C. *Look up the words in a dictionary. Are your answers close to the dictionary definitions? Correct your answers if necessary. Then check your answers with your teacher.*

A. *Read the sentences. Write the part of speech and the general meaning of each underlined word. Use the context to help you.*

1. Sondra didn't understand everything the man said. He was speaking too quickly. But she got the <u>gist</u>. She understood that she'd better leave because it was dangerous there.

   Part of speech: _____

   General meaning: _____

2. I sat down on the grass to rest. Then I felt something on my leg. It was a little black <u>ant</u>. There were a lot of them running all over my socks.

   Part of speech: _____

   General meaning: _____

3. A lot of ancient Greek art shows <u>naked</u> men and women. The Greeks believed that the human body was beautiful. They showed it in their art.

   Part of speech: _____

   General meaning: _____

4. When the wolf caught a deer, it <u>struggled</u> to get free. But the wolf was too strong. In a short time, the deer was dead, and the wolf was eating it.

   Part of speech: _____

   General meaning: _____

5. In old houses, you often find only one or two <u>outlets</u> in each room. New buildings usually have many more because people today have lots of electrical things.

   Part of speech: _____

   General meaning: _____

B. *Talk about your answers with another student. Are they the same?*

C. *Look up the words in a dictionary. Are your answers close to the dictionary definitions? Correct your answers if necessary. Then check your answers with your teacher.*

Guessing the Meaning of Phrases

The following exercises include some phrases. Phrases are groups of words that work together. You should read them the same way you read single words. (See Part 2, Unit 5, page 70.)

Note: In these exercises, the phrases work just like single words in the sentences. Think about the part of speech the same way you do for a single word.

EXAMPLE

1. I <u>found out</u> that the train leaves at nine o'clock.

   Part of speech: *verb*

   General meaning: *learned*

2. The birds flew away, <u>one by one.</u>

   Part of speech: *adverb*

   General meaning: *first one, then another*

EXERCISE 7

A. **Read the sentences. Write the part of speech and the general meaning of each underlined word or phrase. Use the context to help you.**

1. This morning, as usual, I brought my cup of coffee to my room. As I was going upstairs, I somehow missed a step. I didn't fall down, but the coffee <u>spilled</u> all over the stairs.

   Part of speech: _____

   General meaning: _____

2. When children have problems at school, teachers alone can't do much. Teachers and parents need to work <u>side by side</u>. Then it may be possible to help the children with their problems.

   Part of speech: _____

   General meaning: _____

3. "Well," said Sara to her brother. "I <u>see your point</u>. Maybe you're right. You know more about this than I do. I'll wait until next week to decide."

Part of speech: _____

General meaning: _____

4. The firefighters arrived <u>promptly</u> and put out the fire. Fortunately, there was very little damage. We had to get a new stove, but everything else was okay.

Part of speech: _____

General meaning: _____

5. Every year thousands of people <u>set off</u> in boats from northern Africa. They hope to reach Europe. Sometimes they get to Spain or Italy, but often they meet bad weather and never get there.

Part of speech: _____

General meaning: _____

6. My grandmother didn't have an easy life. Her husband died in the war, and she had three small children to <u>bring up</u>. She worked hard for many years.

Part of speech: _____

General meaning: _____

B. *Talk about your answers with another student. Are they the same?*

C. *Look up the words and phrases in a dictionary. Are your answers close to the dictionary definitions? Correct your answers if necessary. Then check your answers with your teacher.*

EXERCISE 8

A. *Read the sentences. Write the part of speech and the general meaning of each underlined word or phrase. Use the context to help you.*

1. The exam had some difficult parts, but <u>on the whole</u> it wasn't very hard. Tamara finished early and checked all her answers.

Part of speech: _____

General meaning: _____

2. There was a large pot on the stove. Ivan lifted the <u>lid</u> to see what was cooking. It was a whole chicken, and it smelled wonderful. There was some rice in another pot and a salad on the table.

   Part of speech: _____

   General meaning: _____

3. Suki <u>burst into tears</u> when her boyfriend left. I tried to talk with her, but she only cried harder. She was afraid she might never see him again.

   Part of speech: _____

   General meaning: _____

4. We usually fly with Lufthansa airlines. The planes are on time, and the <u>flight attendants</u> are always nice. They really try to make you feel comfortable on the plane.

   Part of speech: _____

   General meaning: _____

5. When she was in Russia, Marnie <u>came down with</u> a bad flu. For weeks afterwards, she had a bad cough and she felt unwell.

   Part of speech: _____

   General meaning: _____

6. Do you know where John is? Is he on vacation? I really need to <u>get hold of</u> him. There's a problem at work, and he's the only one who can help.

   Part of speech: _____

   General meaning: _____

B. *Talk about your answers with another student. Are they the same?*

C. *Look up the words and phrases in a dictionary. Are your answers close to the dictionary definitions? Correct your answers if necessary. Then check your answers with your teacher.*

Word Parts

Words are often made of different parts. If you know the meaning of some of the parts, you can better understand the meaning of the whole word.

The **root** is the most important part of a word.
    Example: pleasant

A **prefix** is a part added before the root.
    Example: *un* + pleasant = unpleasant

A **suffix** is a part added after the root.
    Example: pleasant + *ly* = pleasantly

Prefixes

A prefix before the root changes the meaning of the word.

EXAMPLE

unpleasant

Prefix: ___*un-*___   Meaning of prefix: ___*not*___

Root: ___*pleasant*___   Meaning of root with prefix: ___*not pleasant*___

> **Note:** There are many prefixes that mean *not*.
> **Examples:** *dis-, im-, non-, un-*
> Sometimes a hyphen (-) is put between the prefix and the root.
> **Examples:** non-native, pre-existing

A. *These words have two parts: a prefix and a root. Write the prefix and its meaning from the box. Then write the roots. (The meaning* not *is used more than once.)*

Prefixes						Meanings			
dis-	non-	un-	mis-	pre-	under-	bad/badly	before/earlier	lower/less	not

1. unpaid   uncover   uncertain   unreal   unwelcome

   Prefix: _____   Meaning of prefix: _____

   Roots: _____

2. underage   undercharge   underpaid   undercooked   undergraduate

   Prefix: _____   Meaning of prefix: _____

   Roots: _____

3. misfortune   misuse   misstep   misadventure   mislead

   Prefix: _____   Meaning of prefix: _____

   Roots: _____

4. preview   prewar   predate   precondition   preheat

   Prefix: _____   Meaning of prefix: _____

   Roots: _____

5. disorganized   disappear   dislike   disable   dishonor

   Prefix: _____   Meaning of prefix: _____

   Roots: _____

6. nonsense   nonfat   non-native   nonpayment   nonfiction

Prefix: _____   Meaning of prefix: _____

Roots: _____

B. *Talk about your answers with another student. Are they the same?*

C. *Look up the meaning of any new words. Write them in your vocabulary notebook.*

EXERCISE 2

A. *These words have two parts: a prefix and a root. Write the prefix and its meaning from the box. Then write the roots. (The meaning **not** is used more than once.)*

Prefixes						Meanings				
dis-	re-	mis-	pre-	in-	out-	not	badly	before/earlier	outside	again

1. indirect   incomplete   inexpensive   inactive   independent

Prefix: _____   Meaning of prefix: _____

Roots: _____

2. reread   review   reappear   redo   recount

Prefix: _____   Meaning of prefix: _____

Roots: _____

3. misprint   misfit   misplace   misread   misjudge

Prefix: _____   Meaning of prefix: _____

Roots: _____

4. prehistoric   prepaid   preteen   pre-existing   prearrange

Prefix: _____   Meaning of prefix: _____

Roots: _____

5. discontinue   disagree   disadvantage   disconnect   disorder

Prefix: _____   Meaning of prefix: _____

Roots: _____

6. outdoors   outhouse   outlaw   outsource   outspoken

Prefix: _____   Meaning of prefix: _____

Roots: _____

B. **Talk about your answers with another student. Are they the same?**

C. **Look up the meaning of any new words. Write them in your vocabulary notebook.**

Suffixes

A suffix after the root usually changes the part of speech of a word, and it sometimes changes the meaning.

EXAMPLE
....

pleasantly

Suffix: _-ly_____   Root: _pleasant_____

Part of speech: root: _adjective____   root with suffix: _adverb_____

> **Notes:** Sometimes the spelling of the root changes when you add a suffix.
> **Example:** happy + *ness* → happiness (y → i)
> Some suffixes don't change the part of speech. They change the meaning.
> **Example:** small + *er* → smaller (both adjectives, smaller = more small)

A. *These words have two parts: a root and a suffix. Write the suffix from the box. Then write the roots and the part of speech.*

Suffixes
-er   -est   -ful   -less   -ly   -ness

1. sweetly   safely   seriously   simply   strangely

   Suffix: _____   Roots: _____

   Part of speech   root: _____   root with suffix: _____

2. highest   closest   fullest   simplest   cheapest

   Suffix: _____   Roots: _____

   Part of speech   root: _____   root with suffix: _____

3. wonderful   powerful   successful   thoughtful   hopeful

   Suffix: _____   Roots: _____

   Part of speech   root: _____   root with suffix: _____

4. thinness   openness   stillness   sickness   softness

   Suffix: _____   Roots: _____

   Part of speech   root: _____   root with suffix: _____

5. hunter   builder   owner   singer   speaker

   Suffix: _____   Roots: _____

   Part of speech   root: _____   root with suffix: _____

6. lifeless   powerless   useless   hopeless   sleepless

   Suffix: _____   Roots: _____

   Part of speech   root: _____   root with suffix: _____

B. *Talk about your answers with another student. Are they the same?*

C. *Look up the meaning of any new words. Write them in your vocabulary notebook.*

EXERCISE 4

A. *These words have two parts: a root and a suffix. Write the suffix from the box. Then write the roots and the part of speech.*

Suffixes
–able   –ize   –ful   –less   –ly   –tion

1. youthful   lawful   peaceful   restful   truthful

   Suffix: _____   Roots: _____

   Part of speech   root: _____   root with suffix: _____

2. addition   operation   prevention   introduction   reservation

   Suffix: _____   Roots: _____

   Part of speech   root: _____   root with suffix: _____

3. usable   enjoyable   noticeable   valuable   likable

   Suffix: _____   Roots: _____

   Part of speech   root: _____   root with suffix: _____

4. rightly   naturally   politely   hopefully   heavily

   Suffix: _____   Roots: _____

   Part of speech   root: _____   root with suffix: _____

5. careless   thoughtless   restless   helpless   nameless

   Suffix: _____   Roots: _____

   Part of speech   root: _____   root with suffix: _____

6. generalize   modernize   realize   personalize   industrialize

Suffix: _____   Roots: _____

Part of speech   root: _____   root with suffix: _____

B. *Talk about your answers with another student. Are they the same?*

C. *Look up the meaning of any new words. Write them in your vocabulary notebook.*

Word Families

A word family is a group of words with the same root. They all belong to the same "family" of meaning, but they are different parts of speech.

EXAMPLE

Noun	Verb	Adjective	Adverb
wonder	wonder	wonderful	wonderfully

The parts of speech in a word family may be formed in different ways, for example:
- With a suffix: wonder + ful → wonderful
- With a prefix: a + live → alive
- By changing the root: strong → strength

> **Note:** The same word form can sometimes be more than one part of speech.
>
>   **Example:** *wonder* (noun and verb)
>
> Some word families have more than one adjective or noun form. Each form has a different meaning.
>
>   **Example:** *useful, useless* (adjectives)
>
> You may not find all the parts of speech in every word family.

EXERCISE 5

A. *Work with another student. Write the* **adverb** *and* **noun** *forms for each adjective. Don't use a dictionary. If you don't know a form, make a guess.*

Adjective	Adverb	Noun
1. strange	_____	_____
2. pleasant	_____	_____
3. warm	_____	_____
4. interesting	_____	_____
5. strong	_____	_____
6. high	_____	_____
7. true	_____	_____
8. serious	_____	_____
9. short	_____	_____
10. wide	_____	_____

B. *Check your work in the dictionary. Correct your answers if necessary. Write any new words in your vocabulary notebook.*

EXERCISE 6

A. *Work with another student. Write the* **adjective** *and* **adverb** *forms for each noun. Don't use a dictionary. If you don't know a form, make a guess.*

Noun	Adjective	Adverb
1. power	_____	_____
2. life	_____	_____
3. youth	_____	_____
4. direction	_____	_____
5. question	_____	_____
6. peace	_____	_____
7. difference	_____	_____
8. play	_____	_____
9. fortune	_____	_____
10. hope	_____	_____

B. *Check your work in the dictionary. Correct your answers if necessary. Write any new words in your vocabulary notebook.*

A. **Work with another student. Write the adjective and adverb forms for each verb. Don't use a dictionary. If you don't know a form, make a guess.**

Verb	Adjective	Adverb
1. fear	_____	_____
2. act	_____	_____
3. help	_____	_____
4. continue	_____	_____
5. notice	_____	_____
6. complete	_____	_____
7. agree	_____	_____
8. love	_____	_____
9. surprise	_____	_____
10. fill	_____	_____

B. **Check your work in the dictionary. Correct your answers if necessary. Write any new words in your vocabulary notebook.**

A. **Work with another student. Write the missing forms for each word. Don't use a dictionary. If you don't know a form, make a guess.**

Noun	Verb	Adjective	Adverb
1. _____	think	_____	_____
2. success	_____	_____	_____
3. _____	_____	general	_____
4. _____	_____	_____	really
5. _____	_____	separate	_____
6. _____	_____	special	_____
7. difference	_____	_____	_____
8. _____	open	_____	_____
9. _____	_____	simple	_____
10. rest	_____	_____	_____

B. **Check your work in the dictionary. Correct your answers if necessary. Write any new words in your vocabulary notebook.**

How Words Are Used Together

People often use certain words together in phrases. When you are reading, you will understand better if you can recognize common phrases quickly.

Common Types of Phrases

Verb + (adjective) + noun:
Do you know how to <u>ride a horse</u>?
<u>Have a good time</u> at the party!

Verb + adjective/adverb:
He <u>got sick</u> last weekend.
Please <u>leave me alone</u>.

Adjective + noun:
Every morning I drink a cup of <u>strong tea</u>.
There's often <u>live music</u> at the café.

Noun + preposition + noun:
Would you like <u>a glass of water</u>?
<u>A lot of people</u> read his blog.

Phrasal verb (verb + preposition):
I'll <u>pick up</u> a DVD on my way home.
He <u>put off</u> doing his homework until Sunday evening.

Prepositional phrase:
<u>At the top of</u> the hill, there was a nice view.
I'll be ready <u>in an hour</u>.

Adverbial phrase:
It rained <u>day after day</u>.
She was <u>all alone</u> in a new country.

Phrases in Different Languages

Different languages often put words together in different ways. Think about your language:

How do you say *pick up*?
Do you use a verb with a preposition as in English?

How do you say *ride a horse*? *ride a bicycle*? *drive a car*?
Do you use the same or different verbs?

A. *Think about the phrases in these sentences. How do you say them in your language? Write the phrase in your language. If you don't know the meaning, check with your teacher.*

Phrase in English	Phrase in Your Language
1. Did you <u>feed the cat</u> this morning?	_____
2. I <u>looked it up</u> in the dictionary.	_____
3. She's coming <u>in a minute</u>.	_____
4. He has <u>big plans</u> for his son.	_____
5. The car <u>broke down</u> again.	_____
6. It was the first time <u>in years</u>.	_____
7. Maria didn't like it <u>at all</u>.	_____
8. He was <u>on his feet</u> all day.	_____

B. *Talk about the phrases with another student. Answer these questions:*

• If you and your partner speak the same language, look at the phrases you wrote. Are they the same?

• If you speak different languages, talk about the phrases in your language. Are they like English or not?

C. *Are any of the phrases in English new for you? Write the new phrases in your vocabulary notebook.*

Choosing Phrases to Learn

There are many, many phrases in English. Since you can't learn all of them, you must decide which ones to learn. As with single words, you should learn the phrases that are most common.

Before you try to learn a group of words, ask yourself these questions:
- Is it a phrase? Think about the words or look in a dictionary.
- Are the words often used together?
- Do they have a special meaning when they are used together?

> **Example:** Every morning, I drink a cup of strong tea.
> *Strong tea* is a phrase. The words are often used together. They mean "dark tea."
> *Drink a* is not a phrase. The words are often used together, but they don't have any meaning without the rest of the sentence.

- If it is a phrase, is it common? Look it up in the dictionary. If you find it in a learner's dictionary, it is probably a common phrase.

Note: Dictionaries usually list phrases under the noun or verb from the phrase.

Examples: ride a motorcycle → *ride*   at the top → *top*

feel better → *feel*   day after day → *after*

strong tea → *strong*   in fact → *fact*

pick up → *pick (up)*   a lot of → *lot*

- You won't find all common phrases in the dictionary. If you don't find one, look for one that is similar. Then try to guess the meaning.
- If you are not sure about the meaning of a phrase, check with your teacher.
- In some dictionaries, phrasal verbs are listed separately from the verbs. In others, they are listed together.

In each sentence, a group of words is underlined. Is it a phrase?

1. She traveled <u>around the world</u> for her job.   Yes _____ No _____

2. They got <u>lost on</u> the way home.   Yes _____ No _____

Explanation
- *Around the world* is a phrase. The words have a special meaning when they are used together.
- The words *lost on* do not have any meaning without the rest of the sentence. It is not a phrase.

EXERCISE 2

A. *In each sentence, a group of words is underlined. Is it a phrase? If you aren't sure, make a guess.*

1. She <u>makes a living</u> as a musician.   Yes _____ No _____

2. Some of my friends play <u>music in</u> a band.   Yes _____ No _____

3. There were flies <u>all over</u> the place.   Yes _____ No _____

4. Pat <u>fell in love</u> with the little grey cat.   Yes _____ No _____

5. The teacher <u>handed out</u> the test to the students.   Yes _____ No _____

6. We couldn't see <u>anything because</u> of the heavy rain.   Yes _____ No _____

7. Small children don't like to <u>sit still</u>.   Yes _____ No _____

8. Fresh <u>vegetables are</u> good for you.   Yes _____ No _____

9. Last <u>week the teacher</u> gave us a lot of homework.   Yes _____ No _____

10. She <u>changed her mind</u> many times.   Yes _____ No _____

B. *Talk about your answers with another student. Are they the same? Check your answers in the dictionary.*

C. *Choose five phrases to learn from part A. Write them in your vocabulary notebook.*

A. *In each sentence, underline a phrasal verb from the box. (The verb may be in a different form: bring up → brought up.)*

> find out   make up   set up   throw away
> give up   point out take over   work out

1. Yesterday I threw away a lot of old school papers.
2. Javier and his friend set up a business on the Internet.
3. My father pointed out the distant tower.
4. He gave up without a fight when his father said no.
5. When Ahmed died, his wife, Asha, took over the business.
6. The teacher never found out about the missing books.
7. Fortunately things worked out very well for Jonas.
8. Ron made up a long story to explain why he was late.

B. *Complete each sentence with a phrasal verb from the box in part A. You may use each one only once. (You may need to change the form of the verb.)*

1. Mina _____ trying to learn Russian. It was too difficult.
2. I don't like to _____ food. There are so many hungry people in the world.
3. The university _____ a new program in public health.
4. Peter didn't always follow the written music. He often _____ his own songs.
5. Their relationship didn't _____ in the end.
6. We _____ later that we were from the same town.
7. Milly _____ the broken window on the fourth floor.
8. A big company _____ the supermarket in our town.

C. *Talk about your sentences with another student. Are they the same? Check your answers in the dictionary.*

D. *Choose five phrasal verbs to learn from part A. Write them in your vocabulary notebook. (Phrasal verbs may have more than one meaning. Choose the meaning that best fits the sentence.)*

A. *In each sentence underline a phrase from the box.*

big decision	close relationship	fresh vegetables	light lunch	quick look
clear day	far north	good health	nice spot	serious illness

1. This is a nice spot for a picnic.
2. Can you take a quick look at this essay? I have to hand it in.
3. Julia has a very close relationship with her mother.
4. We had a light lunch, so we could continue working afterwards.
5. My father enjoyed good health for 80 years.
6. They live in the far north of Scotland.
7. On a clear day, you can see for miles.
8. We heard that Roberta had a serious illness.
9. Fresh vegetables taste better than frozen vegetables.
10. Lou had to make a big decision, and he needed some help.

B. *Complete each sentence with a phrase from the box in part A. There may be more than one possible answer.*

1. We stopped and had a _____ on our way here.
2. The doctor took a _____ at his leg and sent him to the hospital.
3. Fortunately it was not a _____, and she got better soon.
4. It was a _____, and the mountains seemed very near.
5. Not many people live in the _____ of the country.
6. Glenn didn't know what to do. It was a _____.
7. We buy _____ from the farmer every week.
8. Jefferson chose a _____ to build his new house.
9. _____ is the most important thing in life.
10. They were sisters, but they didn't have a very _____.

C. *Talk about your sentences with another student. Are they the same? Check your answers in the dictionary.*

D. *Choose five phrases to learn from part A. Write them in your vocabulary notebook.*

EXERCISE 5

A. In each sentence, underline a phrase from the box.

all over	as usual	at least	by the time	in the past
almost always	at all	at once	every time	once in a while

1. She saw the movie five times and cried every time.
2. In the past, people used to walk a lot more.
3. Radha almost always took the train to work.
4. The ticket will cost at least one hundred dollars.
5. Don't all speak at once!
6. We see each other once in a while.
7. As usual, the food was terrible.
8. I really don't want to go at all.
9. By the time we get there, it'll be dark.
10. He left the window open, and there were papers all over the floor.

B. Complete each sentence with a phrase from the box in part A. You may use each one only once. There may be more than one possible answer.

1. Mara was asleep _____ we arrived that evening.
2. We looked _____ the house for her ring, but we didn't find it.
3. _____ we go out for a walk, it rains.
4. _____, the bus was late.
5. American children ate a healthier diet _____.
6. I think she's _____ 90 years old.
7. We go out for dinner _____.
8. Don't put onion in the salad. George doesn't like it _____.
9. All the children began to cry _____.
10. The children _____ have sandwiches for lunch.

C. Talk about your sentences with another student. Are they the same? Check your answers in the dictionary.

D. Choose five phrases to learn from part A. Write them in your vocabulary notebook.

A. *In each sentence, underline a phrase from the box. The verbs may be in a different form.*

> catch a cold   get much sleep   keep (someone) company   meet the needs
> deal with it   get some rest   make a living   stay in shape

1. We need to get some rest this afternoon before we go out.
2. He makes a living as a farmer.
3. Every time I go on vacation, I catch a cold.
4. Susanna is not young. She exercises a lot to stay in shape.
5. The company tries to meet the needs of its customers.
6. My cat likes to keep me company. She follows me around the house.
7. She wasn't getting much sleep, and she was very tired.
8. His parents knew about the problem, but they didn't want to deal with it.

B. *Complete each sentence with a phrase from the box in part A. You may use each one only once. You may need to change the form of the verb.*

1. It's better to _____ now. If we wait, the problem may get worse.
2. Jean stayed to _____ her mother _____ over the weekend.
3. Jake _____ on Friday and felt terrible all weekend.
4. I didn't _____ last night because of the noise.
5. The doctor said I should exercise and _____.
6. Teachers should try to _____ of all of their students.
7. After a busy week, I finally _____ on Sunday.
8. It's not easy to _____ as an artist or a writer.

C. *Talk about your sentences with another student. Are they the same? Check your answers in the dictionary.*

D. *Choose five phrases to learn from part A. Write them in your vocabulary notebook.*

A. *In each sentence, underline a phrase from the box. The verbs may be in a different form.*

change your mind	have a meeting	make an appointment	take a trip
do a good job	keep in touch	take a break	take your time

1. Maureen kept in touch with the Farringtons for years.
2. Let's take a break in five minutes. I'm getting tired.
3. If you change your mind, please tell me.
4. Rashid made an appointment for his father at the hospital.
5. This summer we're going to take a trip to Washington.
6. Alma did a good job on her presentation.
7. He had a meeting this morning and was late for lunch.
8. Please take your time. There's no hurry.

B. *Complete each sentence with a phrase from the box in part A. You may use each one only once. You may need to change the form of the verb.*

1. I must _____ with the dentist. I have a terrible toothache.
2. Rosy _____ from her studying and called her friend Yvonne.
3. You can _____. It's still early.
4. I can't have lunch with you tomorrow because I _____.
5. It's too late to _____. We've already bought the tickets.
6. After the trip, Shanna _____ with her new friends by e-mail.
7. If Tom _____ on the windows, I'll pay him $200.00.
8. We _____ to the mountains last weekend. It was beautiful.

C. *Talk about your sentences with another student. Are they the same? Check your answers in the dictionary.*

D. *Choose five phrases to learn from part A. Write them in your vocabulary notebook.*

A. *In this passage from Unit 2, some words are missing from common phrases. The first letter is given. Complete the word.*

Reducing Stress

    Everyday life can be full of stress. There are many possible causes: work or family problems, exams at school, traffic, or noise. This stress can have many bad effects on your body and mind. It can make you unhappy and even ill.

    What can you do to reduce s_____₁? Psychologists say that the most important t_____₂ is not to get a_____₃ or upset about something. Instead you should try to laugh. If you can make a j_____₄ and laugh, you'll feel b_____₅. In f_____₆, doctors say that laughter is good f_____₇ your mental h_____₈. It also makes your body stronger, too, so you are less likely to get s_____₉.

    Another way to r_____₁₀ stress is to do s_____₁₁ you enjoy. It doesn't matter what activity you choose. Some people relax by watching a m_____₁₂, others by playing b_____₁₃ or cooking a nice d_____₁₄. According to doctors, even a very small a_____₁₅ of enjoyment can help. If you like chocolate, for e_____₁₆, you should eat a small p_____₁₇ when you feel stressed.

B. *Look back at the passage on page 45 to check your answers.*

A. *In this passage from Unit 2, some words are missing from common phrases. The first letter is given. Complete the word.*

Pets for Better Health

If an animal can be a pet, someone has it in the United States. Today 61 percent of American families own pets. The most c_____ animals are

1

cats and dogs, of c_____. But people keep all k_____ of other

2   3

animals, from birds to mice, goats, rabbits, turtles, and even snakes.

Why do so many people have pets? According to psychologists, the main

r_____ is loneliness. In the United States today, people are often very

4

alone. Many p_____ live by t_____, with no family nearby.

5   6

They often change jobs and move to new neighborhoods, which means they

can't develop close r_____ with their coworkers or their neighbors. But

7

people need c_____, and they need someone to l_____. A pet

8   9

can fill that n_____.

10

In f_____, pets are g_____ for people's mental health.

11   12

Pet owners often develop c_____ relationships with their animals.

13

According to one study, 99 percent of dog and cat owners talk to their pets. For

m_____ people, their pet is like a member of the f_____. They

14   15

keep pictures of their pets with them. They have parties on their pets' birthdays.

Doctors say that pets are also good f_____ people's physical health.

16

Pet owners have lower heart rates and blood pressure. Studies show that they live

b_____ and longer than people who live alone.

17

B. *Look back at the passage on page 46 to check your answers.*

A. *In this passage from Unit 2, some words are missing from common phrases. The first letter is given. Complete the word.*

Europeans Stand Tall

Who are the tallest people on Earth? For most of the 20th century, American men and women could look down on everyone e_____. But in the 1970s, people in northern Europe began to grow taller. They reached the same height as Americans and then grew taller. Now the Dutch are the tallest in the w_____, followed by the Norwegians and the Danes. Why is this? Why did Americans stop growing? There are two possible reasons.

According t_____ scientists, one reason is related t_____ diet. In the 1980s, Americans began to eat a lot of meat and a lot of junk f_____. This is still true today. Many Americans, especially young people, don't eat a healthy d_____. Their bodies don't get the vitamins and m_____ that they need. On the other h_____, they get a lot o_____ unhealthy sugar and fat. Not surprisingly, many Americans are overweight and have health p_____. Compared with Americans, Europeans generally have a healthier diet. They eat less meat and less junk food, and they eat more fruit and v_____.

The other reason why Europeans are taller is because they get better health c_____. In the United States, the health care system is private, and it's very expensive. Because of this, many p_____ who need medical c_____ don't get it. Pregnant women and children often don't get good care. In Europe, the health care system is public. Doctors' v_____ are free and there are many free health services for families, especially for pregnant women and children. This has generally helped Europeans to stay h_____—and grow taller.

B. *Look back at the passage on page 48 to check your answers.*

How Words Work in Sentences

Understanding a sentence means more than just knowing the words in the sentence. You also need to be able to:

- find the key parts of sentences
- understand the referents of pronouns
- recognize words and phrases that refer to the same thing

Key Parts of Sentences

The key parts of a sentence are the subject and the verb.

> The **subject** tells who or what the sentence is about.

> The **verb** tells what the subject does (in the past, present, or future).

EXAMPLE

> ***Underline the subject and verb in each sentence. Write S under the subject and V under the verb.***

> Last weekend <u>the students</u> <u>went</u> to a concert in Shanghai. <u>A popular new singer</u>
>   S   V   S
> <u>was</u> the star of the concert. <u>Her name</u> <u>was</u> Shen. <u>There</u> <u>were</u> thousands of people at
> V   S   V   S   V
> the concert. <u>Shen</u> <u>can sing</u> many kinds of songs, but <u>she</u> <u>likes</u> traditional Chinese
>   S   V   S   V
> songs best. <u>She</u> <u>doesn't like</u> singing modern western music.
>   S   V

Notes:

- The subject can be a pronoun: *I, you, he, she, it, we, they, this, there, who*
- The subject can be more than one word: *The students, A popular new singer*
- The verb can include a modal: *can sing, should go, must be*
- The verb can be negative: *isn't, doesn't like, didn't have*
- Some sentences have more than one subject and verb: <u>*Shen*</u> <u>*can sing*</u> *many kinds*
                                                              S   V
  of songs, but <u>*she*</u> <u>*likes*</u> *traditional Chinese songs best.*
                 S   V

A. *Underline the subject(s) and verb(s) in each sentence in the passage. Write S under the subjects and V under the verbs.*

The Boston Marathon

Every year in the middle of April, thousands of people go to Boston. They go to run in the Boston Marathon. This is one of the oldest road races in the world. It began in 1897. The racers started out in the countryside in Hopkinton, Massachusetts. They ran all the way to the center of Boston—26.2 miles (42 km).

5   The route is the same today, but the race has changed a lot since 1897. That year there were only a few runners. In the 2009 marathon, there were 23,163 runners who started the race. Of those, nearly 22,849 finished it. In the early years, the runners were only men. Then in 1972, women began to run in the race. In 1975, people in wheelchairs joined them.

10 These days, the runners and wheelchair racers come from all over the world. Many of them are very serious about the race. They prepare for it for months. The best runners start first. They are the people who are most likely to win. In recent years, the winners have come from many different countries, including Kenya, Japan, Russia, England, Ethiopia, Italy, Finland, and the United States.

B. *Talk about your answers with another student. Are they the same?*

A. *Underline the subject(s) and verb(s) in each sentence in the passage. Write S under the subjects and V under the verbs.*

Pets for Better Health

If an animal can be a pet, someone has it in the United States. Today 61 percent of American families own pets. The most common animals are cats and dogs, of course. But people keep all kinds of other animals, from birds to mice, goats, rabbits, turtles, and even snakes.

5   Why do so many people have pets? According to psychologists, the main reason is loneliness. In fact, in the United States today, people are often very alone. Many people live by themselves, with no family nearby. They often change jobs and move to new neighborhoods, which means they can't develop close relationships with their coworkers or their neighbors. But people need company,
10 and they need someone to love. A pet can fill that need.

     In fact, pets are good for people's mental health. Pet owners often develop close relationships with their animals. According to one study, 99 percent of dog and cat owners talk to their pets. For many people, their pet is like a member of the family. They keep pictures of their pets with them. They have parties on their
15 pets' birthdays.

     Doctors say that pets are also good for people's physical health. Pet owners have lower heart rates and blood pressure. Studies show that they live better and longer than people who live alone.

B. *Talk about your answers with another student. Are they the same?*

Pronouns

Pronouns are small but important words. They are often important in the meaning of sentences.

Personal Pronouns and Possessive Adjectives

Personal Pronouns							
Subject pronouns:	I	you	he	she	it	we	they
Object pronouns:	me	you	him	her	it	us	them
Possessive adjectives:	my	your	his	her	its	our	their

A personal pronoun takes the place of a noun or noun phrase.

It can be the *subject* of the sentence.
> **Example:** Do you know where John is? Is <u>he</u> on vacation?

Or it can be the *object* of a verb or preposition.
> **Example:** Is he on vacation? I really need to get hold of <u>him</u>.

A possessive adjective shows that something belongs to someone (or something).
> **Example:** <u>My</u> computer's broken, and he's the only one who can fix it.

EXAMPLE
....

> *Underline the personal pronouns and possessive adjectives in the sentences. Write S under the subject pronouns, O under the object pronouns, and P under the possessive adjectives.*

1. Do <u>you</u> know where John is? Is <u>he</u> on vacation? <u>I</u> really need to get hold of <u>him</u>.
       S   S   S   O

   <u>My</u> computer is broken, and <u>he</u>'s the only one who can help.
   P   S

2. A lot of ancient Greek art shows naked men and women. The Greeks believed that the human body was beautiful. <u>They</u> wanted to show the whole body in
                            S

   <u>their</u> art.
   P

A. *Underline the personal pronouns and possessive adjectives in the passage. Write S under the subject pronouns, O under the object pronouns, and P under the possessive adjectives.*

The Past Under Ice

In very cold parts of the world, scientists are studying the ice. This is one way to get information about the past. Sometimes, for example, they find plants and animals frozen in the ice. When plants and animals are frozen, they don't change. They stay the same for thousands of years.

5   Russian scientists recently found an animal called a mammoth in the ice. There are no mammoths alive today. They lived many thousands of years ago. This animal looked a lot like an elephant, with a long nose and long tusks.[1] But it was even larger than an elephant, and it had fur all over its body.

The scientists kept the mammoth frozen and studied it closely. It still had hair 10 and skin on its body. From these things, scientists could learn a lot about how it lived. The mammoth also still had food in its stomach. This told the scientists a lot about the plants that grew in those days.

On the mammoth, the scientists also found some injuries. They decided that the mammoth had probably been killed by humans. That helped the scientists 15 understand more about the humans in the past and about how they hunted big animals like the mammoth.

---

[1]**tusks** long teeth that stick out of an animal's mouth

B. *Talk about your answers with another student. Are they the same?*

Referents for Personal Pronouns

A personal pronoun usually takes the place of a noun in a sentence. The noun is called the *referent*. To understand a sentence with a pronoun, you need to know the referent.

Example: There were no more ⟨leaves⟩ on the tree. <u>They</u> were all on the ground.

Explanation
The word *leaves* is the referent for the pronoun *They*.

EXAMPLE
Circle the referent for each underlined pronoun. Then draw a line to the pronoun.
(There may be more than one pronoun for a referent.)

When <u>she</u> was six years old, (Oprah) was sent to live with <u>her</u> mother in
Milwaukee, Wisconsin.

EXERCISE 4

A. *Circle the referent for each underlined pronoun. Then draw a line to the*
pronoun. (There may be more than one pronoun for a referent.)

The Boston Marathon

Every year in the middle of April, thousands of people go to Boston. <u>They</u>
go to run in the Boston Marathon. This is one of the oldest road races in the
world. <u>It</u> began in 1897. The racers started out in the countryside in Hopkinton,
Massachusetts. <u>They</u> ran all the way to the center of Boston—26.2 miles (42 km).

5   The route is the same today, but the race has changed a lot since 1897. That
year there were only a few runners. In the 2009 marathon, there were 23,163
runners who started the race. Of these, nearly 22,849 finished <u>it</u>. In the early
years, the runners were only men. Then, in 1972, women began to run in the race.
In 1975, people in wheelchairs joined <u>them</u>.

10   These days, the runners and wheelchair racers come from all over the world.
Many of <u>them</u> are very serious about the race. They prepare for it for months. The
best runners start first. <u>They</u> are the people who are most likely to win. In recent
years, the winners have come from many different countries, including Kenya,
Japan, Russia, England, Ethiopia, Italy, Finland, and the United States.

B. *Talk about your answers with another student. Are they the same?*

Demonstrative Pronouns

These words can take the place of a phrase or an idea. Writers use them to refer to
something they have already mentioned. Sometimes they are used like adjectives, together
with nouns.

	Demonstrative Pronouns	Demonstrative Adjectives
Singular	this, that	this book, that band
Plural	these, those	these people, those years

Circle the referent for each underlined word. (The referent is the phrase or idea the writer has already mentioned.) Then draw a line from the referent to the word.

1. Wild animals are everywhere in Alaska. Some large animals, like the caribou, live in groups, and (you can see hundreds of them.) <u>This</u> can be very exciting.

2. There are also (bears and wolves) in Alaska. <u>These</u> animals are not as dangerous as people think. If you stay away from them, they will usually stay away from you.

EXERCISE 5

A. *Circle the referent for each underlined word. Then draw a line from the referent to the word.*

1. Tourists in New York may think it's one big city, but it's not all the same. Each neighborhood is very different. Some neighborhoods are full of people from one country. <u>These</u> are often good places to find interesting restaurants.

2. In Chinatown, the shop signs are all written in Chinese. The shops all sell Chinese products, and the shopkeepers all speak Chinese. <u>This</u> is one of the most crowded and colorful neighborhoods of the city.

3. Many Italians moved to New York in the early 1900s. In <u>those</u> days, it was a very poor neighborhood. Now it is called "Little Italy." There aren't many Italians left, but tourists come to the Italian cafés and restaurants.

4. Greenwich Village is another kind of neighborhood. It is one of the oldest parts of the city. For many years, <u>this</u> was where writers and students lived. Famous books were written in the neighborhood and about the neighborhood.

5. Soho is an area that used to have a lot of factories. Then the factories closed, and people began to live in the factory buildings. <u>These</u> buildings became popular places for artists because they were large and cheap.

6. Harlem was known in the early 20th century as the center of African-American cultural life. People from all over the city went to hear jazz musicians play in the night clubs. Many of <u>those</u> musicians became famous around the world.

7. Later in the 20th century, Harlem became a very poor neighborhood with many problems. There was a lot of crime and violence. Because of <u>this</u>, many people moved out of the neighborhood, and buildings were left empty.

8. These days, people are moving back to Harlem. They are fixing the empty buildings and starting new businesses. Among <u>these</u> are a big new supermarket, a shopping mall, and a cinema.

B. *Talk about your answers with another student. Are they the same?*

EXERCISE 6

A. *Circle the referent for each underlined word or phrase. Then draw a line from the referent to the word.*

The Past Under the Ice

In very cold parts of the world, scientists are studying the ice. <u>This</u> is one way to get information about the past. Sometimes, for example, they find plants and animals frozen in the ice. When plants and animals are frozen, they don't change. They stay the same for thousands of years.

5   Russian scientists recently found an animal called a mammoth in the ice. There are no mammoths alive today. They lived many thousands of years ago. <u>This</u> animal looked a lot like an elephant, with a long nose and long tusks. But it was even larger than an elephant, and it had fur all over its body.

The scientists kept the mammoth frozen and studied it closely. It still had hair
10   and skin on its body. From <u>these</u> things, scientists could learn a lot about how it lived. The mammoth also still had food in its stomach. <u>This</u> told the scientists a lot about the plants that grew in those days.

On the mammoth, the scientists also found some injuries. They decided that the mammoth had probably been killed by humans. <u>That</u> helped the scientists
15   understand more about the humans in the past and about how they hunted big animals like the mammoth.

B. *Talk about your answers with another student. Are they the same?*

Relative Pronouns

Relative pronouns connect several ideas in one sentence. The pronoun takes the place of a noun or an idea already mentioned in the sentence. See the examples in the box below.

Relative Pronouns: *who*   *which*   *that*

Who and *that* refer to people.
> **Examples:**
> She's the woman <u>who</u> lives next door.
> She's the woman <u>that</u> lives next door. (spoken English)
> (who/that = woman)

That and *which* refer to things.
> **Examples:**
> I like dogs <u>that</u> don't make noise.
> I like dogs <u>which</u> don't make noise.
> (that/which = dog)

Which refers to ideas.
> **Example:**
> He was late again, <u>which</u> made her very angry.
> (which = the fact that he was late again)

EXAMPLE
....

Underline the relative pronoun in each sentence. Then write the pronoun and the referent.

1. Katherine moved to Sheffield, <u>which</u> is in the north of England.

    which = Sheffield

2. The suit <u>that</u> he bought is very nice.

    that = suit

EXERCISE 7

A. Underline the relative pronoun in each sentence. Then write the pronoun and the referent.

1. The teacher chose students who had good grades.

_____

2. The house that my brother built is for sale.

_____

3. We found out Mr. Haydock is married, which was a big surprise.

_____

4. Haymer is writing a new book, which is why he's so busy.

_____

5. The country needs a president who will bring people together.

_____

6. The book that I'm reading is about Turkey.

_____

7. Last summer we saw the house that Mozart lived in.

_____

8. The students speak many different languages, which makes the teacher's job very difficult.

_____

B. Talk about your answers with another student. Are they the same?

Synonyms

A synonym is a word or phrase that has the same or similar meaning as another word or phrase. Writers often use synonyms in order not to repeat words.

Sometimes the synonymous word or phrase is very similar in meaning.

Examples:

little = small   store = shop
enjoy = like   recently = just last week

Writers can also use words or phrases that have a similar meaning but are more specific or more general.

Examples:

General	→	→	→	**Specific**
animal	cat		Siamese	my cat Lou-lou
business	store		supermarket	Joe's Market

EXAMPLE

Read the sentences. Circle the word or phrase that has a similar meaning to the underlined word.

1. The people at the concert were mostly <u>teenagers</u>. These (young people) were happy to hear their favorite singer.

2. Professor Lukas's office was full of (reading material.) The walls were covered with books. There were piles and piles of <u>newspapers</u> on the floor. The professor was sitting at his desk reading (*The New York Times.*)

EXERCISE 9

A. *Read the sentences. Circle the words or phrases that have a similar meaning to the underlined words.*

1. When George's father found out about the test, he was very <u>angry</u>. George didn't want to go home. He said, "My Dad will really be mad when he learns I failed by one point."

2. In the <u>summer months</u>, many families go to the seaside. Sometimes in July and August there is more traffic near the beach than in the city.

4. We saw a lion with three little cubs at the <u>wild animal</u> park. They were lying on the rocks in the warm afternoon sun. It was nice to see a whole family of these beautiful cats.

5. Many astronauts have a <u>problem</u>: They get motion sickness. Their illness causes them to have difficulty in their work. Doctors and scientists are working on ways to prevent this issue.

6. A tornado hit a small town in Kansas yesterday in the early afternoon. The very high winds destroyed several homes and stores, and cars were thrown off the road. Fortunately no one was hurt in the <u>storm</u>.

7. Many people don't have a real breakfast every day. They say they don't feel like eating <u>food</u> at that hour, and so they only have coffee. This is a mistake. The human body needs a meal in the morning.

8. Every spring, thousands of people come to the Arboretum in Boston to see the lilacs. These <u>bushes</u> have beautiful purple, pink, or white flowers that smell wonderful.

B. *Talk about your answers with another student. Are they the same?*

A. *Read the passage. Circle the words or phrases that have a similar meaning to the underlined words.*

The Hebrides Islands

If you like unusual places, you should go sometime to the <u>Hebrides Islands</u>. Not many people live on these islands in the northwest of Scotland. The land is not good for farming. The winters are long, cold, and wet. It is hard to make a living there. But for the visitor, this can be a very special place.

5　　It's not for everyone, however. Even summer days are cool and often windy. The water is too cold for swimming. The <u>landscape</u> is strange. There are no forests and few green fields, only a few trees here and there, and lots of rocks and bushes. The hills, too, are nothing but rocks. Some areas are so rocky, they don't seem to belong on Earth, but rather on the moon.

10　　But there is unforgettable beauty in this wild place. On a clear day, you can look back from the beaches at the villages and the hills. Or you can look out over the water to the other islands. The views all around are memorable.

The <u>colors</u> are also wonderful. Blue is everywhere. It's in the sky, the ocean, and the distant mountains. It's in the tiny flowers that grow between the rocks.

15　In the spring, the land around the villages is green, and there's some green on the hills. In the summer and fall, they're more purple. And often the air is soft and gray with clouds and rain.

On the Hebrides, the rest of the world seems far away. You can forget about <u>city problems</u>. There are no crowds, noise, dirt, or crime here. This is a quiet

20　place, not a tourist hot spot. The villages have few shops and no museums. The restaurants close very early. There isn't much nightlife, just a few pubs that also close early. As for <u>places to stay</u>, there aren't many hotels. Visitors stay in guesthouses or in private homes. These are often called a "Bed and Breakfast."

In fact, the people who come to the Hebrides aren't interested in shopping or

25　sightseeing or nightlife. They come to walk in the clean, cool air. They come for the quiet beauty and for the views.

B. *Talk about your answers with another student. Are they the same?*

A. *Read the passage. Circle the words or phrases that have a similar meaning to the underlined words.*

Health Tips for Travelers

Travel is fun. Travel is exciting, but it's not fun or exciting if you get <u>sick</u>. You may think this can't happen to you. But many people come down with a cold or flu just when they want to enjoy themselves. What can you do to prevent health problems? Three things are the key to good health while traveling: relax, sleep
5   enough, and eat well.

A vacation is supposed to be a <u>time for relaxing</u>, but very often it isn't. There are so many places to visit: museums, monuments, parks, and shops. You probably spend most days on your feet. By the afternoon, your feet will hurt and your head will ache. If this is the way you feel, you should take a rest. A tired body means a
10   weak body, and a weak body gets sick easily. So sit down for a while in nice spot and watch the people go by.

<u>Sleep</u> is also important for your health. When traveling, you may not get enough rest at night. A noisy hotel room or an uncomfortable bed might be the reason. Or maybe you are the kind of person who likes to stay out late. In many
15   cities, the nightlife can be very exciting. However, if you aren't getting enough rest at night, you should plan to nap during the day. An hour of "siesta" can make a big difference.

Finally, if you don't want to get sick, you must <u>eat well</u>. That means eating the right kinds of foods. When you are in a new country, you may want to try new
20   foods, but you should be careful about how much you eat. Small amounts of rich food are okay, but a lot is bad for you, especially if you have heart problems or high blood pressure. It's important to make sure you get enough fresh fruit and vegetables. You can buy fruit to eat as a snack and order salads or vegetables at your meals.

B. *Talk about your answers with another student. Are they the same?*

Comprehension Skills

Previewing

What Is Previewing?

Previewing is when you look at something quickly before you read it. You preview when you want to get information.

Previewing is a common skill in daily life. You can preview many kinds of reading material.

For example, you might preview:
- the newspaper by reading the headlines
- a letter by looking at the envelope
- a new book by reading the front and back cover

Why Preview?

Previewing can help you make decisions. It can help you decide:
- which articles to read in the newspaper
- whether to open the letter (it might be junk mail you would throw out)
- if the book is interesting, and if you want to read it

In the same way, previewing can help you with your reading. When you preview a passage, you get some ideas about it. This way, your brain is already thinking about the topic when you start reading. You can understand better and read faster.

Previewing can help you with all of your reading. It is particularly helpful at school, for reading assignments and for tests.

How Do You Preview?

When you preview, you ask yourself questions about the passage.

The questions you ask depend on many things: what you are reading, why you are reading, and what you need to find out.

Some common previewing questions:
- What is it? (Is it an e-mail message, a news article, a piece of fiction?)
- Who wrote it and who is it for?
- What is it about?
- How long is it?

(continued)

- It is difficult or easy to read?
- Is it interesting or useful?
- What will come next?

In these exercises, you will learn how to preview, and you will practice previewing in different ways.

Read these first lines from a piece of writing. Then answer the questions.

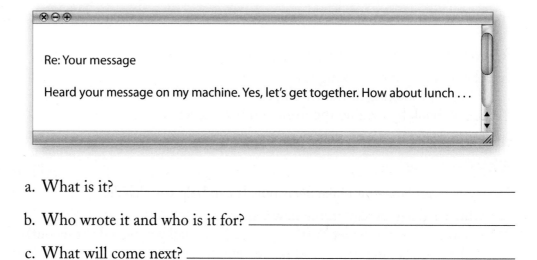

Re: Your message

Heard your message on my machine. Yes, let's get together. How about lunch . . .

a. What is it? _____

b. Who wrote it and who is it for? _____

c. What will come next? _____

Explanation
- We can tell from the way the writing starts (Re:) that it's probably an e-mail message.
- We can also guess that this person is writing to a friend because it's very informal. (An incomplete sentence, and expressions such as *let's* and *how about* . . .)
- This person will probably give a time and place for them to have lunch together.

A. *Read these first lines from different kinds of writing. Then answer the questions.*

1.
> # Ready to Go, Ready to Show!
> 1993 Corvette Chevrolet
> Miles: 53,777   Condition: Like new   Asking Price: $14,400

a. What is it? _____ advertisement for senrond-hand car
b. Who wrote it and who is it for? _____ seller _____ buyer .
c. What will come next? _____

2.
> Dear Sir/Madam,
>
> With reference to your advertisement on the JobFinders.com website, I am interested in . . .

a. What is it? _____
b. Who wrote it and who is it for? _____
c. What will come next? _____

3.
> **The Dark Knight**
>
> Dark, complex, and unforgettable, this new Batman movie, directed by Christopher Nolan . . .

a. What is it? _____
b. Who wrote it and who is it for? _____
c. What will come next? _____

B. *Talk about your answers with another student. Are they the same?*

Using Titles to Make Questions

The title of a piece of writing is very important when you are previewing. You can use it to make questions about the passage.

Work with another student. Read the title of a newspaper article. Then write three questions about it.

Peacekeepers Attacked

a. _____

b. _____

c. _____

Explanation

Many questions are possible. Here are some possibilities:

- Who were the peacekeepers?
- Where were they attacked?
- Why were they attacked?
- Who attacked them?

EXERCISE 2

A. *Work with another student. Read these titles of newspaper articles. Then write three questions for each title.*

1.
88 Die in Crash

a. _____

b. _____

c. _____

2.

Gulf Coast Hit Hard

a. _____

b. _____

c. _____

3.

Milk Powder Deaths in China

a. _____

b. _____

c. _____

4.

Channel Tunnel Slowdown

a. _____

b. _____

c. _____

5.

Butterflies Losing Winter Home

a. _____

b. _____

c. _____

🕐 **B.** ***Preview the articles. (Read only the first lines and look <u>quickly</u> through the text.) Write the number of a title from part A above each article. You will have 45 seconds.***

1. _____

> Millions of monarch butterflies in central Mexico are in danger. Every year the butterflies travel from the Rocky Mountain area of the United States to the Mariposa Monarca Biosphere Reserve. This year illegal cutting has removed many trees from the reserve. If the butterflies can't return to the same area of forest as in the past, they may perish.

2. _____

> The Chinese government is checking the safety of milk powder and says it will punish the criminals responsible for contamination. At least two babies have died, and tens of thousands have been hospitalized. According to the Chinese news agency, laboratory tests have found melamine contamination in some milk powder. Melamine is a chemical used in plastics.

3. _____

> An Aeroflot passenger jet crashed yesterday as it was preparing to land at the airport in Perm, Russia. All 88 people on board were killed. The plane had flown in from Moscow to this city in the Ural Mountains. Russian officials said that the crash was probably caused by failure in one of the plane's two engines.

4. _____

Train service through the Channel tunnel is likely to be slow for months because of work on the tunnel following last week's fire. The fire was the worst accident ever in the tunnel. It burned for 17 hours before fire fighters could put it out, and it caused serious damage to the north tunnel. The Eurostar trains and shuttle service will now run on reduced schedules.

5. _____

Millions of people in Texas and Louisiana were left without water and electricity over the weekend after the passage of Hurricane Ike. The coastal areas were particularly hard hit. The city of Houston, which is the fourth largest in the United States, was almost completely shut down and empty. Around 2 million Texans obeyed orders to leave the coastal areas.

C. *Now read the articles and look for the answers to the questions you wrote in part A.*

D. *Talk with another student. Which questions were answered? Which ones weren't answered?*

Previewing a Passage

When you preview a passage, you read only small parts of it.

Which parts should you read? You should read the ones that will help you answer your questions about the passage.

Every passage is a little different, but you can usually find out a lot by:
- reading the title
- looking at any pictures or graphics
- quickly reading the first and last lines of each paragraph
- noticing names of people and places

A. *Work with a partner. Read the title below and write two previewing questions on a separate piece of paper. Then show your questions to your teacher.*

A One-Woman Show in New York

B. *Preview the article by reading only the underlined parts. You will have 30 seconds.*

The <u>artist Maria Arroyo is having her first one-woman show in New York</u>. <u>Born in Oaxaca, Mexico</u>, Maria attended art school first in <u>Mexico City</u> and then in <u>Madrid, Spain</u>, where she studied with well-known artists such as <u>Orozco</u>, <u>Velasco, and Murillo</u>.

5   <u>In the 1980s, she moved to New York and had several shows at smaller</u> downtown galleries. Then in <u>1985</u>, she went to live in <u>Brazil</u> with her <u>husband</u>, a journalist. Her work in those years included many beautiful landscapes. They showed tropical forests, animals, and mountains in very bright Brazilian colors.

    <u>Two years ago Maria moved back to New York</u>. <u>She</u> now teaches at the
10 <u>New York School of Art</u>. Last year some of her Brazilian paintings were included in a show with other young artists. She has also shown her work in <u>Houston and Chicago</u>.

    <u>This new show includes some earlier work, as well as many new paintings</u>. She has continued to paint landscapes, but now they are less realistic. The artist
15 is more interested in the colors and shapes than in real places. <u>The new work is remarkably suggestive, and it proves that she is an important artist</u>.

C. *Work with your partner. Don't look back at the article. Can you answer your previewing questions?*

D. *Now go back and underline the words or phrases that helped you answer your questions.*

A. *Work with a partner. Read the title and write two previewing questions on a separate piece of paper. Then show your questions to your teacher.*

Accident at the Brookfield Zoo

B. *Preview the article. You will have 45 seconds.*

Yesterday, a small boy was hurt in an accident at the Brookfield Zoo in Chicago. Thomas Kemper, 3, is at the City Hospital, but the doctors say he is doing well and will go home in a few days.

Thomas was at the zoo yesterday with his parents, Janet and Kevin Kemper, and his baby sister, Sally, 6 months old. Janet Kemper says that Thomas loves going to the zoo, and he especially loves watching the gorillas. They went first to the gorilla area yesterday.

There are six adult gorillas and a three-month-old baby gorilla at the Brookfield Zoo. These animals aren't kept in cages. They're kept in large areas dug out of the ground. These areas look very natural with rocks, bushes, and trees, but they have fences to keep the animals in and the people out.

According to Kevin Kemper, Thomas loves climbing and he'll climb anything. At the gorilla area, the Kempers were busy for a moment with their baby. In that moment, Thomas started climbing the fence.

Other people saw him and tried to stop him, but he was already at the top. Then when he looked down, he became fearful and he fell—into the gorilla area. He fell at least 18 feet, but fortunately, he didn't fall head first.

At this point, something remarkable happened. Before a zoo worker could arrive, one of the gorillas went over to Thomas. It was Binti Jua, the mother gorilla, with her baby on her back. With one arm she picked up the little boy and carried him over to a door. Then she put him down so the zoo worker could get him.

Scientists at the zoo say they are not surprised about Binti Jua. A mother gorilla is not so different from a human mother in many ways. The director of the zoo has said that they will make some changes in the fences at the zoo, so accidents like this cannot happen again.

C. *Work with your partner. Don't look back at the article. Can you answer your previewing questions?*

D. *Now go back and underline the words or phrases that helped you answer your questions.*

A. *Read the title and write two previewing questions on a separate piece of paper. Then show your questions to your teacher.*

Children Can't Stop Talking

B. *Preview the article. You will have 45 seconds.*

Two Spanish children are getting treatment for addiction[1] to mobile phones. The children, ages 12 and 13, went to a special center for problems of addiction. Their parents said they could not live without using their phones all the time. These are the first cases like this in the country.

The children were spending about six hours a day talking, sending text messages, or playing video games on their phones.

Dr. Maite Utgès, director of the center, said it was the first time they had treated children for addiction to mobile phones. She said that both children weren't getting along with other children and were failing at school. The children are now learning to live without their phones. Utgès said they might need at least a year of treatment to get them off the mobile phone "drug."

Before they started treatment, both children had their own phones for 18 months. Their parents did not limit the time their children spent on the phones. The children paid for their phones by getting money from a grandmother and other family members. They didn't explain what they were doing with the money.

Governments in other countries are also concerned about the way children use mobile phones. The Japanese government asked parents to limit the time children could use their phones. In Britain, doctors have reported several cases of children with problems because of mobile phones. In these cases, the young people became very unhappy when they didn't receive enough phone calls.

A study in Spain found that 65 percent of children between ages 10 and 15 in Spain had a mobile phone in 2007.

---

[1] **addiction** when you are unable to stop taking something (i.e., alcohol or a drug) or to stop doing something

C. *Don't look back at the article. Can you answer your previewing questions?*

D. *Now go back and underline the words or phrases that helped you answer your questions.*

A. *Read the title and write two previewing questions on a separate piece of paper. Then show your questions to your teacher.*

The Answer to Aging and Disease?

B. *Preview the article. You will have 45 seconds.*

A new report about Coenzyme Q10 (CoQ10) appeared last week in *Science Review*. It questioned the websites of companies that make these popular food supplements.[1] These companies say that the supplements slow down aging and prevent many diseases.

5   Scientific studies have shown that CoQ10 is important in the human body. This substance works like a vitamin in your body and may help keep your body healthy. According to Duncan Walgren, a scientist at the University of Oregon, it may have a positive effect on some genetic processes.

Scientists are planning more studies of these effects. They are particularly
10   interested in the effects of CoQ10 on some diseases. The makers claim that it can help prevent cancer, diabetes, obesity, and heart failure. However, so far, studies have not proven anything.

According to Sara Forman, a scientist at Boston University, it may not be a good idea to take CoQ10 supplements.

15   "Don't believe the websites," says Forman. "These companies say that their supplements are good for any health problem, but they don't have scientific proof for this claim."

She also says that there have not yet been any studies about the possible negative effects of the supplements. In general, she says, it is better to get your
20   vitamins—and CoQ10—from whole foods, not supplements. That way you get all the vitamins, minerals, and other substances you need. CoQ10 can be found in many foods, including beef, soy oil, oily fish, as well as nuts, whole grains, and some vegetables, such as spinach, broccoli, carrots, and cabbage.

---

[1]**food supplement** vitamins or other things you take in addition to your regular meals

C. *Don't look back at the article. Can you answer your previewing questions?*

D. *Now go back and underline the words or phrases that helped you answer your questions.*

Focus on Vocabulary

A. *Do you know the meanings of these words? Read each word aloud. Then put a ✓ (you know), ? (you aren't sure), or X (you don't know).*

_____ treatment   _____ director   _____ fail   _____ limit   _____ report
_____ case   _____ get along   _____ concerned _____ effect   _____ receive

B. *Read the passage to the end.*

Children Can't Stop Talking

Two Spanish children are getting treatment for addiction to mobile phones. The children, ages 12 and 13, went to a special center for problems of addiction. Their parents said they could not live without using their phones all the time. These are the first cases like this in the country.

5   The children were spending about six hours a day talking, sending text messages, or playing video games on their phones.

    Dr. Maite Utgès, director of the center, said it was the first time they had treated children for addiction to mobile phones. She said that both children weren't getting along with other children and were failing at school. The children

10 are now learning to live without their phones. Utgès said they might need at least a year of treatment to get them off the mobile phone "drug."

    Before they started treatment, both children had their own phones for 18 months. Their parents did not limit the time their children spent on the phones. The children paid for their phones by getting money from a grandmother and

15 other family members. They didn't explain what they were doing with the money.

    Governments in other countries are also concerned about the way children use mobile phones. The Japanese government asked parents to limit the time children could use their phones. In Britain, doctors have reported several cases of children with problems because of mobile phones. In these cases, the young people became

20 very unhappy when they didn't receive enough phone calls.

    A study in Spain found that 65 percent of children between ages 10 and 15 in Spain had a mobile phone in 2007.

C. *Look back at the passage and circle the words from the list in part A. (Some words may be in a different form: case → cases.) Then underline words in the passage that are new to you.*

D. *Look up the underlined words in the dictionary. Write them in your vocabulary notebook with the parts of speech, the sentences, and the meanings. (See Part 2, Unit 1, page 41.)*

E. *Check your understanding of the passage. Read it again if you need to. Write T (True) or F (False) after each sentence.*

1. Many children have been treated for addiction to mobile phones in Spain. _____

2. The two Spanish children had problems in school. _____

3. The treatment for phone addiction takes a long time. _____

4. The children got money for their phones from their parents. _____

F. *Talk about your answers with another student. Are they the same? Then check all your work with your teacher.*

EXERCISE 7

A. *Read each sentence and circle the best meaning for the underlined word(s).*

1. Two Spanish children are getting <u>treatment</u> for addiction to mobile phones.
   a. extra schoolwork   b. a lot of money   c. medical care

2. These are the first <u>cases like</u> this in the country.
   a. examples of   b. centers for   c. chances of

3. Dr. Maite Utgès, <u>director</u> of the center where the children are being treated, said, "It's the first time we have treated children for addiction to mobile phones."
   a. doctor   b. manager   c. owner

4. "Both children had difficulties <u>getting along</u> with other children and were failing at school," said Utgès, a child psychiatrist.
   a. making phone calls   b. being happy   c. having fights

5. "Both children had difficulties getting along with other children and <u>were failing</u> at school," said Utgès, a child psychiatrist.
   a. weren't happy   b. were successful   c. had bad grades

6. Their parents did not <u>limit</u> the time their children spent on the phone.
   a. stop   b. know about   c. pay for

7. Governments in other countries are also <u>concerned</u> about mobile phone addiction among children.

    a. surprised   b. worried   c. confused

8. The Japanese government asked parents to limit phone use because of the negative <u>effects</u> on children who use them too much.

    a. fears   b. news   c. changes

9. In Britain, psychologists have <u>reported</u> at least two cases of young people who became very unhappy when they didn't get enough phone calls from friends.

    a. written about   b. asked about   c. looked at

10. In Britain, psychologists have reported at least two cases of young people who became very unhappy when they didn't <u>receive</u> enough phone calls from friends.

    a. make   b. give   c. get

B. *Talk about your answers with another student. Are they the same?*

EXERCISE 8

A. *Complete the sentences with the words from the box. Use each word only once. Change the form of the word for the sentence if necessary (plural, past tense, etc.).*

treatment	director	fail	limit	report
case	get along	concerned	effect	receive

1. We spoke to the _____ of the language center about the problem.

2. Most people know about the negative _____ of smoking.

3. Miriam and James didn't _____ very well as children.

4. You should _____ the amount of chocolate you eat every day.

5. Rest was an important part of the _____ for his illness.

6. The doctor said this was the first _____ of the illness in the town.

7. If you _____ the exam, you have to take the course again.

8. After he won the Nobel Prize, he _____ a phone call from the president.

9. The teachers are _____ about Julio's health.

10. Journalists _____ that fighting had started again.

B. *Talk about your answers with another student. Are they the same?*

EXERCISE 9

A. *Write a sentence for each word in the box. Look at the sentences in Exercises 7 and 8 if you need help.*

case	director	fail	limit	report
concerned	effect	get along	receive	treatment

1. _____
2. _____
3. _____
4. _____
5. _____
6. _____
7. _____
8. _____
9. _____
10. _____

B. *Check your work with your teacher.*

A. *Write the other parts of speech for each word. More than one word may be possible for each part of speech. (See Part 2, Unit 4, page 67.)*

Noun	Verb	Adjective	Adverb
concern	*concern*	concerned	
director			
effect			
	fail		
	limit		
	receive		
	report		
treatment			

B. *Talk about your answers with another student. Are they the same? Then check your answers with your teacher.*

C. *Write the new words from Exercises 6–10 in your vocabulary notebook. Then make study cards. Study them alone and then with another student.*

UNIT 2

Scanning

What Is Scanning?

Scanning is a very fast kind of reading.

When Do You Scan?

You scan when you want to find information quickly. For example, you might scan a telephone book, a menu, a dictionary, or a Web article.

How Do You Scan?

When you scan you move your eyes very quickly over the page. You don't read all the words. You read only the words that help you find the information.

Scanning practice will help you recognize words faster and move your eyes more quickly across the page. This way, you can read faster and with better comprehension.

There are two groups of exercises in this unit.
- In Exercises 1–5 you will practice recognizing common words and phrases.
- In Exercises 6–11 you will scan for information in different kinds of writing.

Scanning for Common Words and Phrases

These exercises will improve your reading in two ways.
- First, you will learn to recognize common words and phrases quickly. This will help you read faster and understand better.
- Second, you will learn to move your eyes more quickly. This will help you do fast kinds of reading like scanning.

Notes:
- The following exercises with a 🕐 have a time limit. You need to work quickly. Your teacher will time you.
- These exercises are for learning to recognize words quickly. They are not vocabulary exercises. Don't stop to think about each word and don't look them up in the dictionary. Move your eyes quickly to look for the key words.

EXAMPLE

 Look for the key word and circle it every time you see it. You will have 10 seconds.

Key Words

1. **about**	above	(about)	abate	(about)	abode
2. **people**	(people)	pepper	(people)	period	purple

EXERCISE 1

 A. Look for the key word and circle it every time you see it. You will have 60 seconds.

Key Words

1. **way**	wag	warp	way	way	why
2. **fast**	fast	fail	fast	fist	fact
3. **right**	rigid	rigor	right	rite	right
4. **with**	white	with	wink	with	witch
5. **best**	best	best	beet	beat	bent
6. **every**	early	evenly	every	envy	every
7. **read**	rend	read	reed	real	read
8. **save**	save	sane	serve	salve	save
9. **down**	dawn	down	done	down	dove
10. **good**	goof	goad	good	good	goal
11. **were**	wire	were	were	ware	where
12. **have**	hare	hair	have	harm	have
13. **back**	bake	back	bark	bask	back
14. **think**	think	thick	thing	thank	think
15. **people**	pepper	people	popular	period	people
16. **there**	there	their	three	there	theme
17. **thought**	through	thorough	thought	thought	though
18. **with**	white	with	wish	wife	wilt

B. Look back at the exercise and check your work.

EXERCISE 2

 A. *Look for the key phrase and circle it every time you see it. You will have 90 seconds.*

Key Phrases

1. **turn over**	turn over	turn on	turn out	turn off
	turn into	turn over	turn into	turn over
2. **go away**	go along	go away	go around	go away
	go after	go about	go away	go ahead
3. **set up**	set out	set off	set up	set in
	set up	set down	set forth	set up
4. **get back**	get better	get by	get back	get behind
	get back	get down	get along	get back
5. **make up**	make out	make off	make for	make up
	make up	make over	make do	make up
6. **look out**	look up	look out	look into	look back
	look over	look on	look out	look out
7. **put off**	put out	put off	put off	put away
	put off	put up	put down	put on
8. **take over**	take over	take away	take out	take over
	take after	take on	take over	take back

B. *Look back at the exercise and check your work.*

EXERCISE 3

 A. *Look for the key phrase and circle it every time you see it. You will have 90 seconds.*

Key Phrases

1. **at all**	attic	a tall	at last	at all
	at all	atlas	at an	altar
2. **every time**	every time	everything	even then	ever taller
	every ten	every time	every one	even true

3. **some day**	one day any day	in a day some day	some day in my day	some day long day
4. **out of date**	in a day on the day	out of date one day	a later date on the day	on a date out of date
5. **as usual**	as usual as used	as usual than usual	a useful in use	is usual as usual
6. **all the time**	a long time all the time	at a time at any time	all the time at the time	it's time all the time
7. **at least**	at last at least	a leash all leaves	are last to lead	at least at least
8. **more or less**	more and more more or less	more or less move a lot	more hours more orders	move a lot more or less

B. *Look back at the exercise and check your work.*

Scanning for Key Words in Passages

In these exercises, you will scan for key words in a passage. These key words are from the titles of the passages.

Remember, you are not working on comprehension. You should just look for the key words as quickly as you can. You will read the passage and think about the ideas later.

EXERCISE 4

 A. *Scan the passage and circle the key word every time you see it. You will have 60 seconds.*

Key Word: pet(s)

Pets for Better Health

If an animal can be a pet, someone has it in the United States. Today 61 percent of American families own pets. The most common animals are cats and dogs, of course. But people keep all kinds of other animals from birds, to mice, goats, rabbits, turtles, and even snakes.

5   Why do so many people have pets? According to psychologists, the main reason is loneliness. In the United States today, people are often very alone. Many people live by themselves, with no family nearby. They often change jobs and move to new neighborhoods,which means they don't develop close relationships with their coworkers or their neighbors. But people need company, and they need
10   someone to love. A pet can fill that need.

In fact, pets are good for people's mental health. Pet owners often develop close relationships with their animals. According to one study, 99 percent of dog and cat owners talk to their pets. For many people, their pet is like a member of the family. They keep pictures of their pets with them. They have parties on their

15 pets' birthdays.

Doctors say that pets are also good for people's physical health. Pet owners have lower heart rates and blood pressure. Studies show that they live better and longer than people who live alone.

B. *Look back at the exercise and check your work.*

EXERCISE 5

A. *Scan the passage and circle the key word every time you see it. You will have 60 seconds.*

Key Word: cold(s)

The Common Cold

Around the world, mothers tell their children, "Dress warmly or you'll catch a cold." This is a common belief. But is it true? Can cold weather cause a cold?

The answer is basically no. Colds are caused by viruses. A cold always comes—directly or indirectly—from another person with the virus. However,

5 there is a connection with the weather. In fact, you are more likely to catch a cold in the winter. One reason is that windows are closed, which makes it easier for the cold virus to spread from one person to another. Another reason is that the body prefers to stay warm. If you get cold—particularly your feet—your body can't fight viruses as well, and you are more likely to get sick.

10 There is no sure way to prevent a cold, but you can reduce the number of colds you catch. The most important thing is to wash your hands often. Wash them before you eat. Wash them every time you come home from school or from work. And when your hands aren't clean, don't touch your mouth, nose, or eyes.

If you do catch a cold, you should be careful not to spread it. Try not to sneeze

15 or cough onto other people, into the air, or into your hands. If you have the virus on your hands, you will leave it on everything you touch. Instead, you should sneeze or cough into a tissue that you throw away.

B. *Look back at the exercise and check your work.*

Scanning for Information

In these exercises, you will scan to find the answers to questions. You don't know exactly what words you are looking for. But you do know what kind of information you need. For example:

> If the question asks, "*When . . . ?*", look for a date.
> If the question asks, "*How many . . . ?*", look for a number.

Some questions may include words that can help you. For example:

> If the question asks, "*What medals . . . ?*", look for the word *medals*.
> If the question asks, "*What . . . in Prague?*", look for the word *Prague*.

> **Note:** You don't need to read or understand everything in these exercises. You only need to look for the words that help you answer the questions.

EXERCISE 6

A. **Scan the Web page on page 123 for the answers to the questions. Write the answers on a separate piece of paper. You will have two minutes.**

1. What year did the Beatles get their first record contract?
2. What are the names of the former members of the band?
3. How many different record labels did they work for?
4. What person was important in 1960–1962?
5. Does the site include a catalogue of their songs?
6. What happened between the years of 1964–1966?

B. **Write three more questions about the Web page. Then ask another student to scan for the answers.**

_____

_____

_____

C. Talk with another student. Discuss these questions.

1. Are your answers to part A the same?
2. Do you know the Beatles' music? If so, do you have a favorite Beatles' song?
3. What kinds of music do you enjoy listening to? Who are your favorite musicians or groups?

The Beatles

Origin: Liverpool, England
Genre(s): Pop, rock, and various others
Record labels: Parlophone, Capitol, Odeon, Apple, Vee-Jay, Polydor, Swan, Tollie
Members: John Lennon, Paul McCartney, George Harrison, Ringo Starr
Former members: Stuart Sutcliffe, Pete Best

Contents
1 History
    1.1 1957–60: Formation
    1.2 1960–62: Hamburg, Cavern Club, and Brian Epstein
    1.3 1962: Record contract
    1.4 1962–63: Fame in the UK
    1.5 1963–64: American success
    1.6 1964–66: Beatlemania crosses the Atlantic
    1.7 1966–69: Studio years
    1.8 1969–70: Let It Be project and breakup
    1.9 1994–1996: Reunion and anthology
    1.10 1996–present: Recent projects and developments

2 Discography
    2.1 Song catalogue
    2.2 Studio albums
    2.3 2009 CD remasters

3 References

A. *Scan the list of cruises on page 125 for the answers to the questions. Write the answers on a separate piece of paper. You will have two minutes.*

1. How much does the sightseeing trip cost?
2. Where do you have lunch on the Hudson River Cruise?
3. How many harbor cruises are there every day?
4. Which cruises have guides on board?
5. On which cruise can you listen to music?
6. How fast does the boat go on the Speed Boat Cruise?
7. How many cruises serve food?
8. Which cruise travels on a luxury boat?

B. *Write three more questions about the cruises. Then ask another student to scan for the answers.*

_____

_____

_____

C. *Talk with another student. Discuss these questions.*

1. Are your answers to part A the same?
2. Which of these cruises would you most like to take? Why?
3. Do you like visiting new cities? What cities have you visited recently?

New York City: Cruises and Trips

Harbor Cruise

Duration: 90 minutes
Price: $26
When: Daily at 10:00 A.M., 11:00 A.M.,
12:00 P.M., 1:00 P.M., 2:00 P.M., 3:00 P.M.
Description: Admire the city from the
water on a high-speed catamaran or a ferry.

Speed Boat Cruise

Duration: 30 minutes
Price: $20
When: Daily, every hour, noon until dusk
Description: Take a wild ride at 45 mph
across the waters of New York! The fastest
and most exciting way to see the city from the water.

Circle Line Cruise

Duration: 2 hours
Price: $30
When: Daily at 11:30 A.M. and 3:30 P.M.
Description: See the highlights of the sights and history of New York from the water,
including the Statue of Liberty. Cruise guides in four languages. Light meals and snacks
on board.

Sightseeing Trip and Cruise

Duration: One day
Price: $50
When: Daily at 7:20 A.M. and 8:20 P.M.
Description: Visit the Statue of Liberty, Intrepid Museum, Empire State Building, Fifth
Avenue, United Nations, Lincoln Center, Times Square, and more. Take a cruise around
Manhattan. Guides in four languages. Light meals and snacks on board.

Hudson River Cruise

Duration: Two hours
Price: $50
When: Daily at 10:00 A.M.
Description: Take a tour up the Hudson River to see the Hudson Valley. Enjoy the water
and the sights as far as West Point. Lunch at Torches on the Hudson Restaurant. Return
by bus.

Lunch and Dinner Cruises

Duration: Lunch: Two hours, Dinner: Three hours
Price: Lunch: $65, Dinner: $75
When: Daily at 12:00 P.M. and 7:30 P.M.
Description: Enjoy gourmet lunch and dinner menus or buffet menu on a luxury boat.
Live jazz music at lunch time. Live music and entertainment in the evening. Parties
welcome (reserve in advance).

A. *Scan the list of books on page 127 for the answers to the questions. Write the answers on a separate piece of paper. You will have two minutes.*

1. How many books take place in the 1800s?
2. Who is the author of the book about Shackleton?
3. How long did Phineas Gage live after his accident?
4. When did Juan Francisco Manzano live?
5. How long is the book about Marley?
6. Which book takes place in Sarajevo?
7. Which book talks about the problems of young black men in America?
8. Which two books are about Jewish people in the Second World War?

B. *Write three more questions about the book list. Then ask another student to scan for the answers.*

_____

_____

_____

C. *Talk with another student. Discuss these questions.*

1. Are your answers to part A the same?
2. Which books seem interesting to you? Why?
3. What kind of books do you like to read?

Extensive Reading Books

The Diary of a Young Girl. Franck, Anne. This well-known book tells the true story of a Jewish girl hiding from the Nazis in World War II Holland. (368 pages)

Letters to a Young Brother: Manifest Your Destiny. Harper, Hill. A young black American writer tells his own story and answers letters from other young men. (192 pages)

Marley: A Dog Like No Other. Grogan, John. As a family dog, Marley is 90 pounds of trouble, fun, and love. (208 pages)

Night. Wiesel, Elie. Taken from his Hungarian village as a boy, the author survived the Nazi death camps. This book asks fundamental questions about life and faith. A masterpiece. (120 pages)

Only the Names Remain: The Cherokees and the Trail of Tears. Bealen, Alex W. The sad history of the Cherokees from 16th century to their removal from Georgia in 1837. (80 pages)

The Perilous Journey of the Donner Party. Calabro, Marian. In 1846, 90 people traveling to California were trapped for the winter—only a few survived. (192 pages)

Phineas Gage: A Gruesome But True Story about Brain Science. Fleischman, John. After an iron rod went through his brain in 1848, a man lived for 11 years. (96 pages)

The Poet Slave of Cuba: A Biography of Juan Francisco Manzano. Engle, Margarita and Qualls, Sean. This biography tells of the suffering and the talent of a 19th-century Cuban poet. (192 pages)

Shipwreck at the Bottom of the World: The Extraordinary True Story of Shackleton and the Endurance. Armstrong, Jennifer. In 1914, the ship *Endurance* was trapped in the Antarctic ice. This is the story of the remarkable survival and rescue. (144 pages)

Zlata's Diary: A Child's Life in Wartime Sarajevo. Filipovish, Zlata. Ten-year-old Zlata tells about the bombings and hardship of life in Sarajevo. (208 pages)

A. *Scan the newspaper article on page 129 for the answers to the questions. Write the answers on a separate piece of paper. You will have two minutes.*

1. What is the name of the new car?
2. How many of these cars has Lamborghini sold?
3. Where are most of the buyers from?
4. Where was the first car shown?
5. When will Lamborghini start making the Reventon?
6. What's the name of the company's chief executive?

B. *Write three more questions about the article. Then ask another student to scan for the answers.*

_____

_____

_____

C. *Talk with another student. Discuss these questions.*

1. Are your answers to part A the same?
2. Do you have or does your family have a car? If so, what kind of car?
3. How do you usually get to school? Do you use public transportation, or do you travel by car? Which do you prefer?

High Speed, Huge Cost: 1 Million Euro Car Sells Out

What's the price for the very best? If you ask Lamborghini, 1 million euros should do it—before taxes, of course.

The Italian carmaker hopes to show the world that it is indeed the best, with its new super luxury sports car, the Reventon, shown for the first time at the Frankfurt International Motor Show this week. This car, which looks more like an arrow than any car you've seen, will be produced in only a very limited number.

With a price tag of $1.4 million, it is the most expensive car ever built. Lamborghini has already sold the 20 cars that it plans to build.

"As soon as people heard about it, we sold out in four days," said Stephan Winkelmann, the company's chief executive. Most of the buyers were men from the United States, some of whom already own a Lamborghini, according to Winkelmann.

Although it is based on another Lamborghini car, the company engineers copied the lines of a fighter jet, and they reworked the carbon fiber car body to make it look more dramatic. The engine is the same as the LP640 model: a 12-cylinder rocket that can move the car from zero to 100 kilometers per hour, or 60 miles per hour, in 3.4 seconds.

Lamborghini, which is run by Volkswagen's Audi division, will start making the Reventon in January and deliver them in October.

Adapted from the International Herald Tribune, *September 13, 2007*

EXERCISE 10

A. **Scan the newspaper article on page 130 for the answers to the questions. Write the answers on a separate piece of paper. You will have two minutes.**

1. Where is Natalie Du Toit from?
2. What was the time for Brian Frasure?
3. How many medals were awarded on Monday?
4. How did Du Toit lose her left leg?
5. How many medals did China have overall?
6. What was Pistorius' personal best time?

B. *Write three more questions about the Paralympics. Then ask another student to scan for the answers.*

_____

_____

_____

C. *Talk with another student. Discuss these questions.*

1. Are your answers to part A the same?
2. Do you know anyone with a physical disability? If so, tell about that person.
3. In your country, do disabled people compete in sports?

Pistorius Opens Bid for 3 Gold Medals

Oscar Pistorius began his campaign to win three gold medals in the Beijing Paralympics, clocking the fastest time Monday in heats of the 100-meter event.

The South African, who failed in an attempt to qualify for the Beijing Olympics, ran a personal-best time of 11.16 seconds in the sprint. The next best times went to three Americans: Jerome Singleton (11.48), Brian Frasure (11.49), and Marlon Shirley (11.77).

Pistorius will also run the 200- and 400-meter, hoping to better his performance from four years ago in the Athens Paralympics, where he won a gold and bronze.

A double amputee known as "Blade Runner" because of the prosthetic legs he races on, Pistorius won a legal battle in May for the right to run in the Olympics, but he subsequently failed to meet the qualifying-time standard.

Forty-one medals were awarded on Monday, the second day of the Paralympics. China had 28 medals overall and 8 gold. The United States also has 8 gold medals and 17 medals overall.

The South African swimmer, Natalie Du Toit, won her second gold in two days, winning the 100-meter freestyle after taking the 100-meter butterfly on Sunday. She's attempting to win five gold medals at the Paralympics. A swimmer with Olympic promise, Du Toit lost her left leg above the knee in a 2001 motorcycle crash.

The United States took 3 of the 18 golds in swimming to lead that count. The medals went to Jessica Long, Erin Popovich, and Anna Eames.

The 10 gold medals on Monday in track and field were scattered around with China taking 2, and Cuba, Australia, Saudi Arabia, Latvia, Algeria, Denmark, Canada, and the Netherlands each taking one.

Based on The Associated Press, *September 8, 2008*

Focus on Vocabulary

A. *Do you know the meanings of these words? Read each word aloud. Then put a ✓ (you know), ? (you aren't sure), or X (you don't know).*

| ____ doubt | ____ substance | ____ process | ____ claim | ____ prove |
| ____ prevent | ____ according to | ____ particularly | ____ so far | ____ negative |

B. *Read the article to the end.*

The Answer to Aging and Disease?

Last week there was a new report about Coenzyme Q10 (CoQ10) in *Science Review*. The writers of this report have serious doubts about these popular food supplements. The companies that make them say that the supplements are good for you because they slow down aging and prevent many diseases. The report said

5   this may not be true.

Scientific studies have shown that CoQ10 is important in the human body. This substance works like a vitamin in your body and may help keep your body healthy. According to Duncan Walgren, a scientist at the University of Oregon, it may have a good effect on some genetic processes.

10   Scientists are planning more studies of these effects. They are particularly interested in the effects of CoQ10 on some diseases. The makers claim that it can help prevent cancer, diabetes, obesity, and heart failure. However, so far, studies have not proven anything.

According to Sara Forman, a scientist at Boston University, it may not be a

15   good idea to take CoQ10 supplements.

"Don't believe the websites," says Forman. "These companies say that their supplements are good for any health problem, but they don't have scientific proof for this claim."

She also says that there have not yet been any studies about the possible

20   negative effects of the supplements. In general, she says, it is better to get your vitamins—and CoQ10—from whole foods, not supplements. That way you get all the vitamins, minerals, and other substances you need. CoQ10 can be found in many foods, including beef, soy oil, oily fish, as well as nuts, whole grains, and some vegetables, such as spinach, broccoli, carrots, and cabbage.

C. *Look back at the passage and circle the words that are on the list in part A. Then underline the words in the passage that are new to you.*

D. *Look up the underlined words in the dictionary. Write them in your vocabulary notebook with the parts of speech, the sentences, and the meanings. (See Part 2, Unit 1, page 41.)*

E. *Check your understanding of the article. Read it again if you need to. Write **T** (True) or **F** (False) after each sentence.*

1. Companies that make CoQ10 supplements say they slow down aging. _____

2. Scientific studies agree with the companies. _____

3. Coenzyme Q10 is a kind of disease. _____

4. Sara Forman says it's better to get CoQ10 in food. _____

F. *Talk about your answers with another student. Are they the same? Then check all your work with your teacher.*

EXERCISE 12

A. *Read each sentence and circle the best meaning for the underlined word(s).*

1. The writers of this article have serious <u>doubts</u> about these popular food supplements.
   a. uncertainties   b. ideas   c. effects

2. These companies say that the supplements slow down aging and <u>prevent</u> many diseases.
   a. pays for   b. keep away   c. make worse

3. This <u>substance</u> works like a vitamin in your body and may help keep your body healthy.
   a. vegetable   b. word   c. thing

4. <u>According to</u> Duncan Walgren, a scientist at the University of Oregon, it may have a good effect on some genetic processes.
   a. Walgren hopes   b. Walgren says   c. Walgren asks if

5. According to Duncan Walgren, a scientist at the University of Oregon, it may have a positive effect on some genetic <u>processes</u>.
   a. studies   b. shapes   c. changes

6. They are <u>particularly</u> interested in the effects of CoQ10 on some diseases.
   a. especially   b. less   c. usually

7. The makers <u>claim</u> that it can help prevent cancer, diabetes, obesity, and heart failure.
   a. believe   b. say   c. know

8. However, <u>so far,</u> studies have not proven anything.
   a. in the end   b. after that   c. until now

9. However, so far, studies have not <u>proven</u> anything.
   a. tested   b. shown   c. seen

10. She also says that there have not yet been any studies about the possible <u>negative</u> effects of the supplements.
    a. bad   b. good   c. unknown

B. *Talk about your answers with another student. Are they the same?*

EXERCISE 13

A. *Complete the sentences with the words from the box. Use each word only once. Change the form of the word for the sentence if necessary (plural, past tense, etc.).*

according to	doubt	particularly	process	so far
claim	negative	prevent	prove	substance

1. The director was _____ angry with one student.
2. The aging _____ seems to happen more slowly in some people.
3. A chemical _____ in the milk powder made children very sick.
4. The film showed the people of New York in a very _____ way.
5. _____ Dr. Thorpe, there was no need for more treatment.
6. She guessed that he wasn't telling the truth, but she couldn't _____ it.
7. The parents have _____ not reported their missing daughter.
8. I have no _____ that we did the right thing.
9. The man _____ that he was visiting friends that evening, but the police didn't believe him.
10. You can _____ some diseases by living in a healthy way.

B. *Talk about your answers with another student. Are they the same?*

EXERCISE 14

A. *Write a sentence for each word in the box in Exercise 13. Look at the sentences in Exercises 12 and 13 if you need help.*

1. _____
2. _____
3. _____
4. _____
5. _____
6. _____
7. _____
8. _____
9. _____
10. _____

B. *Check your work with your teacher.*

EXERCISE 15

A. *Write the other parts of speech for each word. More than one word may be possible for each part of speech. (See Part 2, Unit 4, page 67.)*

Noun	Verb	Adjective	Adverb
	doubt		
	claim		
		negative	
			particularly
	prevent		
process			
	prove		
substance			

B. *Talk about your answers with another student. Are they the same? Then check your answers with your teacher.*

C. *Write the new words from Exercises 11–15 in your vocabulary notebook. Then make study cards. Study them alone and then with another student.*

Making Inferences

How Do You Make an Inference?

An inference is a kind of guess. When you read a passage, you get information from it. Then you can make an inference (guess) about other information and ideas that are not in the passage.

When Do You Make Inferences?

In everyday life, you often make inferences.

Examples:

- A friend from Chicago is supposed to arrive by plane this afternoon. You hear that there are terrible snow storms in Chicago. You make an inference from this:
  - ➢ Planes will probably not be able to fly out of Chicago, and your friend won't come today.

- You read an article in the newspaper about tourism in Turkey. It says that the number of foreign visitors has increased greatly. You make an inference from this:
  - ➢ Turkey might be a good place to look for a job in the tourist industry.

Readers also make inferences.

- They may need to infer the general meaning of new words. (See Part 2, Unit 3.)
- They sometimes infer information or ideas that aren't in the passage. Writers don't or can't always tell everything to the reader. There may be gaps (holes) in the reader's knowledge about something. The reader may need to try to fill in these gaps by making inferences.

Making Inferences from Conversations

In these exercises, you will make inferences about the people in the conversations.

A. Read the conversation. Make inferences to answer the questions. More than one answer may be possible.

A: Do you think it'll be late?
B: Stop worrying, dear. It'll be just fine.
A: But look at all that rain and wind.
B: They didn't say anything when you checked in.
A: I know, but the weather's getting worse. Let's go ask again.
B: We don't need to. See, it says up there that your flight's on time.
A: I'm sorry, honey. You know I don't like flying! And I'm nervous about my meeting.
B: Why don't you take the train next time?

1. Where are these people? _____
2. Who are they? _____
3. What are they doing? _____
4. Do you think A is the husband or the wife? _____
5. What can you infer about A? _____
6. What do you think will happen next? _____

B. Talk about your answers with another student. Are they the same? What words helped you get your answers?

Note: There may be more than one possible answer for many of the questions in these exercises. You should be ready to explain your answer.

Explanation
1. They're at the airport. (*checked in, it says up there that your flight's on time*)
2. They're probably husband and wife. (*stop worrying, dear, honey*),
3. Waiting for A's flight. A is going away on a business trip. (*I don't like flying. And I'm nervous about my meeting.*)
4. Both answers are possible.
5. She worries a lot. She's not very sure of herself.
6. Many answers are possible. For example:
   She will get on her flight and everything will be fine.
   Her flight will be delayed and she will miss her meeting.
   Her husband will get angry with her and they will have a fight.

A. Read the conversation. Make inferences to answer the questions.

A: Excuse me. Can you tell me what you think about this?

B: Hmm. Well, the color is perfect on you.

A: What about the style?

B: It's very popular. We sell a lot of those.

A: Does it look alright? It's so hard to find something that fits me right.

B: It looks great on you. It looks great on everyone.

A: You're sure it doesn't look a bit funny. I mean, the style's not too young for me?

B: No-o-o. You look very nice. Really.

1. Where are these people? _____

2. Who are they? _____

3. What are they doing? _____

4. What can you infer about A? _____

5. What can you infer about B? _____

6. What do you think will happen next? _____

B. Talk about your answers with another student. Are they the same? What words helped you get your answers?

A. Read the conversation. Make inferences to answer the questions.

> A: I've got to tell you what happened yesterday.
>
> B: What?
>
> A: You know I had to stay late to finish that report? Well, I was here at my computer, and guess who came along . . . Sheila!
>
> B: Sheila? You mean Sheila Gifford from the top floor?
>
> A: That's right. She went right into Paul's office with a big pile of papers and stayed in there for about an hour.
>
> B: You're kidding!
>
> A: No, I'm serious. I could hear them talking. When she came out, she gave me a strange look. I thought she was going to say something, but she went straight to the elevator.
>
> B: Oh, no. Do you think we've got bad news coming?
>
> A: Well, if Sheila's in it, anything's possible.

1. Where are these people? _____
2. Who are they? _____
3. What are they talking about? _____
4. Who do you think Paul is? _____
5. How do the speakers feel about Sheila? _____
6. What do you think will happen next? _____

B. Talk about your answers with another student. Are they the same? What words helped you get your answers?

A. *Read the conversation. Make inferences to answer the questions.*

> A: Hey you!
> B: I'm sorry.
> A: There's a stop sign!
> B: I said I'm sorry . . .
> A: You didn't even look!
> B: I guess I wasn't thinking.
> A: Yeah, I'll say. You know how much this is going to cost?
> B: I don't know. It looks pretty bad.
> A: I want all your info now. You know, registration, insurance, everything.
> B: Jeez, what's my Dad going to say . . . ?
> A: That's your problem. Come on. Let's get this done. I'm going to call the police, too. I don't want any trouble about this later.

1. Where are these people? _____

2. Who are they? _____

3. What are they talking about? _____

4. What can you infer about A? _____

5. What can you infer about B? _____

6. What do you think will happen next? _____

B. *Talk about your answers with another student. Are they the same? What words helped you get your answers?*

A. *Read the conversation. Make inferences to answer the questions.*

A: Excuse me. Do you have the time?
B: Nine o'clock.
A: Already? Are you sure?
B: Look, my watch says nine o'clock.
A: Then where's the Number 13?
B: The Number 13? It's probably downtown by now.
A: What do you mean?
B: It probably came about fifteen minutes ago. It always comes at fifteen minutes before the hour.
A: So, the next one isn't until nine forty-five?
B: There's no next one. That was the last one.
A: The last one?
B: Yeah. After nine o'clock, there aren't any more.
A: Oh, no! What's Trudy going to say! . . . But wait a minute. What are you doing here?
B: I'm waiting for a taxi . . . Where are you going? I'm going downtown, to Tremont Street. Are you heading that way? We could share.

1. Where are these people? _____
2. Who are they? _____
3. What are they talking about? _____
4. What can you infer about A? _____
5. What can you infer about B? _____
6. What do you think will happen next? _____

B. *Talk about your answers with another student. Are they the same? What words helped you get your answers?*

Making Inferences from Stories

In each of these exercises, there is a passage from a book. You will try to infer more about the story from the information in the passage. There may be more than one possible answer for some questions.

> **Note:** More than one answer is often possible in these exercises, too. You should be ready to explain your answers.

A. *Read the passage from* Anne of Green Gables, *by L. M. Montgomery. Make inferences to answer the questions. More than one answer may be possible.*

When Anne woke up the next morning, she felt happy. She jumped out of bed and ran to the window.

It was a beautiful morning. The sun shone and the sky was blue. Anne opened the window. Outside, there was a fruit tree with beautiful flowers. Anne could see
5 many other trees and flowers, and a small river, too.

"This is a wonderful place!" she thought. Then, suddenly, she remembered. She felt very sad again. "But I can't stay here," she thought. "They don't want me because I'm not a boy."

Marilla came into the room. "Good morning Anne," she said. "Breakfast is
10 waiting. Wash your face and put on your clothes."

"I'm feeling very hungry," Anne said. "I can never be sad in the mornings. I love mornings."

After breakfast, Anne washed the plates and cups. Marilla watched carefully, but Anne did the job well.

15 "This afternoon I'm going to drive to White Sands," Marilla said. "You'll come with me, Anne, and we'll talk to Mrs. Spencer."

Matthew didn't say anything, but he looked very sad. Later, he got the horse and buggy ready for Marilla. Marilla drove, and Anne sat next to her.

"Is it a long way to White Sands?" asked Anne.
20 "About eight kilometers," answered Marilla. "I know you like to talk, Anne. So tell me your story."

"It isn't very interesting," said Anne. I was born in Bolingbroke in Nova Scotia, and I was 11 last March. My parents were teachers. But they died when I was a baby. So their cleaner, Mrs. Thomas, and her husband took me into their house.

25 "Mrs. Thomas had four children. I helped her with them. But then Mr. Thomas died in an accident. Mrs. Thomas and the children went to Mr. Thomas's parents. They didn't want me.

"Then Mrs. Hammond, Mrs. Thomas's friend, took me into her house. She had eight children. They were very hard work. Then Mrs. Hammond moved away. I had
30 to go to the orphanage because nobody wanted me. I was there for four months."

1. Where are these people? _____
2. Who are they? _____
3. When do you think this takes place? _____
4. What is happening? _____
5. How do the people probably feel? _____
6. What do you think will happen next? _____

B. *Talk about your answers with another student. Are they the same? What words helped you get your answers?*

EXERCISE 6

A. *Read the passage from* **Sarah, Plain and Tall,** *by Patricia MacLachlan. Make inferences to answer the questions. More than one answer may be possible.*

5 "You don't sing anymore," he said. He said it harshly. Not because he meant to, but because he had been thinking of it for so long. "Why?" he asked more gently.

Slowly, Papa straightened up. There was a long silence, and the dogs looked up, wondering at it.

"I've forgotten the old songs," said Papa quietly. He sat down. "But maybe
10 there's a way to remember them." He looked at us.

"How?" asked Caleb eagerly.

Papa leaned back in his chair. "I've placed an advertisement in the newspapers. For help."

"You mean a housekeeper?" I asked, surprised.

15 Caleb and I looked at each other and burst out laughing, remembering Hilly, our housekeeper. She was round and slow and shuffling. She snored in a high whistle at night, like a teakettle, and let the fire go out.

"No," said Papa slowly. "Not a housekeeper." He paused. "A wife."

Caleb stared at Papa. "A wife? You mean a mother?"

20 Nick slid his face onto Papa's lap, and Papa stroked his ears.

"That, too," said Papa. "Like Maggie."

Mathew, our neighbor to the south, had written to ask for a wife and mother for his children. And Maggie had come from Tennessee. Her hair was the color of turnips, and she laughed.

Papa reached into his pocket and unfolded a letter written on white paper. "And I have received an answer."

1. Where are these people? _____

2. Who are they? _____

3. How old do you think Caleb is? _____

4. What happened before this in the story? _____

5. When do you think this takes place? _____

6. Why doesn't Papa remember the old songs? _____

7. What is in Papa's letter? _____

8. What do you think will happen next? _____

B. *Talk about your answers with another student. Are they the same? What words helped you get your answers?*

A. *Read the passage from* Gentlehands, *by M.E. Kerr. Make inferences to answer the questions.*

I tried to convince Skye to let me drive to Beauregard with her that night and hitch a ride back to my house, but she wouldn't hear of it. She dropped me and took off like a rocket. I saw my father standing in our driveway by his Toyota, smoking a cigarette, watching me. He was in uniform because he was working
5   nights that week.
"That was a Jensen she was driving," I said. "Did you ever hear of a Jensen?"
"Did she ever hear of a speed limit?"
"Oh, *Dad*."
"It isn't funny, Buddy," he said.
10 I stood there and he stood there, and then he said, "Where'd you go?"
I didn't want to tell him then. He wasn't in the greatest mood, and I didn't want to open that whole can of worms at the end of a beautiful evening.
"We just rode around."
"Rode around at eighty miles an hour?"
15 "She wasn't doing eighty."
"She was close to it," he said. He took a drag on his cigarette and twirled his car keys in his hand. "Buddy, if your social calendar isn't too full, I'd appreciate it if you'd do something with Streaker tomorrow."
"I work until two," I said.
20 "And after two?"
"I was going clamming¹ with Ollie."
"Take Streaker with you," he said. "Okay?"
"Okay," I agreed.
"Streaker hangs around his mother too much," my father said.
25 "I know that. Okay."
He gave me one of his friendly punches and opened his car door. "I've never even heard of a Jensen," he said.
"Neither had I," I said.
"Well, anyway, did you have a good time?"
30 "Yeah."

---

¹ **clamming** looking for clams at the seaside; *clams* are a kind of shellfish

1. Where are these people? _____
2. Who are they? _____
3. How old do you think Buddy is? _____
4. Who do you think Streaker is? _____
5. What happened before this in the story? _____
6. What do you think will happen after this? _____

B. *Talk about your answers with another student. Are they the same? What words helped you get your answers?*

EXERCISE 8

A. *Read the next part of the story from* **Gentlehands.** *Make inferences to answer the questions.*

She was all in blue, right down to her sandals. I guess she specialized in wearing all one color, and she had this great perfume on, and that smile, and she just stood there and I just stood there, and the jukebox was roaring out some rock number, and the whole place was babbling around us, waiters calling out: "Two

5   over easy, o.j., and one black."

"I came to get you," she said.

"I'm working," I said.

"I'm shopping," she said. "What time are you through working?"

"Two," I said.

10   "I'm going to take you for a swim," she said. "Would a swim make you happy, Buddy?"

"I guess it would," I said.

"Don't guess with me, Buddy," she said.

"BUDDY!" I could hear Kick behind me.

15   "Someone's calling you," she said. "I'll be parked outside at two sharp. Okay?"

"Okay," I said.

Before I'd left the house that morning, I'd stuck a note up in Streaker's bunk telling him to be ready at two thirty.

So much for promises, and clamming.

1. Where are the people? _____

2. What can you infer about Buddy after reading both passages? _____

    _____

3. What can you infer about his family? _____

4. What can you infer about the girl? _____

5. What is meant by "So much for promises, and clamming"? _____

    _____

6. What do you think will happen next? _____

B. *Talk about your answers with another student. Are they the same? What words helped you get your answers?*

Focus on Vocabulary

A. *Do you know the meanings of these words? Read each word aloud. Then put a* ✓ *(you know),* ? *(you aren't sure), or* X *(you don't know).*

_____ respect   _____ population   _____ including   _____ attack   _____ destroy

_____ nation   _____ throw out   _____ tear   _____ trouble   _____ increase

B. *Read the article to the end.*

A Crow Problem in Japan

Until recently, the Japanese loved and respected crows. They believed that these big, black birds were messengers from the gods. In fact, there is a crow on the shirts of the Japanese soccer team. But today, many Japanese people have very different feelings about these birds.

5 Across the nation, the crow population has grown very fast, particularly in cities. The reason is simple: They have more to eat. Where do they find food? In the garbage that the Japanese put on the streets in the evening. As the Japanese begin to live more like Westerners, they buy more and throw out more, including food. Trucks pick up the garbage in the morning, but the crows often get there

10 first. They tear holes in the garbage bags and throw the garbage all over the usually clean streets.

The birds also take food right out of people's hands. This happens in city parks, as well as in school playgrounds. At times, they even attack people. These birds are very big with long, sharp beaks and claws, and they can cause serious

15 injury.

The birds are also causing trouble in other ways. They build their nests on electricity poles, which can cause blackouts. They tear up fiber optic cables,[1] so they can use pieces of the cables for their nests.

Some Japanese cities are now trying to limit the crow population. In

20 Kagoshima, city officials are destroying the nests. But this doesn't seem to be very effective. They have destroyed 600 nests, but the number of crows is still increasing. In Tokyo, bird catchers catch and kill crows—93,000 in Tokyo in six years. In fact, now there are fewer reports of problems with crows in Tokyo.

---

[1] **fiber optic cables** a special kind of wire for the telephone or Internet

C. *Look back at the passage and circle the words that are on the list in part A. Then underline the words in the passage that are new to you.*

D. *Look up the underlined words in the dictionary. Write them in your vocabulary notebook with the parts of speech, the sentences, and the meanings. (See Part 2, Unit 1, page 41.)*

E. *Check your understanding of the passage. Read it again if you need to. Write T (True) or F (False) after each sentence.*

1. The Japanese never liked crows. _____

2. There are more crows because there is more garbage on the streets. _____

3. Crows are afraid of people. _____

4. Japanese cities can't do anything about the crows. _____

F. *Talk about your answers with another student. Are they the same? Then check all your work with your teacher.*

EXERCISE 10

A. *Read each sentence and circle the best meaning for the underlined word(s).*

1. Until recently, the Japanese loved and <u>respected</u> crows.
   a. were afraid of   b. had a good opinion of   c. had a poor opinion of

2. Across the <u>nation</u>, the crow population has grown very fast, particularly in cities.
   a. country   b. world   c. island

3. Across the nation, the <u>crow population</u> has grown very fast, particularly in cities.
   a. area of crows   b. size of crows   c. number of crows

4. As the Japanese begin to live more like Westerners, they buy more and <u>throw out</u> more, including food.
   a. pay a lot for   b. put in the garbage   c. keep at home

5. As the Japanese begin to live more like Westerners, they buy more and throw out more, <u>including</u> food.
   a. but not   b. even   c. except

6. They <u>tear</u> holes in the garbage bags and throw the garbage all over the usually clean streets.
   a. see   b. find   c. break

7. At times, they even <u>attack</u> people.
   a. try to hurt   b. try to help   c. try to get near

8. The birds are also causing <u>trouble</u> in other ways.
   a. fear   b. surprise   c. problems

9. In Kagoshima, city officials are <u>destroying</u> the nests.
   a. pulling down   b. building up   c. checking on

10. They have destroyed 600 nests, but the number of crows is still <u>increasing</u>.
    a. the same   b. becoming larger   c. becoming smaller

B. *Talk about your answers with another student. Are they the same?*

EXERCISE 11

A. *Complete the sentences with the words from the box. Use each word only once. Change the form of the word for the sentence if necessary (plural, past tense, etc.).*

| attack | including | nation | respect | throw out |
| destroy | increase | population | tear | trouble |

1. I had to _____ a whole bottle of milk because it wasn't good to drink.

2. Italy became a _____ in 1863. Before then, it was made up of several smaller countries.

3. The price of meat _____ a lot last year.

4. Bears are usually afraid of people and don't _____ them.

5. Young people today often don't _____ their teachers.

6. Tim had a lot of _____ with his new computer. He had to bring it back several times.

7. When George climbed over the fence, he _____ a hole in his pants.

8. The storm _____ many houses along the coast.

9. The _____ of Europe is not growing any more.

10. There were forty people on the bus, _____ the driver.

B. *Talk about your answers with another student. Are they the same?*

A. Write a sentence for each word in the box. Look at the sentences in Exercises 10 and 11 if you need help.

attack	including	nation	respect	throw out
destroy	increase	population	tear	trouble

1. _____

2. _____

3. _____

4. _____

5. _____

6. _____

7. _____

8. _____

9. _____

10. _____

B. Check your work with your teacher.

A. **Write the other parts of speech for each word. More than one word may be possible for each part of speech. (See Part 2, Unit 4, page 67.)**

Noun	Verb	Adjective	Adverb
	attack		
	destroy		
	increase		
nation			
population			
	respect		
	tear		
trouble			

B. **Talk about your answers with another student. Are they the same? Then check your answers with your teacher.**

C. **Write the new words from Exercises 9–13 in your vocabulary notebook. Then make study cards. Study them alone and then with another student.**

Focusing on the Topic

What Is a Topic?

A topic is a word or phrase that tells what something is about.

Examples:

- You are talking with a friend about a person you both know. You say to your friend, "He's always talking about baseball." In other words, baseball is his favorite *topic* of conversation.
- You are reading a book, and a friend asks, "What is it about?" You answer, "It's about mountain climbing." Mountain climbing is the *topic* of the book.

The topic is important in written English. Writers think about the topic as they are writing, and their ideas follow from that topic. If you want to understand the ideas, you must start by looking for the topic.

Finding the Topic

In these exercises, you will look for the topic of a list of words. One word is the topic for the other words. The topic is the most general word. It can be a thing, a person, or an idea. The other words all belong to the topic and are more specific.

EXAMPLE

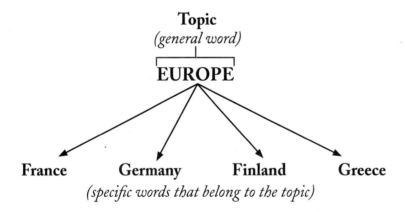

Topic
(general word)

EUROPE

France   Germany   Finland   Greece
(specific words that belong to the topic)

Kinds of Topics

There are three kinds of topics:

1. The topic can be the name of a group of things or people.

    Example: Topic: __*meat*__

        beef   chicken   lamb   pork   turkey   rabbit

    Explanation
    All the words are specific kinds of meat.

2. The topic can be the name of a thing with many parts.

    Example: Topic: __*apartment*__

        bedroom   closet   bathroom   kitchen   hall   balcony

    Explanation
    All the words are parts of an apartment.

3. The topic can be the name for a general idea or thing. It can include more specific things.

    Example: Topic: __*party*__

        music   food   people   games   drinks   dancing

    Explanation
    All the words are specific things that are often included at a party.

> **Notes:** In these exercises, you don't need to know the meaning of every word. You just need to find the general word that tells the topic.
>
> Do each exercise without using a dictionary. Look up words you want to know after you finish the exercise.

PRACTICE
. . . .

Find the topic in each list. Then circle it and write it on the line.

1. Topic: _____
   minute   hour   day   time   week   second

2. Topic: _____
   lunch   meal   brunch   supper   dinner   breakfast

Explanation
- The topic of the first group of words is *time*. All the other words are about time.
- The topic of the second group is *meal*. All the other words are names of different meals.

A. *Find the topic in each list. Then circle it and write it on the line.*

1. Topic: _____

    nose   ear   eye   mouth   head   chin

2. Topic: _____

    dog   mouse   fish   bird   cat   pet

3. Topic: _____

    shirt   skirt   clothing   sock   suit   dress

4. Topic: _____

    carrot   vegetable   potato   pea   onion   bean

5. Topic: _____

    dollar   euro   yen   ruble   peso   money

6. Topic: _____

    eighty   sixteen   seventy-seven   number   nine   thirty-two

7. Topic: _____

    family   mother   sister   uncle   brother   aunt

8. Topic: _____

    table   sofa   bed   chair   furniture   desk

9. Topic: _____

    Sudan   Africa   Kenya   Nigeria   Egypt   Zimbabwe

10. Topic: _____

    refrigerator   oven   microwave   stove   sink   kitchen

B. *Talk about your answers with another student. Are they the same?*

A. *Find the topic in each list. Then circle it and write it on the line.*

1. Topic: _____

    milk   juice   coffee   drink   water   tea

2. Topic: _____

    engine   car   window   door   brake   tire

3. Topic: _____
   river   lake   sea   pond   ocean   water

4. Topic: _____
   school   bank   house   building   factory   supermarket

5. Topic: _____
   computer   keyboard   mouse   monitor   software   hard drive

6. Topic: _____
   happy   feeling   excited   angry   upset   bored

7. Topic: _____
   oxygen   nitrogen   helium   neon   hydrogen   gas

8. Topic: _____
   map   reservation   suitcase   travel   guidebook   hotel

9. Topic: _____
   plant   tree   bush   flower   grass   seed

10. Topic: _____
    doctor   hospital   bed   patient   nurse   medicine

B. *Talk about your answers with another student. Are they the same?*

Thinking of the Topic

In these exercises, the topic is not included in the lists. You must think of a topic for each list. The topic should be just right for the words in the list. It should not be too general (too big) or too specific (too small).

PRACTICE

Read the list. Then write a topic.

Topic: _____
baseball   rugby   tennis   soccer   cricket   football

Explanation
- This topic tells us that all the words are names of sports played with a ball.
- The topic *sports* is too general. It includes many other kinds of sports that are not on the list.
- The topic *sports played with a ball in the United States* is too specific. One of the sports on the list (cricket) is not played in the United States.

A. *Read each list. Then write a topic.*

1. Topic: _____
   sheep   cow   horse   goat   chicken   pig

2. Topic: _____
   knife   spoon   cup   bowl   fork   chopsticks

3. Topic: _____
   Buenos Aires   Caracas   Lima   Rio de Janeiro   La Paz   Montevideo

4. Topic: _____
   subway   train   bus   tram   taxi   limousine

5. Topic: _____
   index   title page   table of contents   chapters   cover pages

6. Topic: _____
   physics   chemistry   biology   astronomy   geology   botany

7. Topic: _____
   purple   hot pink   orange   beige   grey   forest green

8. Topic: _____
   cheese   milk   ice cream   yogurt   butter   cream

9. Topic: _____
   morning   afternoon   noon   midnight   dawn   evening

10. Topic: _____
    papaya   banana   mango   pineapple   coconut   avocado

B. *Talk about your answers with another student. Are they the same?*

EXERCISE 4

A. *Read each list. Then write a topic.*

1. Topic: _____
   Seoul   Bankok   Saigon   Rangoon   Jakarta   Kuala Lumpur

2. Topic: _____
   Mercury   Venus   Saturn   Mars   Jupiter   Uranus

3. Topic: _____
   dollar   quarter   penny   dime   nickel   half dollar

4. Topic: _____
   driveway   street   highway   lane   avenue   motorway

5. Topic: _____
   Kennedy   Washington   Clinton   Bush   Lincoln   Roosevelt

6. Topic: _____
   roof   wall   window   floor   stair   door

7. Topic: _____
   war   hunger   sickness   poverty   unemployment   crime

8. Topic: _____
   Louisiana   Florida   Texas   Mississippi   Georgia   Alabama

9. Topic: _____
   heavy   fat   skinny   slim   thin   overweight

10. Topic: _____
    Pelé   Maradona   Beckham   Gullit   Platini   Von Basten

B. Talk about your answers with another student. Are they the same?

EXERCISE 5

A. Read each list and write a topic. Then add one more word to the list.

1. Topic: _____
   wing   seat   pilot   seatbelt   tail   _____

2. Topic: _____
   sports   movie   soap opera   cartoon   _____

3. Topic: _____
   gloves   hat   scarf   sweater   coat   _____

4. Topic: _____
   rain   wind   sun   fog   snow   _____

5. Topic: _____
   run   jump   walk   kick   hop   _____

6. Topic: _____
   Amazon   Ganges   Danube   Nile   Yangtze   _____

7. Topic: _____
   candy ice cream pie pudding cookies _____

8. Topic: _____
   desert mountains wetland prairie forest _____

9. Topic: _____
   book letter Web page article e-mail _____

10. Topic: _____
    Mexico Honduras Guatemala El Salvador _____

B. **Talk about your answers with another student. Are they the same?**

EXERCISE 6

A. **One word in each list doesn't belong to the topic. Cross out the word that doesn't belong. Then write the topic.**

1. Topic: _things we use to go up_
   road   ladder   elevator   stairs   ~~wall~~   escalator

2. Topic: _____
   teacher   doctor   taxi driver   scientist   lawyer   engineer

3. Topic: _____
   box   table   bag   pocket   basket   suitcase

4. Topic: _____
   truck   tractor   car   van   motorcycle   jeep

5. Topic: _____
   warm   nice   freezing   cold   cool   hot

6. Topic: _____
   runway   gate   shops   tracks   security   waiting area

7. Topic: _____
   look   shout   say   speak   scream   laugh

8. Topic: _____
   hand   leg   heart   arm   knee   foot

9. Topic: _____
   actor   camera   director   producer   costume   paint

10. Topic: _____
    farmer   nurse   road worker   gardener   baseball player   police officer

B. *Talk about your answers with another student. Are they the same?*

EXERCISE 7

A. *Think of words for these topics and write them on the lines.*

1. Well-paid jobs

   _____
   _____
   _____
   _____
   _____

2. Places to visit in your city

   _____
   _____
   _____
   _____
   _____

3. Problems at your school/university

   _____
   _____
   _____
   _____
   _____

4. _____
   (your own topic)

   _____
   _____
   _____
   _____

B. *Talk about your answers with another student. Are they the same?*

Focus on Vocabulary

A. *Do you know the meanings of these words? Read each word aloud. Then put a ✓ (you know), ? (you aren't sure), or X (you don't know).*

____ get down to	____ connected	____ charge	____ customer	____ access
____ power	____ equipment	____ offer	____ settle	____ join

B. *Read the passage to the end.*

Hungry for Power

Michelle Lebrun was in Chicago, and she didn't know what to do. She wanted to work, but her computer's battery[1] was dead. It was mid morning, and she had to get ready for a meeting. Then she saw a coffee shop. She went in and looked around. She soon saw what she needed and sat down. Under her table, there was a
5 power outlet.[2] Now she could get down to work.

These days, more and more people are looking for outlets. They are away from their office or home, and they need power. Until recently, most electronic equipment stayed in the office or at home. It was connected to power all the time. But now, people carry all kinds of electronic equipment with them. Computers, cell
10 phones, personal organizers, cameras, music players, games—all these things run on batteries. Sooner or later, the batteries die and need to be charged.

Many coffee shops allow customers to use outlets for free. It's good for business. Some are adding more outlets to their walls and are offering free wireless Internet access. Airports are also adding outlets and offering Internet access.
15 Business travelers in particular need power. You sometimes see them sitting on the floor of the airport if there are no chairs near an outlet.

Occasionally there are arguments about outlets, but they are usually settled quickly. Everyone knows the rules: First, you should never take up all the outlets. Second, if someone else needs the outlet, you should limit your time.
20 The next time your computer or your cell phone battery dies, what will you do? Will you join the crowd looking for an outlet? Or will you make a different choice? You could turn off all your equipment, and, instead, you could open a book or go for a walk.

---

[1]**battery** an object that provides electricity for something
[2]**outlet** a place on a wall where you can connect electrical things to the electricity supply

C. *Look back at the passage and circle the words that are on the list in part A. Then underline words in the passage that are new to you.*

D. *Look up the underlined words in the dictionary. Write them in your vocabulary notebook with the parts of speech, the sentences, and the meanings.*

E. *Check your understanding of the passage. Read it again if you need to. Write T (True) or F (False) after each sentence.*

1. Michelle Lebrun didn't need a power outlet. _____

2. To charge a battery, you need to plug it into an outlet. _____

3. More and more places offer Internet access. _____

4. In public places, you can use an outlet for as long as you want. _____

F. *Talk about your answers with another student. Are they the same? Then check all your work with your teacher.*

EXERCISE 9

A. *Read each sentence and circle the best meaning for the underlined word(s).*

1. Now she could <u>get down to</u> work.
   a. continue   b. start   c. finish

2. They are away from their office or home, and they need <u>power</u>.
   a. electricity   b. control   c. lights

3. Until recently, most electronic <u>equipment</u> stayed in the office or at home.
   a. typewriters   b. news   c. machines

4. It was <u>connected</u> to the power all the time.
   a. turned on   b. attached   c. closed

5. Sooner or later, the batteries die and need to be <u>charged</u>.
   a. opened   b. used   c. refilled

6. Many coffee shops allow <u>customers</u> to use outlets for free.
   a. people who   b. people who   c. people who
      sell things   work there   buy things

7. Some are adding more outlets to their walls and are <u>offering</u> free wireless Internet access.
   a. selling   b. giving   c. using

8. Some are adding more outlets to their walls and are offering free wireless Internet <u>access</u>.

    a. programs   b. news   c. entry

9. Occasionally, there are arguments about outlets, but they are usually <u>settled</u> quickly.

    a. ended   b. started   c. paid

10. Will you <u>join</u> the crowd looking for an outlet?

    a. stay away from   b. become part of   c. look at

B. ***Talk about your answers with another student. Are they the same?***

EXERCISE 10

A. ***Complete the sentences with the words from the box. Use each word only once. Change the form of the word for the sentence if necessary (plural, past tense, etc.).***

access	connected	equipment	join	power
charge	customer	get down to	offer	settle

1. Mihoko _____ the photography club at the university.
2. Is there _____ to the building for people in wheelchairs?
3. At 9:00 A.M., there weren't many _____ in the shop.
4. They decided to _____ their argument and work together again.
5. Good skiing _____ can be very expensive.
6. The battery in my cell phone was _____ but it still didn't work.
7. Now that we agree about the conditions, we can _____ business.
8. The telephone company _____ a free phone to new customers.
9. The machine is not working because it's not _____ to anything.
10. Yesterday evening the _____ was out for almost three hours.

B. ***Talk about your answers with another student. Are they the same?***

EXERCISE 11

A. *Write a sentence for each word in the box in Exercise 10. Look at the sentences in Exercises 9 and 10 if you need help.*

1. _____
2. _____
3. _____
4. _____
5. _____
6. _____
7. _____
8. _____
9. _____
10. _____

B. *Check your work with your teacher.*

EXERCISE 12

A. *Write the other parts of speech for each word. More than one word may be possible for each part of speech. (See Part 2, Unit 4, page 67.)*

Noun	Verb	Adjective	Adverb
access			
		charged	
		connected	
customer			
equipment			
	join		
	offer		
power			
	settle		

B. *Talk about your answers with another student. Are they the same? Then check your answers with your teacher.*

C. *Write the new words from Exercises 8–12 in your vocabulary notebook. Then make study cards. Study them alone and then with another student.*

Understanding Paragraphs

What Is a Paragraph?

A paragraph is a group of sentences that are all about one thing or idea.

PRACTICE

*Read these passages. Are they paragraphs? Check (✓) **Paragraph** or **Not a Paragraph**.*

1. Sports stars in the United States make a lot of money. This is especially true for the most popular team sports, such as basketball, football, and baseball. The best players in these sports get millions of dollars from their teams. They can make even more money from companies that make sports clothes or shoes. These companies will pay a star a lot of money to wear the clothes or shoes that they make.

   Paragraph _____   Not a Paragraph _____

2. In the United States, many college students eat in the college dining hall. Millions of people around the world also eat at McDonald's every day. The most popular foods there are the hamburgers and French fries. However, fresh fruit and vegetables are very expensive in the United States. Poor families often don't have enough money to buy them. Finally, a Japanese restaurant paid $231 per pound for a whole tuna fish. This was the highest price ever paid for a fish.

   Paragraph _____   Not a Paragraph _____

   Explanation
   - The first passage is a paragraph because all the sentences are about *sports stars* and *money*.
   - The second passage is **not** a paragraph because the sentences are about many different things. A paragraph is about one thing or idea.

A. *Read these passages. Are they paragraphs? Check (✓) Paragraph or Not a Paragraph.*

1. A doctor's job is not easy. Doctors have to work long hours, all day and often at night, too. During the day, they spend a lot of time with patients in their office. They may also visit other patients in the hospital. Some doctors do operations that take many hours. Other doctors work on studies of new medicines and new treatments. Doctors also have read a lot, and they have to write reports about their patients.

    Paragraph _____   Not a Paragraph _____

2. In England, tea is a drink, and it is also a meal. There are many different ways to make coffee. Florida is a big producer of oranges for juice. In East Asia, rice is the most important food. People make rice in many different ways. In some countries in the Middle East, people make bread that is round and flat. The Turkish language is not at all like the Arabic language.

    Paragraph _____   Not a Paragraph _____

3. Many musical instruments are made of wood. For example, violins, cellos, pianos, clarinets, and oboes are all made of wood. Scott Joplin played ragtime piano music. It was very popular in the early 20th century. Many children play musical instruments in Venezuela. There are also hundreds of orchestras for young people. Chinese opera is completely different from Italian opera.

    Paragraph _____   Not a Paragraph _____

4. Around the world, many people travel to work—commute—by train. Commuting by train can be more relaxing than driving to work. On a train, you don't have to think about the road. You can read, work, sleep, or talk with other passengers. However, sometimes there can be problems with trains. They may be crowded or late. At times, the passengers can also be unpleasant. For example, some people talk loudly on their cell phones, so it's impossible to read or sleep.

    Paragraph _____   Not a Paragraph _____

B. *Talk about your answers with another student. Are they the same?*

Topics of Paragraphs

In English, most paragraphs (and longer passages) have a topic. The topic of a paragraph tells what the paragraph is about. When you are reading, you should **always look for the topic**. If you know the topic, you will understand better.

In these exercises, the topic is a word or phrase that fits the paragraph. It's not too general or too specific. In other words:
- all the facts and ideas in the paragraph will fit in the topic
- it doesn't refer to facts and ideas that are not in the paragraph

PRACTICE

A. **Read this paragraph from Exercise 1 again. What is it about? Circle the best topic.**

A doctor's job is not easy. Doctors have to work long hours, all day and often at night, too. During the day, they spend a lot of time with patients in their office. They may also visit other patients in the hospital. Some doctors do operations that take many hours. Other doctors work on studies of new medicines and new treatments. Doctors also have read a lot, and they have to write reports about their patients.

a. doctors in hospitals _____

b. a doctor's job _____

c. difficult jobs _____

B. **Check your answer with your teacher.**

C. **Now decide which topic is too specific and which topic is too general. Write too general *or* too specific *next to those topics.***

Explanation
- Topic *a. doctors in hospitals* is too specific. Not all the sentences are about doctors in hospitals. Some sentences talk about doctors in their offices.
- Topic *c. difficult jobs* is too general. The paragraph only talks about a doctor's job. It doesn't talk about any other kinds of jobs.

> **Notes:**
> - Writers often put the topic in the first sentence.
> - The topic is usually repeated several times in the paragraph.

A. *Read each paragraph and circle the best topic. Write* too general *or* too specific *after the other topics.*

Forests

1. The redwood trees in California are very special. They are some of the tallest trees in the world. How did they grow so tall? Scientists say there are several reasons. The most important reason is the weather. In this part of California, it is never very hot or very cold and it rains often. These are good conditions for growing. There is also not a lot of wind because of the mountains nearby. With no strong winds, the young trees are not blown over in storms. Finally, these trees grow slowly, but they live for a very long time. Some of them are over 2,000 years old.

   a. trees in the United States _____

   b. redwood trees in California _____

   c. growing conditions for trees _____

2. Large forests are important to us in many ways. They give us wood for paper, building, and heating. For many city people, forests are a place to go on vacation. Forests are also home for many kinds of plants and animals. But there is one more reason why forests are important: They help clean the air. Air pollution is a problem in many parts of the world. It has many bad effects—on people and on the Earth. Scientist believe that air pollution is causing global warming. Without large forests, these problems would be even worse.

   a. wildlife in forests _____

   b. large forests _____

   c. the importance of forests _____

3. The land in Scotland was once mostly forest, but now it is nearly treeless. Five thousand years ago, forests covered the area. Then around 3,900 years ago, people arrived and began farming. As the population grew, they needed more space for farms, so they cut down trees or burned large areas of forests. By the time the Romans arrived (in about 100 C.E.), half the forests were already gone. The destruction continued after that. By the 19th century, there were few forests left in Scotland. Today, the Scottish government wants to protect the last forests. It also wants to increase the forest areas by planting new trees.

    a. new forests in Scotland _____

    b. forests in Scotland _____

    c. the history of forests _____

B. *Talk about your answers with another student. Are they the same?*

EXERCISE 3

A. *Read each paragraph and circle the best topic. Write* **too general** *or* **too specific** *after the other topics.*

The History of Chemistry

1. Before the 1600s, alchemy was an important science. In some ways it was like modern chemistry. For example, chemists often mix substances together and heat them over fire. In the same way, alchemists also mixed different substances and heated them. But their reasons for doing this were very different. Modern chemists mix things so they can find out something about the substances. They want to have a better understanding of the world. Alchemists, however, believed they could make something new by mixing things. In particular, they believed they could make gold. They were never successful, of course.

    a. scientists _____

    b. making gold _____

    c. alchemists and chemists _____

2. Robert Boyle began as an alchemist and became the first modern chemist. He was born in Ireland in 1627. He studied philosophy, religion, and mathematics in England. Afterwards, he traveled in France and Italy and taught at Oxford University. At first he believed in alchemy, but

he soon began to think differently. He began to study substances more scientifically. In the late 1650s, he discovered the elements.[1] This work opened the way for modern chemistry. In 1662, Boyle made another important discovery, now called Boyle's Law. In his later years, he was mostly interested in philosophy and religion. He died in 1691.

a. Robert Boyle's life and work _____
b. Robert Boyle's discoveries _____
c. English scientists _____

3. The French chemist Antoine Lavoisier (1743–1794) made several important discoveries. The most important was the Law of Conservation of Mass. According to this law, nothing really goes away. It just changes into something else. For example, when water is heated and it boils, it becomes steam. Lavoisier discovered what happens when we breathe. He also found out that people breathe in oxygen and breathe out carbon dioxide. Finally, Lavoisier showed that all substances can change their form. They can all become solid, liquid, or gas. For example, water can also become ice or steam.

a. the Law of Conservation of Mass _____
b. Lavoisier's life _____
c. Lavoisier's discoveries _____

B. *Talk about your answers with another student. Are they the same?*

Writing the Topic of a Paragraph

When you write the topic of a paragraph, you have to think carefully about the paragraph. This is the first step in understanding it.

Remember
• The topic should tell what the paragraph is about. • It shouldn't be too general or specific.

[1] **elements** the basic substances that things are made of

Read the paragraph and write the topic.

Around the world, many people commute (travel) to work by train. Commuting by train can be more relaxing than driving to work. On a train, you don't have to think about the road. You can read, work, sleep, or talk with other passengers. However, sometimes there can be problems with trains. They may be crowded or late. At times, the passengers can also be unpleasant. For example, some people talk loudly on their cell phones, so it's impossible to read or sleep.

Topic: _____

Explanation
- *Commuting by train* is a good topic because it tells what the paragraph is about. All the sentences are about that topic.
- The topic *commuting to work* is too general. A paragraph with this topic can be about commuting by car or by bicycle. But this paragraph talks only about commuting by train.
- The topic *problems with trains* is too specific. The paragraph doesn't talk only about the problems with trains. It also talks about the good things about train travel.

EXERCISE 4

A. Read each paragraph and write the topic.

Galileo Galilei

1. Galileo Galilei is often called the father of modern science. He was born in Pisa, Italy, in 1564. His father wanted him to become a doctor, so at first, he studied medicine in Florence. Then he followed his true interests, studying mathematics and astronomy. In 1592, he became professor of mathematics at the University of Padua. Then in 1610, he returned to Florence and remained there until he died at the age of 78 in 1642. Galileo made many important scientific discoveries. Even more important was his method—the way he worked. He didn't just guess how things happened. He did experiments and then looked at the results of the experiments.

Topic: _____

2. One of Galileo's most important discoveries was about gravity. This is the force that makes things fall down. Before Galileo, there were no scientific studies of gravity. People generally believed that heavy things fell faster than light things. Galileo showed that this was not true. In his most famous experiment, he used a heavy ball and a light ball. He let them both go at the same time so they rolled down a board. The heavy ball didn't roll faster than the light ball. They both rolled at the same speed. From this experiment, Galileo understood an important law of physics: the law of falling bodies.

   Topic: _____

3. Some of Galileo's ideas caused him problems during his life. The Catholic Church in particular didn't accept his ideas about astronomy. In one of his books, he agreed with Copernicus, a German astronomer. Copernicus said that the sun didn't go around the earth, as most people thought. Instead, it was the earth that went around the sun. This went against Catholic religious beliefs at the time. Galileo tried to explain his ideas to Catholic leaders, but they were not pleased. First, they made it difficult for him to work. Then, in 1633, they kept him imprisoned in his home. He was not allowed to leave his home for the rest of his life.

   Topic: _____

B. *Talk about your answers with another student. Are they the same? Then check your answers with your teacher.*

EXERCISE 5

A. *Read each paragraph and write the topic.*

Earth Sciences

1. The shape of the earth is always changing. These changes have many different causes. Some come from forces below ground. These forces can cause a volcano, an earthquake, or a tsunami. And afterwards, the land often looks very different. Changes also happened because of the weather. Many years of rain, for example, can wash away dirt and change the shape of rocks. In the desert, the wind blows the sand and changes the shapes of the hills. Finally, water can also change the shape of the land. For example,

a river can make a deep cut into a mountain. At the seaside, waves can move the shore inland.

Topic: _____

2. Mt. Vesuvius in Italy and Mt. Pinatubo in the Philippines are both famous volcanoes, and they are similar in many ways. The Roman city of Pompeii was very close to Mt. Vesuvius. When it erupted[1] in 79 C.E., it killed thousands of people, and the city was destroyed. Many people also lived on the sides of Mt. Pinatubo. When it erupted in 1991, about 800 people were killed and 100,000 lost their homes. Both volcanoes also put a lot of ashes into the air. According to scientists, about 10 feet (3 meters) of ashes fell on Pompeii. After Mt. Pinatubo erupted, about 1 foot (33 cm) of ash fell on the area around the mountain.

Topic: _____

3. New technology has helped scientists learn a lot about the earth. For example, they now understand what a volcano is. They also know what kinds of rocks and chemicals usually come out of a volcano. And they understand the effects on the land and on the air. Scientists have also learned a lot about earthquakes. They understand many things about the forces underground that can cause an earthquake. They can also tell when an earthquake is likely. But there are still some important things that scientists don't know about the earth. For example, they can't say when a volcano or an earthquake will happen.

Topic: _____

B. *Talk about your answers with another student. Are they the same? Then check your answers with your teacher.*

Main Ideas in Paragraphs

The main idea is the writer's idea about the topic. The main idea gives you a more complete understanding of the topic. When you are reading, you should first find the topic. Then ask yourself, "What does the writer want to say about this topic?"

---

[1] **erupt** when a volcano sends out smoke, ashes, or rocks into the sky

For any topic, different main ideas are possible. For example:

Topic: The redwood trees in California

Possible main ideas:
a. There are several reasons why the redwood trees in California are so tall.
b. The redwood trees in California are protected in state and national parks.
c. There are much fewer redwood trees in California today than in the past.

PRACTICE

Read the paragraph and circle the best main idea sentence.

The land in Scotland was once mostly forest, but now it is nearly treeless. Five thousand years ago, forests covered the area. Then around 3,900 years ago, people arrived and began farming. As the population grew, they needed more space for farms, so they cut down trees or burned large areas of forests. By the time the Romans arrived (in about 100 C.E.), half the forests were already gone. The destruction continued after that. By the 19th century, there were few forests left in Scotland. Today, the Scottish government wants to protect the last forests. It also wants to increase the forest areas by planting new trees.

a. Five thousand years ago, forests covered Scotland.
b. Scotland was once mostly forest, but now it is nearly treeless.
c. Scotland has changed a lot over the years.

Explanation
- The answer is *b.* This is the writer's main idea about Scotland. All the sentences in the paragraph talk about the forests.
- Sentence *a.* is too specific. Only one part of the paragraph is about forests 5,000 years ago.
- Sentence *c.* is too general. It tells about change in Scotland, but it doesn't say what kind of change. It could be economic or social change, but this paragraph talks only about the land has changed.

A. Read each paragraph and circle the best main idea.

The History of Chemistry

1. Before the 1600s, alchemy was an important science. In some ways it was like modern chemistry. For example, chemists often mix substances together and heat them over fire. In the same way, alchemists also mixed different substances and heated them. But their reasons for doing this were very different. Modern chemists mix things so they can find out something about the substances. They want to have a better understanding of the world. Alchemists, however, believed they could make something new by mixing things. In particular, they believed they could make gold. They were never successful, of course.

    a. Modern chemists mix substances together to find out more about them.
    b. Alchemists believed they could make something new—gold.
    c. Alchemists were like chemists in some ways, but very different in others.

2. Robert Boyle began as an alchemist and became the first modern chemist. He was born in Ireland in 1627. He studied philosophy, religion, and mathematics in England. Afterwards, he traveled in France and Italy and taught at Oxford University. At first he believed in alchemy, but he soon began to think differently. He began to study substances more scientifically. In the late 1650s, he discovered the elements. This work opened the way for modern chemistry. In 1662, Boyle made another important discovery, now called Boyle's Law. In his later years, he was mostly interested in philosophy and religion. He died in 1691.

    a. Robert Boyle became the first great modern chemist.
    b. Robert Boyle was the scientist who discovered the elements.
    c. Robert Boyle was also interested in philosophy and religion.

3. The French chemist Antoine Lavoisier (1743–1794) made several important discoveries. The most important was the Law of Conservation of Mass. According to this law, nothing really goes away. It just changes into something else. For example, when water is heated and it boils, it becomes steam. Lavoisier also discovered what happens when we breathe. He found out that people breathe in oxygen and breathe out carbon dioxide. Finally, Lavoisier showed that all substances can change their form. They can all become solid, liquid, or gas. For example, water can also become ice or steam.

a. French chemists have made important discoveries.
b. Lavoisier showed that substances are not fixed in one form.
c. The French chemist Antoine Lavoisier made several important discoveries.

B. *Talk about your answers with another student. Are they the same?*

Writing the Main Idea of a Paragraph

The first sentence in a paragraph often, but not always, includes the main idea. You may need to use parts of several sentences to write the main idea.

When you write a main idea sentence, it should:
• tell the writer's idea about the topic
• be general enough for all the ideas and information in the paragraph
• not refer to ideas or information that are not in the paragraph

PRACTICE

Read each paragraph and write a main idea sentence.

Sports stars in the United States make a lot of money. This is especially true for the most popular team sports, such as basketball, football, and baseball. The best players in these sports get millions of dollars from their teams. They can make even more money from companies that make sports clothes or shoes. These companies will pay a star a lot of money to wear the clothes or shoes that they make.

Main idea: _____

Explanation
The main idea sentence is the first sentence in this paragraph. It gives the topic—*sports stars* and *money*—and tells the writer's idea about the topic. All the other sentences in the paragraph tell about this idea.

Main Idea Sentences

• The main idea sentence expresses the writer's idea about the topic.
• It should include all the ideas and information in the paragraph.
• It should not include other ideas or information that aren't in the paragraph.
• The first sentence of a paragraph is often a good main idea sentence—but not always. Sometimes it does not give the complete idea and you need to add something else from the paragraph.

A. *Read these paragraphs again (from Exercise 4, page 168). Now write the main idea sentence.*

Galileo Galilei

1. Galileo Galilei is often called the father of modern science. He was born in Pisa, Italy, in 1564. His father wanted him to become a doctor, so at first, he studied medicine in Florence. Then he followed his true interests, studying mathematics and astronomy. In 1592, he became professor of mathematics at the University of Padua. Then in 1610, he returned to Florence and remained there until he died at the age of 78 in 1642. Galileo made many important scientific discoveries. Even more important was his method—the way he worked. He didn't just guess how things happened. He did experiments and then looked at the results of the experiments.

   Main idea: _____

2. One of Galileo's most important discoveries was about gravity. This is the force that makes things fall down. Before Galileo, there were no scientific studies of gravity. People generally believed that heavy things fell faster than light things. Galileo showed that this was not true. In his most famous experiment, he used a heavy ball and a light ball. He let them both go at the same time so they rolled down a board. The heavy ball didn't roll faster than the light ball. They both rolled at the same speed. From this experiment, Galileo understood an important law of physics: the law of falling bodies.

   Main idea: _____

3. Some of Galileo's ideas caused him problems during his life. The Catholic Church in particular didn't accept his ideas about astronomy. In one of his books, he agreed with Copernicus, a German astronomer. Copernicus said that the sun didn't go around the earth, as most people thought. Instead, it was the earth that went around the sun. This went against Catholic religious beliefs at the time. Galileo tried to explain his ideas to Catholic leaders, but they were not pleased. First, they made it difficult for him to work. Then, in 1633, they kept him imprisoned in his home. He was not allowed to leave his home for the rest of his life.

   Main idea: _____

B. *Talk about your answers with another student. Are they the same? Then check your answers with your teacher.*

A. Read these paragraphs again (from Exercise 5, page 169) and write the main idea sentence.

Earth Sciences

1. The shape of the earth is always changing. These changes have many different causes. Some come from forces below ground. These forces can cause a volcano, an earthquake, or a tsunami. And afterwards, the land often looks very different. Changes also happened because of the weather. Many years of rain, for example, can wash away dirt and change the shape of rocks. In the desert, the wind blows the sand and changes the shapes of the hills. Finally, water can also change the shape of the land. For example, a river can make a deep cut into a mountain. At the seaside, waves can move the shore inland.

   Main idea: _____

2. Mt. Vesuvius in Italy and Mt. Pinatubo in the Philippines are both famous volcanoes, and they are similar in many ways. The Roman city of Pompeii was very close to Mt. Vesuvius. When it erupted in 79 C.E., it killed thousands of people, and the city was destroyed. Many people also lived on the sides of Mt. Pinatubo. When it erupted in 1991, about 800 people were killed and 100,000 lost their homes. Both volcanoes also put a lot of ashes into the air. According to scientists, about 10 feet (3 meters) of ashes fell on Pompeii. After Mt. Pinatubo erupted, about 1 foot (33 cm) of ash fell on the area around the mountain.

   Main idea: _____

3. New technology has helped scientists learn a lot about the earth. For example, they now understand what a volcano is. They also know what kinds of rocks and chemicals usually come out of a volcano. And they understand the effects on the land and on the air. Scientists have also learned a lot about earthquakes. They understand many things about the forces underground that can cause an earthquake. They can also tell when an earthquake is likely. But there are still some important things that scientists don't know about the Earth. For example, they can't say when a volcano or an earthquake will happen.

   Main idea: _____

B. Talk about your answers with another student. Are they the same? Then check your answers with your teacher.

Finding Supporting Facts and Ideas

A paragraph also includes facts and ideas that support (explain or relate to) the main idea. They help make the writer's ideas stronger and clearer. Supporting facts and ideas can be examples of something or parts of an explanation.

Note: In these exercises, you should underline only the supporting facts and ideas. There may be other information in the paragraph, but you should look for the parts that explain or relate closely to the main idea.

PRACTICE

Read each paragraph and write a main idea sentence. Then underline the supporting facts and ideas.

The land in Scotland was once mostly forest, but now it is mostly treeless. Five thousand years ago, forests covered the area. Then around 3,900 years ago, people arrived and began farming. As the population grew, they needed more space for farms, so they cut down trees or burned large areas of forests. By the time the Romans arrived (in about 100 C.E.), half the forests were already gone. The destruction continued after that. By the 19th century, there were few forests left in Scotland. Today, the Scottish government wants to protect the last forests. It also wants to increase the forest areas by planting new trees.

Main idea: _____

Explanation
These are the important facts and ideas. They should be underlined:

Five thousand years ago, forests covered the area.
3,900 years ago, people arrived
they cut down trees or burned large areas of forest
(in about 100 C.E.), half the forests were already gone
By the 19th century, there were few forests left

Note: When different people read a passage, they may have different ideas about what is important in the passage. For this reason, there is never one right way to underline supporting facts and ideas.

But remember:

• Don't underline too much. That way, you can't tell what is important.
• Think carefully about what is important and be ready to explain your underlining.

A. *Read these paragraphs and main idea sentences again. Then underline the supporting facts and ideas.*

The History of Chemistry

1. Before the 1600s, alchemy was an important science. In some ways it was like modern chemistry. For example, chemists often mix substances together and heat them over fire. In the same way, alchemists also mixed different substances and heated them. But their reasons for doing this were very different. Modern chemists mix things so they can find out something about the substances. They want to have a better understanding of the world. Alchemists, however, believed they could make something new by mixing things. In particular, they believed they could make gold. They were never successful, of course.

   Main idea: *Alchemists were like chemists in some ways, but very different in others.*

2. Robert Boyle began as an alchemist and became the first modern chemist. He was born in Ireland in 1627. He studied philosophy, religion, and mathematics in England. Afterwards, he traveled in France and Italy and taught at Oxford University. At first he believed in alchemy, but he soon began to think differently. He began to study substances more scientifically. In the late 1650s, he discovered the elements. This work opened the way for modern chemistry. In 1662, Boyle made another important discovery, now called Boyle's Law. In his later years, he was mostly interested in philosophy and religion. He died in 1691.

   Main idea: *Robert Boyle became the first great modern chemist.*

3. The French chemist Antoine Lavoisier (1743–1794) made several important discoveries. The most important was the Law of Conservation of Mass. According to this law, nothing really goes away. It just changes into something else. For example, when water is heated and it boils, it becomes steam. Lavoisier also discovered what happens when we breathe. He found out that people breathe in oxygen and breathe out carbon dioxide. Finally, Lavoisier showed that all substances can change their form. They can all become solid, liquid, or gas. For example, water can also become ice or steam.

   Main idea: *The French chemist Antoine Lavoisier made several important discoveries.*

B. *Talk about your answers with another student. Are they the same? Then check your answers with your teacher.*

A. *Read these paragraphs and main ideas again. Then underline the supporting facts and ideas.*

Galileo Galilei

1. Galileo Galilei is often called the father of modern science. He was born in Pisa, Italy, in 1564. His father wanted him to become a doctor, so at first, he studied medicine in Florence. Then he followed his true interests, studying mathematics and astronomy. In 1592, he became professor of mathematics at the University of Padua. Then in 1610, he returned to Florence and remained there until he died at the age of 78 in 1642. Galileo made many important scientific discoveries. Even more important was his method—the way he worked. He didn't just guess how things happened. He did experiments and then looked at the results of the experiments.

   Main idea: *Galileo, the father of modern science, lived a long and full life.*

2. One of Galileo's most important discoveries was about gravity. This is the force that makes things fall down. Before Galileo, there were no scientific studies of gravity. People generally believed that heavy things fell faster than light things. Galileo showed that this was not true. In his most famous experiment, he used a heavy ball and a light ball. He let them both go at the same time so they rolled down a board. The heavy ball didn't roll faster than the light ball. They both rolled at the same speed. From this experiment, Galileo understood an important law of physics: the law of falling bodies.

   Main idea: *One of Galileo's most important discoveries was about gravity.*

3. Some of Galileo's ideas caused him problems during his life. The Catholic Church in particular didn't accept his ideas about astronomy. In one of his books, he agreed with Copernicus, a German astronomer. Copernicus said that the sun didn't go around the earth, as most people thought. Instead, it was the earth that went around the sun. This went against Catholic religious beliefs at the time. Galileo tried to explain his ideas to Catholic leaders, but they were not pleased. First, they made it difficult for him to work. Then, in 1633, they kept him imprisoned in his home. He was not allowed to leave his home for the rest of his life.

   Main idea: *Some of Galileo's ideas caused him problems during his life.*

B. *Talk about your answers with another student. Are they the same? Then check your answers with your teacher.*

A. *Look back at Unit 4, Exercise 7, on page 174. Choose one of the topics and write it below. Then write a main idea sentence.*

Topic: _____

Main idea: _____

B. *Now write three supporting facts or ideas for your main idea sentence.*

1. _____
2. _____
3. _____

C. *Check your main idea sentence and your supporting facts and ideas with your teacher. Then write a paragraph about your main idea. Use the supporting facts and ideas in your paragraph.*

_____

_____

_____

_____

_____

_____

_____

_____

_____

D. *Work with a partner. Read each other's paragraphs. Did you write about the same thing? What did you learn from your classmate?*

E. *Check your work with your teacher.*

Focus on Vocabulary

A. *Do you know the meanings of these words? Read each word aloud. Then put a ✓ (you know), ? (you aren't sure), or X (you don't know).*

_____ local	_____ experienced	_____ effort	_____ actually	_____ missing
_____ human	_____ sight	_____ manage	_____ right away	_____ otherwise

B. *Read the passage to the end.*

Five Divers and a Dragon[1]

Five European divers were found on the Indonesian island of Rinca. Local officials say they are very lucky to be alive. This island is home to the Komodo dragon.[2]

The day before, they were diving from a boat near the island of Flores. This is
5 an area of great beauty, but it is also dangerous for divers. There are often sharks[3] and strong ocean currents.[4] All five of these divers were experienced.

When they came up again, the boat was far away. It soon moved out of sight. According to the captain of the boat, he had lost sight of the divers.

They were in the water for twelve hours. With high waves and strong currents,
10 it was very difficult to swim. They saw several islands, but couldn't get close to them. In the evening, they made one last effort. This time they managed to reach land.

But they had no chance to rest. Out of the dark appeared one of the dragons. These Komodo dragons do not actually breathe fire, of course. But they are very big—10 feet long (3 meters) and 365 pounds (166 kg)—and very dangerous. They
15 eat any meat they can find, even humans.

This dragon attacked right away. The divers threw stones at it and managed to fight it off. The next day, it attacked again, and again they threw stones.

The whole next day, they didn't sleep for fear of the dragons. They found some shellfish to eat, but no water to drink. Then, towards evening, they were seen and
20 picked up by a boat. The five divers had been missing for more than 24 hours. They were very tired, thirsty, and hungry, but otherwise they were all right.

---

[1] **dragon** a large, imaginary animal that has wings and a long tail, and can breathe out fire
[2] **Komodo dragon** the largest living reptile
[3] **shark** a large sea fish with sharp teeth
[4] **current** movement of the water or air

C. *Look back at the passage and circle the words that are on the list in part A. Then underline the words in the passage that are new for you.*

D. *Look up the underlined words in the dictionary. Write them in your vocabulary notebook with the parts of speech, the sentences, and the meanings.*

E. *Check your understanding of the passage. Read it again if you need to. Write* **T** *(True) or* **F** *(False) after each sentence.*

1. The water near the island of Flores is a safe place for diving. _____

2. The boat moved away because the captain didn't see the divers. _____

3. The divers saw other islands but didn't want to land on them. _____

4. The divers killed the Komodo dragon. _____

F. *Talk about your answers with another student. Are they the same? Then check all your work with your teacher.*

EXERCISE 13

A. *Read each sentence and circle the best meaning for the underlined word(s).*

1. <u>Local</u> officials say they are very lucky to be alive.
   a. international   b. from the city   c. from the area

2. All five of these divers were <u>experienced</u>.
   a. skilled   b. young   c. strong

3. It soon moved out of <u>sight</u>.
   a. water   b. time   c. view

4. In the evening, they made one last <u>effort</u>.
   a. call   b. time   c. try

5. This time they <u>managed</u> to reach land.
   a. succeeded   b. wanted   c. hoped

6. They eat any meat they can find, even <u>humans</u>.
   a. animals   b. plants   c. people

7. These Komodo dragons do not <u>actually</u> breathe fire, of course.
   a. often   b. really   c. usually

8. This dragon attacked <u>right away</u>.
   a. immediately   b. in a while   c. later

9. The five divers had been <u>missing</u> for more than 24 hours.
   a. found   b. seen   c. lost

10. They were very tired, thirsty, and hungry, but <u>otherwise</u> they were all right.
   a. in all ways   b. except that   c. fortunately

B. *Talk about your answers with another student. Are they the same?*

EXERCISE 14

A. *Complete the sentences with the words from the box. Use each word only once. Change the form of the word for the sentence if necessary (plural, past tense, etc.).*

actually	experienced	local	missing	right away
effort	human	manage	otherwise	sight

1. Please come home _____. There's a problem with the heat.
2. To our surprise, sales _____ increased last month.
3. Our cat is _____. She's black and white. Have you seen her?
4. The apartment is a bit dark, but _____ it's very nice.
5. He _____ to answer all the questions, but he didn't have time to check them.
6. Joyce made an _____ to remember his name. Was it George? Or John?
7. An _____ teacher, she knew just what to do with the difficult new child.
8. Our _____ post office is not open on Saturday.
9. The ability to speak is the biggest difference between _____ and animals.
10. At the _____ of his mother, the baby stopped crying.

B. *Talk about your answers with another student. Are they the same?*

EXERCISE 15

A. *Write a sentence for each word in the box. Look at the sentences in Exercises 13 and 14 if you need help.*

actually	experienced	local	missing	right away
effort	human	manage	otherwise	sight

1. _____
2. _____
3. _____
4. _____
5. _____
6. _____
7. _____
8. _____
9. _____
10. _____

B. *Check your work with your teacher.*

EXERCISE 16

A. *Write the other parts of speech for each word. More than one word may be possible for each part of speech. (See Part 2, Unit 4, page 67.)*

Noun	Verb	Adjective	Adverb
			actually
effort			
		experienced	
human			
		local	
	manage		
		missing	
sight			

B. *Talk about your answers with another student. Are they the same? Then check your answers with your teacher.*

C. *Write the new words from Exercises 12–16 in your vocabulary notebook. Then make study cards. Study them alone and then with another student.*

Identifying the Pattern

What Is a Pattern?

It's a regular way that something is organized or done. Many things around us are organized into patterns in some way. In fact, people usually prefer things to be organized. For example:

- At home, the things in your kitchen are organized in a certain way. This plan or pattern helps you put things away faster and find them again.
- At school, you have a schedule for the semester. This is another kind of pattern. It organizes your time and tells you when to go to classes.

There are patterns in English writing, too. When you are reading in English, you should look for the pattern. It will help you understand and remember the ideas. In this unit you will learn about four common patterns in English writing.

Common Patterns in Paragraphs	
• The Listing Pattern	• The Comparison Pattern
• The Sequence Pattern	• The Cause/Effect Pattern

Signal Words

Writers often use certain words to signal (show) the main idea and the supporting facts and ideas. These signal words help you notice the pattern and follow the ideas.

For each pattern in this unit, there is a list of common signal words. Writers can use other signal words, too. (Sometimes they don't use any signal words.)

The Listing Pattern

In this pattern, the main idea tells you about a list of things or ideas. The paragraph tells about each of the things or ideas on the list.

A. *This paragraph has a listing pattern. Read the paragraph and write the main idea. Then underline the supporting facts and ideas.*

There are many ways you can enjoy yourself in Rome, Italy. First, it's a good city for walking. There are lots of beautiful streets, plazas, and parks. It's also a great city for looking at art. You can enjoy the art in many lovely old churches and museums, including St. Peter's. Another enjoyable thing about Rome is the ancient history. Every year millions of people visit the Colisseum, the Forum, and other places from ancient Rome. Finally, there's the food. On almost every street, you can find a restaurant—a *trattoria*—where you can get a wonderful meal.

Main idea: _____

B. *Talk about your answer with another student. Did you write the same main idea? Check your answer with your teacher. Then talk about these questions:*

1. What words in the main idea tell you there will be a list?

   _____

2. What signal words are used?

   _____

Explanation
- The first sentence is also the main idea sentence.
- The words *many ways* tell us there will be a list.
- The signal words are *first*, *also*, *another*, *finally*.

Common Signal Words for the Listing Pattern

For the main idea:
many, several, a lot of, lots of, some, a few

For the supporting facts and ideas:
first, third, one, other, another, in addition, last, finally, second, and, also, too, yet another, for example

---

A. *Read these listing pattern paragraphs. Write the main ideas. Circle the signal words and phrases. Then underline the supporting facts and ideas.*

Successful Companies

1. Nintendo® is a Japanese company that has many well-known products. First, there are the video games, in particular, Donkey Kong® and Super Mario.® These were big international hits almost thirty years ago, and they are still popular. When they came out, they were played on big video machines. Then Nintendo also invented the Game Boy.® This was the first hand-held video game player. Another successful product is the Wii.® In Wii games, it's not just the picture on the screen that moves. The player moves, too.

   Main idea: _____

2. The Bic® company is famous for its ballpoint pens. Bic didn't invent the ballpoint, but in 1950, it was the first to produce ballpoint pens. Bic pens were very popular for several good reasons. First of all, they didn't tear the paper. That was one problem the old pens had. Second, ballpoint pens didn't get ink all over the paper. That was another problem with the old pens. In addition, the ink from a ballpoint pen dried very quickly. With the old pens, people often got ink on their hands. But not with a ballpoint.

   Main idea: _____

3. The beauty care products of the Body Shop® are special. For one thing, they aren't tested on animals. Most other companies that make beauty products do test them on animals. This sometimes means hurting or killing the animals. Also, all Body Shop products are made from natural substances. There are no man-made chemicals in them. Another special thing about the company is the way it gets the materials. In fact, all the materials come directly from the farmers or producers. This helps the producers and means the materials are fresher.

   Main idea: _____

B. *Talk about your answers with another student. Are they the same? Then check your answers with your teacher.*

The Sequence Pattern

In this pattern, the main idea tells you about a sequence (things that happen in order). The paragraph tells you about the events or the steps of the sequence.

- It can be a sequence of events.
  Examples: events in the life of a person, dates in history

- It can also be a sequence of steps in a process.
  Examples: instructions for how to do something, directions for going somewhere

PRACTICE

A. **These paragraphs have a sequence pattern. Read each paragraph and write the main idea. Then underline the supporting facts and ideas.**

1. The history of the island of Cuba began a very long time ago. The first people came to the island from South America in about 3,500 B.C.E. They lived by hunting meat and gathering plants in the forests. Two thousand years later, a new group of people came to the island. They knew how to farm and fish and how to build simple houses. Then in about 1,100 C.E., another group of people arrived (the Taino). They built villages, had a government, and could make boats and clothing. Columbus saw these people on October 27, 1492 during his famous first trip to the New World.

   Main idea: _____

2. Would you like to learn how to surf? First, swim out from the beach with your board. Then wait for a strong ocean wave. When a good wave comes to you, stand up on the board. As the wave rises under the board, try not to fall down. While you ride the wave, use your feet to control the direction of the board. Try to keep it heading for the beach. If you're lucky, you can ride the wave all the way to the beach. If you can't stay on the board the first time, keep trying. Surfing is not easy, but it's fun and exciting.

   Main idea: _____

B. **Work with another student. Answer these questions for each paragraph.**

1. a. What words in the main idea tell you there will be a sequence?

   _____

   b. Is it a sequence of events or steps in a process?

   _____

   c. What signal words are used?

   _____

2. a. What words in the main idea tell you there will be a sequence?

_____

b. Is this paragraph about a sequence of events or steps in a process?

_____

c. What signal words are used?

_____

Explanation

1. The first sentence is also the main idea sentence.
   - The words *history* and *a long time ago* tell us there will be a list.
   - It's a sequence of events.
   - The signal words are *about 3,500 B.C.E.*, *Two thousand years later*, *about 1,100 C.E.*, *October 27, 1492*.

2. The main idea sentence is something like: *Here are the steps for learning how to surf.*
   - The words *learn how to* tell us there will be a sequence.
   - It's a sequence of steps in a process.
   - The signal words are *first, then, when, as, while, finally.*

Common Signal Words for the Sequence Pattern

For the main idea:
- A date or time phrase and words such as *history* or *life*
- Words that tell about a process such as *how, make, do, learn, the way to, process*

For the supporting facts and ideas:
- A date, a time, the age of a person
- Phrases with time:
  for a year, in a month, the same day, at this time, today, last week, many years, later, by the 1950s
- Phrases that tell about the order of events or steps:
  first, second, before, soon, while, now, at last, finally, when, at first, then, now, next, last, after, during

---

A. *Read these sequence pattern paragraphs. Write the main ideas. Circle the signal words and phrases. Then underline the supporting facts and ideas.*

Popular Toys

1. The Lego® company was started in the 1930s by a Danish toymaker. At first, the company made wooden blocks. In the 1940s, they changed from wood to plastic. Then, in 1958, they invented the famous Lego blocks that stay together. At that time, they also began selling sets of blocks to build dinosaurs, spaceships, castles, and so on. By the 1990s, many sets also included electronic parts. Over the years, the company has made many different kinds of toys, but the blocks are the same. In fact, blocks made today can be used with blocks from 1958.

   Main idea: _____

2. All children love playing with toys. Making the toy can be fun, too. One thing that is easy to make is playdough.[1] First, you take a cup of flour and a half cup of salt. Put them in a bowl. Now add two large spoonfuls of cream of tartar[2] and mix it with the flour and salt. Next add one cup of water and two spoonfuls of oil. Mix everything together. Then put the mixture in a small pot. Cook it on the stove, mixing slowly. When it is harder to mix, take it off the stove. Put it on a plate and let it cool. Finally, work the mixture with your hands. You can add vegetable juice (from carrots, beets, or spinach) to give it natural color.

   Main idea: _____

3. Scrabble,® a popular board game, was invented by Alfred Mosher Butts. In the mid-1930s, he had an idea for a new board game, but at first, no one was interested in his idea. Fifteen years later, he called his game Scrabble and he found a partner, James Brunot. That same year, they began to make Scrabble sets. At first, they didn't sell many sets. But then the president of a big store in New York played Scrabble on vacation, and he ordered many sets for the store. Other stores did, too. Soon everybody wanted to have a Scrabble set. Today Scrabble is a favorite game for children and adults around the world.

   Main idea: _____

B. *Talk about your answers with another student. Are they the same? Then check your answers with your teacher.*

---

[1] **playdough** a soft material that can be shaped to make different things
[2] **cream of tartar** an ingredient used in baking cakes

The Comparison Pattern

In this pattern, the main idea tells you about two things, people, or ideas. It tells how they are similar, different, or both. The paragraph tells about the ways they are similar or different.

PRACTICE

A. **These paragraphs have a comparison pattern. Read each paragraph and write the main idea. Then underline the supporting facts and ideas.**

1. Modena and Ferrara are both interesting, smaller Italian cities, and they are similar in many ways. First, they are in the same area in the north of Italy, in the Po River valley. Both cities also have long histories and have central streets with many old buildings. Some of the buildings in Modena even look similar to those in Ferrara. Finally, the streets in both Modena and Ferrara are always full of bicycles. Many people use bicycles in these cities to go to work or to go shopping.

   Main idea: _____

2. Though there are many similarities, Modena and Ferrara are different in some ways. Modena is a little larger than Ferrara. Modena is also better known outside of Italy because Ferrari cars are made nearby. Some of the buildings are very different, too. The biggest building in Modena is the Ducal Palace. It looks very different from the biggest building in Ferrara, the Estense Castle. Another difference is in the food. They both make a kind of pasta that is filled with meat. In Modena, this pasta is called *tortellini*, but in Ferrara, it's called *capelletti*.

   Main idea: _____

B. _Work with another student. Answer these questions for each paragraph._

1. a. What words in the main idea tell you there will be a comparison?

   _____

   b. Does it tell about similarities, differences, or both?

   _____

   c. What signal words are used?

   _____

2. a. What words in the main idea tell you there will be a comparison?

   _____

   b. Does it tell about similarities, differences, or both?

   _____

   c. What signal words are used?

   _____

Explanation

1. The first sentence is also the main idea sentence.
   - The words _both_ and _similar_ tell us there will be a comparison.
   - It tells about similarities.
   - The signal words are _same, similar, a lot like, both._

2. The first sentence is the main idea sentence.
   - The words _are different in some ways_ tell us there will be a comparison.
   - It tells about differences.
   - The signal words are _larger, better known, very different, difference, but._

Common Signal Words for the Comparison Pattern

For the main idea:
- The main idea sentence usually includes the two things that will be compared.
- Any of the signal words below may be included in the main idea.

For the supporting facts and ideas:
- Words that show similarity: *alike, like, similar, same, also, both, too*
- Words that show difference: *different, unlike, but, however, while, on the other hand*
- Comparatives: *more than, less than, bigger, smaller, more beautiful*

Note: Writers may include a kind of list (of similarities or differences) in a comparison paragraph. They may use some listing signal words with the comparison/contrast signal words.
   Example: They also taste a little different.

EXERCISE 3

A. *Read these comparison pattern paragraphs. Write the main ideas. Circle the signal words and phrases. Then underline the supporting facts and ideas.*

1. People sometimes think that lemons and limes are the same fruit. But in fact, they are quite different. First of all, they are a different color. Lemons are green at first, but then they become yellow. However, limes remain green. Limes also taste different from lemons. Finally, lemons are grown all over the world, but limes are grown in only a few places. This is because lemons are a very old fruit. People have grown them for thousands of years. Limes, on the other hand, are a new fruit. Scientists made them from lemons only about 70 years ago.

    Main idea: _____

2. In Paris today, people can shop for food at supermarkets or at small shops. They are similar in some ways. In both places, you can buy meat, bread, fruit, vegetables, and other foods. Both supermarkets and small shops are found in every neighborhood. However, there are important differences. While the supermarkets are open all day and until late, small shops close at midday and in the evening. There is also a difference in their prices. The small shops are often more expensive. But many Parisians believe that the food in small shops is better than the food in supermarkets.

    Main idea: _____

3. The food in India and China tastes very different, but there are also some similarities. In both countries, people eat a lot of rice. In fact, it is served at almost every meal. In the same way, they also eat a lot of vegetables in both countries. When they eat meat, it's often cut in small pieces and mixed with vegetables. Another similarity is in the variety of dishes. This is because both India and China are very large. Each area of these countries has its own special dishes. Finally, in both India and China, there is an area where people like to eat very spicy dishes.

Main idea: _____

B. *Talk about your answers with another student. Are they the same? Then check your answers with your teacher.*

The Cause/Effect Pattern

In this pattern, the main idea tells you that something causes something else (or is caused by something else). The paragraph tells about the causes and/or the effects.

Sometimes the cause comes first and sometimes the effect comes first. For example:

       cause   effect

A. Shoes with high heels <u>can cause</u> foot problems.

       effect   cause

B. Foot problems <u>are caused by</u> shoes with high heels.

PRACTICE

A. *These paragraphs have a cause/effect pattern. Read each paragraph and write the main idea. Then underline the supporting facts and ideas.*

1. Why did many people from other European countries move to Ireland after 2001? One important cause was economic. Many big international companies moved to Ireland and there was lots of work. There were also political reasons. New laws made it easier for people to move around Europe, so people from Eastern Europe could go to work in Western Europe. They didn't have to get special papers anymore. Many of these Eastern Europeans knew some English. Because of this, some went to England, but many went to Ireland.

Main idea: _____

2. The immigrants had both good and bad effects on Ireland. First, the new people helped the Irish economy. They did the hard jobs that young Irish people didn't want to do anymore. The arrival of all these people also brought changes to Irish cities and towns. Irish people learned about other religions, other foods, and other ways of life. At the same time, however, all these changes caused some problems. Some Irish people became afraid of the immigrants. This fear led to anger and to some attacks on the foreigners.

Main idea: _____

B. *Work with another student. Answer these questions for each paragraph.*

1. a. What words in the main idea tell you there is a cause/effect pattern?

   _____

   b. Does it tell about causes, effects or both?

   _____

   c. What signal words are used?

   _____

2. a. What words in the main idea tell you this is a cause/effect pattern?

   _____

   b. Does it tell about causes, effects or both?

   _____

   c. What signal words are used?

   _____

Explanation
1. The first sentence is the main idea sentence.
   • The word *why* tells us there will be a cause/effect pattern.
   • It tells about the causes.
   • The signal words are *cause, reasons, because of.*

2. The first sentence is the main idea sentence.
   • The word *effects* tells us there will be a cause/effect pattern.
   • It tells about effects.
   • The signal words are *helped, brought, as a result of, caused, led to.*

Common Signal Words for the Cause/Effect Pattern

For the main idea:
Any of the signal words below may be included in the main idea.

For the supporting facts and ideas:
* When the cause comes first:
  so, help, stop, become, result in, reason for, have an effect on, cause, make, lead to, as a result, the cause of, bring

* When the effect comes first:
  because, be due to, be caused by, result from, because of, be the effect of, be made by, reason why

Note: Writers may also include a kind of list (of causes and effects) in a cause/effect paragraph. They may use some listing signal words with the cause/effect signal words.
Example: They also may become very tired and sleepy.

EXERCISE 4

A. *Read these cause/effect pattern paragraphs. Write the main ideas. Circle the signal words and phrases. Then underline the supporting facts and ideas.*

Health and Medicine

1. Why do so many people in the United States take vitamins? Americans spend millions of dollars on them every month, more than in any other country. One reason for this is the unhealthy lifestyle of many Americans. In fact, many people don't exercise much and don't eat good food. But they want to stay healthy, so they take vitamins. It's easier than changing their lives. The big spending of Americans on vitamins is also the effect of advertising. Big companies advertise vitamins as the quick and easy way to take care of health problems. These ads are not always true, but many people believe them. As a result, people buy more and more vitamins.

Main idea: _____

2. Aspirin is a simple drug, but it's very useful. It can stop a headache or an earache. It helps take away pain in the fingers or knees. Aspirin can stop a fever if you have the flu, and it can make you feel better if you have a cold. Furthermore, aspirin can help prevent heart disease. Doctors often tell people to take an aspirin a day to protect their heart. However, aspirin may also cause problems for some people. If you take aspirin often, it may lead to stomachaches and even to serious stomach problems. To prevent this, you should always take aspirin after a meal.

   Main idea: _____

3. When people take diet pills, they often get the effect they wanted: they lose weight quickly. But that result may not last long. Very often they gain the weight back again later. Furthermore, some diet pills can have unpleasant side effects. Some of these pills may cause stomach problems. Others can cause anxiety and trouble sleeping. Some diet pills may even have serious effects on your heart. Before you start taking diet pills, you should talk to your doctor.

   Main idea: _____

B. *Talk about your answers with another student. Are they the same? Then check your answers with your teacher.*

Recognizing the Pattern

In these exercises, each paragraph has a different pattern. As you read each paragraph, think about the main idea and look for the signal words. Then decide on the pattern.

Here's a recap of the four patterns you learned about on page 184.

• The Listing Pattern	• The Comparison Pattern
• The Sequence Pattern	• The Cause/Effect Pattern

A. *Turn to Unit 5, Exercise 2, on page 165. Read the paragraphs again and write the pattern for each one here.*

1. Pattern: _____

2. Pattern: _____

3. Pattern: _____

B. *Turn to Unit 5, Exercise 6, on page 172. Read the paragraphs again and write the pattern for each one here.*

1. Pattern: _____

2. Pattern: _____

3. Pattern: _____

C. *Turn to Unit 5, Exercise 7, on page 174. Read the paragraphs again and write the pattern for each one here.*

1. Pattern: _____

2. Pattern: _____

3. Pattern: _____

D. *Talk about your answers with another student. Are they the same?*

A. *Complete each of these paragraphs about Shakespeare with a sentence from the box. (There is one extra sentence.) Then write the pattern.*

> ### Missing Sentences
>
> a. Yet another kind of play was the comedy.
> b. When he was only 18, he married Ann Hathaway.
> c. Shakespeare wrote poetry, but he is best known for his plays.
> d. In fact, Shakespeare wrote many plays, but Marlowe only finished four.

1. Shakespeare wrote many plays, but they were all very different. In fact, he wrote three kinds of plays. One kind was the history play. Most of his history plays were about kings. For example, his play called *Henry V* is about a king of England. Another kind of play was the tragedy. In fact, some of Shakespeare's most famous plays are tragedies. These include *Macbeth*, *Othello*, *Hamlet*, and *King Lear*. _____ _____ One of his comedies that is still very popular is *A Midsummer Night's Dream*.

   Pattern: _____

2. Two great writers were born in England in 1564. One was William Shakespeare. The other was Christopher Marlowe. Shakespeare lived until the age of 52, but Marlowe died suddenly when he was only 29. This is one reason why Shakespeare produced a lot more work than Marlowe. _____ Both writers were famous in their time, but Shakespeare is much better known today. People around the world know Shakespeare's plays, but not many people know Marlowe's plays.

   Pattern: _____

3. Not much is known about Shakespeare's life except the basic facts. He was born in Stratford-on-Avon on April 16, 1564. For a few years, he studied at a school near home. _____ _____ Then he moved to London to work as an actor and a writer. By the age of 35, he was already well known. He continued to work in London until about 1613. He returned to Stratford that year and lived there until his death in 1616.

   Pattern: _____

B. *Talk about your answers with another student. Are they the same?*

A. *Complete each of these paragraphs about zoos with a sentence from the box. (There is one extra sentence.) Then write the pattern.*

Missing Sentences

a. They don't just show people how they eat and sleep.
b. Soon many other countries will have new zoos, too.
c. The new zoos still have cages, but they are very big.
d. For the first few days, he just sat in one place.

---

1. Zoos in the United States today are different from zoos in the past. The old zoos had lots of cages. Even large animals were kept in cages. Often the cages had nothing in them except an animal, and the animal looked very sad and lonely. _____
_____ Many animals live together in these cages. In fact, they're not like cages at all. They look like real wild areas, with trees, flowers, rocks, and water.

   Pattern: _____

2. The new zoos teach people a lot about animals. They show people how the animals really live. _____
_____ They also show the way animals have families, and how the mothers take care of the babies. These zoos even show how animals form groups and live together. In addition, the animals in the new zoos don't look sad. Are they really happy? They can't tell us, of course, but they look healthier.

   Pattern: _____

3. Zoo workers say that some animals change after they come to the big new cages. For example, a young gorilla named Timmy was born at the Cleveland Zoo. For years he lived in a small cage in a dark building. Then he was moved to the Bronx Zoo in New York, to a large cage outside.

   _____

   He sat on some rocks because he didn't like the feeling of the grass on his feet. Then he started to move around a lot. Later he became very friendly with the other gorillas in the cage. After only a few months, he became a father.

   Pattern: _____

B. *Talk about your answers with another student. Are they the same?*

Focus on Vocabulary

A. *Do you know the meanings of these words? Read each word aloud. Then put a ✓ (you know), ? (you aren't sure), or X (you don't know).*

_____ standard   _____ certainly   _____ fair   _____ quite   _____ choice

_____ suggestion   _____ deal with   _____ quality   _____ wish   _____ point at

B. *Read the passage to the end.*

I Wore Shorts to Work, and They All Laughed
by Eric Wilson

In the 1890s, Oscar Wilde tried to change the way men dressed. In summer, he said, the standard dark suits were too heavy and hot. Instead men should wear light shirts and shorts.

Did anyone follow his suggestion? Certainly not. They just laughed.

5 Last week, Mayor Bloomberg of New York tried again. He said he was concerned about New Yorkers in the heat. He suggested dressing comfortably.

His words were not meant for the women. They already know how to deal with hot weather—in light clothing and little dresses. But what about the men? Have they made any changes? Of course not. The mayor himself continues to go
10 to work in a dark suit.

It didn't seem fair. The women all looked so cool, while the men were all suffering.

So the next day, I put on shorts. They were the latest thing, top quality—and they just reached my knee. As I walked down the street, I felt quite cool and very
15 strange. Everybody looked at me. Some people took pictures.

At noon I went to the park. As usual in summer, there were lots of people eating lunch. The temperature was around 100 degrees. Some men had taken off their jackets and ties, but they all were wearing long pants. I sat beside two men eating sandwiches. One of them asked me, "What country are you from?"

20 He was surprised at my answer. "I wish I could wear shorts, too," he said. "But all the other men in my office are wearing long pants, so I have no choice."

After lunch, two young men were pointing at my shorts and laughing. I guess some things haven't changed since Oscar Wilde.

The next day I wore long pants again.

Adapted from The New York Times, *August 6, 2006*

C. *Look back at the passage and circle the words that are on the list in part A. Then underline the words in the passage that are new to you.*

D. *Look up the underlined words in the dictionary. Write them in your vocabulary notebook with the parts of speech, the sentences, and the meanings.*

E. *Check your understanding of the passage. Read it again if you need to. Write* **T** *(True) or* **F** *(False) after each sentence.*

1. In the 1890s, men started wearing lighter clothes in summer. ____
2. The men in New York didn't listen to Mayor Bloomberg. ____
3. The man in the park thought the writer was a foreigner. ____
4. Men in offices in New York often wear shorts. ____

F. *Talk about your answers with another student. Are they the same? Then check all your work with your teacher.*

EXERCISE 9

A. *Read each sentence and circle the best meaning for the underlined word(s).*

1. In summer, he said, the <u>standard</u> dark suits are too heavy and hot.
   a. usual   b. cotton   c. special

2. Did anyone follow his <u>suggestion</u>?
   a. order   b. step   c. idea

3. Did anyone follow his suggestion? <u>Certainly</u> not.
   a. sometimes   b. maybe   c. of course

4. They already know <u>how to deal with</u> hot weather—in light little dresses.
   a. where to go in   b. what to do in   c. what to eat in

5. It didn't seem <u>fair.</u>
   a. right   b. true   c. pleasant

6. They were the latest thing, <u>top quality</u>—and they just reached my knee.
   a. the largest size   b. the best kind   c. the highest price

7. As I walked down the street, I felt <u>quite</u> cool and very strange.
   a. a little   b. not at all   c. very

8. "I <u>wish I could</u> wear shorts, too," he said.

    a. would like to   b. will probably   c. would never

9. "But all the other men in my office are wearing long pants, so I have no <u>choice</u>."

    a. different ideas   b. other possibility   c. difficulty

10. After lunch, two young men were <u>pointing at</u> my shorts and laughing.

    a. talking about   b. looking towards   c. showing with a finger

B. *Talk about your answers with another student. Are they the same?*

EXERCISE 10

A. *Complete the sentences with the words from the box. Use each word only once. Change the form of the word for the sentence if necessary (plural, past tense, etc.).*

certainly	deal with	point at	quite	suggestion
choice	fair	quality	standard	wish

1. Roger _____ he could get in the boat and sail away.
2. "That's not _____!" shouted Vince. "He got two, and I only got one."
3. My friend Jane sings _____ well.
4. I have a _____ for a way to make more money.
5. You have a _____ between potatoes or rice with your meal.
6. My father only bought good _____ clothes or tools.
7. Your husband _____ knows how to cook!
8. You shouldn't _____ people. It's not nice.
9. Amelia was so unhappy she couldn't _____ the problems at school.
10. Televisions are _____ in most hotel rooms.

B. *Talk about your answers with another student. Are they the same?*

EXERCISE 11

A. **Write a sentence for each word in the box. Look at the sentences in Exercises 9 and 10 if you need help.**

certainly	deal with	point at	quite	suggestion
choice	fair	quality	standard	wish

1. _____

2. _____

3. _____

4. _____

5. _____

6. _____

7. _____

8. _____

9. _____

10. _____

B. **Check your work with your teacher.**

A. **Write the other parts of speech for each word. More than one word may be possible for each part of speech. (See Part 2, Unit 4, page 67.)**

Noun	Verb	Adjective	Adverb
		certain	
choice			
	deal		
		fair	
	point		
quality			
		standard	
suggestion			
	wish		

B. *Talk about your answers with another student. Are they the same? Then check your answers with your teacher.*

C. *Write the new words from Exercises 8–12 in your vocabulary notebook. Then make study cards. Study them alone and then with another student.*

Thinking in English

Introduction

When you read in English, are you thinking about what will come next? For example, in the following passage, what word do you think will come next?

> When our little cat died, we were all very sad. The house seemed very empty. "What should we do?" we asked the children. "Should we get another _____?"

The next word must be *cat*. Why?

- From the first sentences, you know the context: A family had a cat that died.
- You can tell the part of speech. Only a noun can follow "another."
- You can understand (from "another") that the word is probably already in the sentences.
- The word can be used with "get." (You can't say "get a baby," for example.)

This is how good readers think when they are reading. They are thinking ahead. That is, they are thinking about the ideas, and about what might come next. If they think about what will come next, their eyes move ahead quickly. In fact, good readers don't have to focus on each word for long. A quick look is enough.

In these exercises, you will practice thinking in English. This will help you understand better and read faster.

PRACTICE

Circle the best answer.

1. The driest place on the earth is the Atacama Desert in Chile. Scientists say that in this desert there is never any _____.
   a. sun   c. rain
   b. wind   d. sand

2. Today we have clocks all around us. We always know what time it is. But before the year 1500, people didn't have clocks. They used the sun to _____.
   a. tell the time   c. make clocks
   b. get places   d. get up early

Explanation
- The sentences in number 1 are about "the driest place on earth." The second sentence includes the word "never." In a desert (a very dry place), you will probably find sun, wind, and sand, but probably not "rain."
- In number 2, answers *b.* and *c.* don't make sense. You can't use the sun to get places or to make clocks. Also, the sentences say that there were no clocks. Answer *d.* is not possible because if you get up early, there may not be any sun. The only answer that makes sense is *a.*

Guidelines for *Thinking in English* Exercises

Follow these guidelines to help you think in English:

1. Work **quickly**.

2. Try to guess the meaning of new words. Look up a word only if you need it for the answer.

3. Remember, your first guess is often the right one!

EXERCISE 1

A. *Circle the best answer.*

1. Parents should not let small children eat candy often. It's not good for their teeth. Lots of candy could mean expensive bills from the _____.
   a. dentist   c. babysitter
   b. supermarket   d. doctor

2. Oranges are a big business in Florida. But the people who work on the orange farms often work in terrible conditions. They are paid very little, and they have to _____.
   a. eat oranges   c. live on farms
   b. pick lemons   d. work hard

3. 1903 is probably the most important year in the history of flying. That year, in Kittyhawk, North Carolina, the Wright brothers flew 120 feet (about 40 meters) in the first _____.
   a. automobile   c. machine
   b. airplane   d. wings

4. Big windows can be dangerous for birds. They don't understand that there is glass. They see sky or trees in the windows, and they crash into _____.
   a. other birds   c. the ground
   b. the glass   d. airplanes

5. In the past, people learned the news from newspapers. Then they started watching the news on television. Now many people don't read newspapers or watch television. They get the news from _____.
a. the Internet   c. movies
b. books   d. the front page

6. Coffee grows only in places with a warm climate. In some parts of the world, the land is good for growing coffee, but the winters are too _____.
a. dry   c. short
b. cloudy   d. cold

B. *Talk about your answers with another student. Are they the same?*

EXERCISE 2

A. *Circle the best answer.*

1. Forest Park is in the city of Portland, Oregon. It's the biggest natural park in a United States city. It doesn't have baseball fields, gardens, or snack bars. The whole park is a _____.
a. city   c. forest
b. building   d. camp

2. Penguins are an unusual kind of bird. They live on or near the ocean. They can dive and swim very well. But they are heavy and have very small wings, so they can't _____.
a. fly   c. sing
b. fish   d. walk

3. We sometimes think of the ocean as a silent place. But this is not true. Many kinds of fish make sounds. They can do this in different ways. For example, some fish use their teeth to _____.
a. get their food   c. move around
b. make a noise   d. bite other fish

4. New York City is one of the biggest cities in the world. It has a population of about seven million. The population of Tokyo is even larger. It is about

_____.
a. a million people   c. the same size
b. thousands of people d. eight million people

5. A bicycle is useful in the city. It's faster than walking, and it can go more places than a car. Also, with a bicycle, you don't have to look for _____.
a. parking   c. traffic
b. a taxi   d. a map

6. Are you going out? The weather report says that a rainstorm is coming later. Before you leave the house, please be sure to _____.
a. watch the news   c. lock the door
b. close the windows   d. turn off the lights

B. *Talk about your answers with another student. Are they the same?*

EXERCISE 3

A. *Circle the best answer.*

1. You can tell a horse's age by looking at its teeth. You can learn about its health by looking at its eyes. So, before you buy a horse, look carefully at its _____.
a. owner   c. head
b. legs   d. nose

2. Many people are afraid of new technology. This is not a new fear. In the 19th century, the first trains terrified people. They said that the trains went too fast and were _____.
a. necessary   c. dirty
b. safe   d. dangerous

3. One hundred years ago, there were no radios, CD players, or MP3 players. If people wanted to hear music, they had to play it themselves or go to _____.
a. a concert   c. the station
b. the city   d. a teacher

4. Franz Joseph Haydn wrote music in the 1700s. He lived to be 77 years old. Many younger musicians loved him, and they learned a lot from him. To them, Haydn was like _____.
a. a son   c. an old man
b. a father   d. a young man

5. Two hundred years ago, corn was grown only in North and South America. Now it's an important food all around the world. It's grown in Europe and also _____.
a. in Asia   c. in France
b. on farms   d. in California

6. Mountains in the distance often look blue. When you get closer, you see that they aren't really blue, of course. They just seem blue when they're _____.
a. nearby   c. in the dark
b. in the west   d. far away

B. *Talk about your answers with another student. Are they the same?*

EXERCISE 4

A. *Circle the best answer.*

1. In cold weather, it's important to wear a hat. It keeps your head and your whole body warm. Without a hat, you lose much of your body heat through your
   _____.
   a. arms
   b. coat
   c. head
   d. body

2. Cooking is different high up in the mountains. You have to cook things longer. For example, it usually takes an hour to bake a potato. But in the mountains, it may take _____.
   a. forty-five minutes
   b. a few minutes
   c. an hour and a half
   d. half an hour

3. Seagulls are birds that usually live near the ocean. But you can also find seagulls near cities. In the wild, their usual food is fish, but they will eat
   _____.
   a. almost anything
   b. only fish
   c. at the beach
   d. nothing else

4. Ninevah was an important city in the Middle East in the 7th century. It was famous for its library, its religious buildings, and its gardens. The rulers of Ninevah were rich and they wanted their city to be _____.
   a. poor
   b. warm
   c. busy
   d. beautiful

5. Why are some people afraid of airplane travel? In fact, it's much more dangerous to travel by car. There are very few airplane accidents, but every year there are
   _____.
   a. many car accidents
   b. airplane accidents
   c. few car accidents
   d. many bicycle accidents

6. Jules Verne is called the "father of science fiction." In the 1800s, he wrote books about things that were discovered much later. For example, he described airplanes and submarine ships. He also told about a trip to _____.
   a. the sun
   b. New York
   c. the moon
   d. the city

B. *Talk about your answers with another student. Are they the same?*

A. Circle the best answer.

1. On weekends, people in Paris like to go away. They go the country, to the mountains, or to the sea. Every Friday evening, the roads going out of Paris are _____.
   a. empty   c. crowded
   b. closed   d. wide

2. The whale swims like a fish and lives in the ocean, but it isn't a fish. A fish stays underwater all the time. A whale must have air. It can stay underwater for many minutes, but after a while, it needs to _____.
   a. come up for air   c. eat a fish
   b. swim a long way   d. go down deep

3. Many people who work on computers don't work in an office. They work at home most of the time. They go to the office only when they need to _____.
   a. read a book   c. have lunch
   b. meet someone   d. use the computer

4. Around the world, the roads near cities are full of cars every day. This traffic causes a number of problems for cities. One of the worst problems is _____.
   a. dirty air   c. fresh air
   b. bus service   d. dirty water

5. When there are high, thin clouds, it will probably rain in a few days. When there are heavy, dark clouds, it will probably rain quite soon. Clouds can tell you a lot about the _____.
   a. time   c. temperature
   b. sky   d. weather

6. The Hebrides Islands are in the northwest of Scotland. The sea is beautiful there, but the water is cold. Even in summer, it's not a good place to go _____.
   a. fishing   c. swimming
   b. shopping   d. walking

B. Talk about your answers with another student. Are they the same?

A. *Circle the best answer.*

1. Tweed is a special kind of woolen cloth. The Scottish island of Harris produces a very good quality tweed. People around the world will pay a lot of money for _____.

    a. Scottish whiskey   c. woolen cloth
    b. a trip to Harris   d. Harris tweed

2. Today many fishing boats are like factories. They can catch and freeze very large amounts of fish. In fact, they are catching too many fish. Some areas of the oceans now have _____.
    a. lots of fish   c. very few fish
    b. lots of ice   d. very dirty water

3. King Louis XIV of France was very rich and powerful, but he was not very clean. Like most people in those days, he didn't wash very often. Some history books say that he had a bath _____.
    a. every day   c. in a gold bathroom
    b. many times   d. only three times

4. Some scientists used to have strange ideas about the size of a person's head. They thought that people with large heads were the smartest, and that people with smaller heads were _____.
    a. not as smart   c. the smartest
    b. even smarter   d. also smart

5. Around the world, people are moving from small towns to big cities. There they hope to find better jobs and better lives. The cities are growing bigger and bigger; the small towns are _____.
    a. also growing   c. getting richer
    b. getting smaller   d. building houses

6. Doctors say that you shouldn't smoke, work too hard, or eat badly. If you do, you may get heart disease. However, some doctors have heart attacks themselves. Maybe they don't do what they _____.
    a. say   c. like
    b. want   d. hear

B. *Talk about your answers with another student. Are they the same?*

A. Circle the best answer.

1. All living things change over time. These changes are often caused by the conditions where they live. For example, some fish live in rivers deep underground. There is no light where they live, so these fish no longer have _____.

   a. food   c. eggs
   b. a heart   d. eyes

2. The Civil War was a difficult time for the United States. The northern states were fighting the southern states. Families who lived in the central states were sometimes divided. In some cases, one son fought for the North and another _____.

   a. for the South   c. stayed home
   b. for the family   d. also for the North

3. Every year the Italian neighborhood in New York City has a special holiday— San Gennaro. On that day, people sell Italian food in the street. There are Italian songs, dances, and games. The streets are full of people from all over New York and from _____.

   a. downtown   c. outside the city
   b. the restaurants   d. neighborhoods

4. World War I ended in 1918. It was a terrible war that killed millions of people. Europeans called it the "war to end all wars." For them at that time, another war seemed _____.

   a. impossible   c. probable
   b. likely   d. near

5. Two thousand years ago, the Roman Empire ruled much of the Western world. The city of Rome was at the center of the Empire. People used to say that "all roads led to _____."

   a. the West   c. the East
   b. Rome   d. Europe

6. Sir Edmund Hillary from New Zealand is famous as the first person to reach the top of Mt. Everest. But he wasn't alone at the top. He was with a man from Nepal named Tenzing Norgay. Many people know about Hillary, but few people have heard of _____.

   a. Nepal   c. Mt. Everest
   b. England   d. Norgay

B. Talk about your answers with another student. Are they the same?

A. *Circle the best answer.*

1. The Koruba people live in Brazil. Their homeland is deep in the jungle near the Amazon River. They live the same way they have always lived. They don't know very much about the _____.
   a. jungle animals
   b. modern world
   c. Amazon River
   d. Koruba language

2. Most European languages are alike in certain ways. In fact, most of them developed from the same ancient language. Hungarian and Finnish are different from all the others because they developed from another _____.
   a. ancient language
   b. part of Europe
   c. way of speaking
   d. time in history

3. One hundred years ago, the British used to say, "The sun never sets on the British Empire." In other words, the Empire spread all the way around the world. When it was nighttime in one part of the Empire, in another part it was

   _____.
   a. raining
   b. English
   c. dark
   d. daytime

4. On average, Americans move to a new home every seven years. However some Americans never move. They live all their lives in the same place. That means there are other Americans who _____.
   a. sell their homes
   b. never move
   c. move very often
   d. work in their homes

5. In the 1840s, the Irish people were very poor. Meat and bread were expensive, so they ate mostly potatoes. Then a disease killed many of the potato plants. With no potatoes to eat, many people _____.
   a. ate meat instead
   b. were happier
   c. became ill
   d. died of hunger

6. Kinkajous are small animals that live in South America. They live in forests, high up in trees, and they sleep during the day. They also usually stay away from people. For this reason, few people have seen _____.
   a. these animals
   b. the people
   c. the trees
   d. this forest

B. *Talk about your answers with another student. Are they the same?*

A. *Circle the best answer.*

1. Mothers used to say to their children, "An apple a day keeps the doctor away." People believed that it was good to eat lots of apples, but they didn't know why. Now scientists have discovered that there is scientific truth behind the saying. In fact, apples are _____.
   a. bad for you   c. good for you
   b. expensive   d. delicious

2. John Logie Baird sent the first television picture in 1925. He didn't send it very far. It went just from one part of London to another. Two years later, he sent a picture from London to Glasgow, Scotland. Then in 1928, he sent a picture much farther away, from London to _____.
   a. London   c. Scotland
   b. New York   d. England

3. The plains zebra lives in large groups in Africa. Every year, these groups travel about 300 miles in a big circle. They follow the seasons and the rain. When one area becomes too dry, they _____.
   a. move to another   c. wait for rain
   b. stay in Africa   d. run far away

4. In the United States, there are many people from Central and South America. All big American cities have neighborhoods full of people from these areas. They come from many different countries, but the largest group comes from _____.
   a. China   c. Miami
   b. Texas   d. Mexico

5. Hong Kong is an interesting mixture of people and ways of life. It's now part of China, but in the past it belonged to Great Britain. In some ways, Hong Kong still seems British, but in many other ways, it's _____.
   a. far away   c. modern
   b. Chinese   d. Western

6. Today, people can run much faster than in the past. Until 1954, the fastest time for running a mile was over four minutes. That year, Roger Bannister ran a mile in less than four minutes. Since then, many other runners have also run _____.
   a. a four-minute mile   c. a whole mile
   b. a five-minute mile   d. more than a mile

B. *Talk about your answers with another student. Are they the same?*

A. *Circle the best answer.*

1. Many English words come from Greek words. For example, the Greek word for *star* is *aster*. We don't talk about *asters* in the sky at night. But we do use the word in other ways. For example, scientists who study the stars are called _____.
   a. philosophers
   b. night watchers
   c. astronomers
   d. architects

2. In the last few years of his life, Beethoven could not hear. When he was younger, he always tried out his music on the piano. Later, however, he couldn't do that. When he wrote music, he had to play it _____.
   a. in his head
   b. to a friend
   c. on the violin
   d. in an orchestra

3. In New York City, the apartments at the top of buildings often have the best views. Everyone would like to live in these apartments, of course, but not everyone has enough money. The top apartments are usually _____.
   a. not very pleasant
   b. the most important
   c. the cheapest
   d. the most expensive

4. In the 1920s, scientists discovered the remains of Peking Man in China. He lived more than 400,000 years ago. He was not a modern human being, but he was very similar. He probably used fire, and he _____.
   a. didn't eat meat
   b. couldn't walk
   c. walked on two feet
   d. lived in trees

5. Strange things happen when there's a full moon. More babies are born. Cats and other pets become more active. Some people can't sleep. So it's not surprising that when the moon is full, there are _____.
   a. fewer cats
   b. more accidents
   c. more stars
   d. fewer storms

6. In the country there's very little light at night, so you can see many things in the night sky. You can find many stars, the Milky Way galaxy, and sometimes other planets. In the city, it's different. You can't see many stars because there's _____.
   a. not enough light
   b. no Milky Way
   c. too much light
   d. not enough time

B. *Talk about your answers with another student. Are they the same?*

Focus on Vocabulary

EXERCISE 11

A. *Do you know the meanings of these words? Read each word aloud. Then put a ✓ (you know), ? (you aren't sure), or X (you don't know).*

____ native   ____ various   ____ advantage   ____ damage   ____ reduce

____ spread   ____ relative   ____ valuable   ____ matter   ____ experiment

B. *Read the passage to the end.*

Squirrel for Dinner?

American grey squirrels are cute little animals with black eyes and big tails. You see them in parks and forests all over North America. Now they're common in England, too, and the English are not happy about this.

In fact, grey squirrels are not native to England. They were brought over in the 19th century. Since then, the squirrels have increased and spread. Now there are millions of them around the country, and they are causing various problems.

For one thing, they are pushing out their relatives, the European red squirrels. Grey squirrels have several advantages over red squirrels. They are bigger and stronger, so they get the food first. They also aren't afraid to live near humans in towns and cities. Red squirrels generally stay in the forests. Finally, grey squirrels will eat almost anything. Like red squirrels, they eat wild nuts and berries. But they also eat birds' eggs, garbage, garden plants, and the new parts of trees in the spring.

This is the other reason why the English don't like grey squirrels. These little animals are destroying valuable plants in the gardens. They are damaging trees in the forests. This is a serious matter, since the English love their gardens and forests.

In North America, squirrels are hunted by many other animals, and this helps limit the population. They are also hunted—and eaten—by humans. In the state of Mississippi, for example, two million squirrels are shot and turned into dishes such as southern-fried squirrel.

This may be the best way to reduce the number of squirrels in England. Some English animal-lovers don't like the idea. But others are already experimenting in the kitchen. They say squirrel is very nice, a bit like lamb and a bit like chicken.

C. *Look back at the passage and circle the words from the list in part A. (Some words may be in a different form: relative → relatives.) Then underline all of the new words in the passage.*

D. *Look up the underlined words in the dictionary. Write them in your vocabulary notebook with the parts of speech, the sentences, and the meanings.*

E. *Check your understanding of the passage. Read it again if you need to. Write T (True) or F (False) after each sentence.*

1. Before the 19th century, there weren't any grey squirrels in England. ____

2. There are more red squirrels now than in the past. ____

3. Grey squirrels eat more things than red squirrels. ____

4. English people are beginning to hunt and eat grey squirrels. ____

F. *Talk about your answers with another student. Are they the same? Then check all your work with your teacher.*

EXERCISE 12

A. *Read each sentence and circle the best meaning for the underlined word(s).*

1. In fact, grey squirrels are not <u>native to</u> England.
   a. around   b. from   c. outside

2. Since then, the squirrels have increased and <u>spread</u>.
   a. left the country   b. become larger   c. moved all over

3. Now there are millions of them, and they are causing <u>various</u> problems.
   a. one   b. several   c. no real

4. For one thing, they are pushing out their <u>relatives</u>, the European red squirrels.
   a. family members   b. enemies   c. friends

5. Grey squirrels <u>have several advantages over</u> red squirrels.
   a. are weaker than   b. are smaller than   c. are stronger than

6. These little animals are destroying <u>valuable</u> plants in the gardens.
   a. cheap   b. expensive   c. large

7. They are <u>damaging</u> trees in the forests.
   a. hurting   b. helping   c. planting

8. This is a serious <u>matter</u>, since the English love their gardens and forests.
   a. difference   b. problem   c. reason

9. This may be the best way to <u>reduce</u> the number of squirrels in England.
   a. count   b. make less   c. increase

10. But others are already <u>experimenting</u> in the kitchen.
   a. eating   b. studying   c. trying

B. *Talk about your answers with another student. Are they the same?*

EXERCISE 13

A. *Complete the sentences with the words from the box. Use each word only once. Change the form of the word for the sentence if necessary (plural, past tense, etc.).*

advantage	experiment	native	relative	valuable
damage	matter	reduce	spread	various

1. He wanted to _____ with different colors in his next painting.
2. Cats and lions are distant _____.
3. My mother bought _____ kinds of cheese for the party.
4. Because he was tall, he had a big _____ over the other players.
5. The museum lost some very _____ paintings in the fire.
6. They had an important _____ to talk about.
7. After Christmas, many stores _____ their prices.
8. The fire _____ some of the clothes in the store.
9. Elephants are _____ to Africa and Asia.
10. The news _____ very quickly around town.

B. *Talk about your answers with another student. Are they the same?*

EXERCISE 14

A. *Write a sentence for each word in the box. Look at the sentences in Exercises 12 and 13 if you need help.*

advantage	experiment	native	relative	valuable
damage	matter	reduce	spread	various

1. _____
2. _____
3. _____
4. _____
5. _____
6. _____
7. _____
8. _____
9. _____
10. _____

B. *Check your work with your teacher.*

EXERCISE 15

A. *Write the other parts of speech for each word. More than one word may be possible for each part of speech. (See Part 2, Unit 4, page 67.)*

Noun	Verb	Adjective	Adverb
advantage			
	damage		
	experiment		
matter			
	reduce		
relative			
	spread		
		valuable	
		various	

B. *Talk about your answers with another student. Are they the same? Then check your answers with your teacher.*

C. *Write the new words from Exercises 11–15 in your vocabulary notebook. Then make study cards. Study them alone and then with another student.*

Reading Faster

Introduction

Why Read Faster?

There are three important reasons for learning to read faster:

1. You can read more in less time.
   - This will help you with homework, class work, and tests.
   - It will also make reading stories and books more enjoyable—so you'll probably read more.

2. You can understand better.

How can you understand when you read faster? Because of the way your memory works. When you read slowly, you read one word at a time. This way, you read separate words. Try reading the sentences below with words separated. Is it easier or harder to read this way?

> What really happens when we read? Many people think we read one word at a time. They think we read a word, understand it, and then move on to the next word.

It's harder to read this way, of course. The separate words are separate pieces of information. They don't stay in your memory for long. You may forget the beginning of a sentence by the time you get to the end.

When you read faster, your short-term memory can work better. It can group more words together and you can understand sentences better.

3. You will improve your general knowledge of English.

If you read faster and understand better, you will be able to read more. This way, you will see a lot of words and sentences. This will help you:
   - learn more vocabulary
   - understand how sentences work
   - learn what words are used together
   - become a better writer

> **Note:** Sometimes you need to read slowly and carefully. This is true when you are reading directions, a cookbook recipe, a poem, or the explanation of a math problem. You shouldn't always try to read faster. But you should be able to speed up or slow down when you want to.

How to Read Faster

1. **Check your reading habits.**

   Some habits can slow you down when you are reading. Think about your own reading habits:

   ➤ *Do you try to pronounce each word as you read?*
   You will probably understand less this way. If you are trying to say and understand the words, your brain has to do two things at the same time. (You can practice saying the sentences <u>after</u> you read them silently.)

   ➤ *Do you move your lips when you read silently?*
   If you do, you are probably thinking each word to yourself. You will have the same problems as someone who pronounces the words.

   ➤ *Do you point at the words with your finger or a pencil?*
   If you do, your eyes will move word by word across the lines. But your eyes need to be free to follow your thinking. You may want to go back and check a word. Or you may want to skip ahead.

   ➤ *Do you try to translate into your native language while you are reading in English?*
   If you do, you will have to stop often to think about the translation. This will make it harder to think about the story or the ideas.

2. **Skip or guess unknown words.**

   ➤ *Skip words that are not necessary for understanding the passage.*
   You don't always need to know the meaning of every new word. You may be able to follow the story or understand the main idea without it. (See Part 1, Unit 1, Exercise 1, page 4.)

   ➤ *Guess the general meaning of the words you need to understand the passage.*
   You can learn a lot about a word from the words or sentences around it (the context). You can often understand the general meaning of the word. With this general meaning, you can continue reading and understanding the passage. (See Part 2, Unit 3, for more about guessing meaning.)

3. **Practice reading faster by timing yourself.**

   Reading rate (speed) is partly habit (what you are used to doing). You are used to reading at a certain rate, so you continue to read at that rate.
   Timed readings can help you break the habit of slow reading. When you read against the clock, you push yourself to read faster. You have to change the way you read.
   First, you will find out how fast you read now and you will learn how to time yourself. Then you will work on improving your reading rate in the timed readings in Units 1–3.

Guidelines for Reading Faster

Follow these guidelines for timed readings:

1. Before you start, write down the *exact* time it says on your watch or clock (minutes and seconds).

2. Preview each passage quickly before reading it.

3. Read the passage and then write down the exact time you finish.

4. Answer the questions without looking back at the passage. Then check your answers with your teacher.

5. Read the passage again. Look for the answers to the questions, especially the ones you answered incorrectly.

6. Find your reading time (finishing time minus starting time) and find your reading rate on the Reading Rate Table on page 229.

7. Write your reading rate and your comprehension score (the number of correct answers) on the progress charts on pages 230–232.

8. After reading four or five passages, check your progress.
   - If your reading rate has stayed the same, you should push yourself to read faster.
   - If you have more than two incorrect answers on any passage, you might be trying to read too quickly. Slow down a little and read more carefully.

EXERCISE 1

A. *Write your starting time. Preview the passage. (See the guidelines above.) Then read the passage to the end.*

Pompeii: The Morning of the Volcano

In 79 C.E., Pompeii was a Roman city of about 20,000 people in southern Italy (near the present city of Naples). On one side of the city was the sea. On the other side was Mt. Vesuvius. This tall mountain was a volcano, but it had been quiet for 800 years. The people in Pompeii lived well. The land near the city was good for
5   farming. The sea was full of fish. Traders did a lot of business by land or by sea with other Roman cities.

On the morning of August 25, the weather was hot, and the marketplace in Pompeii was busy. Farmers came in from the country with chickens, fruit, and vegetables. The shops sold oil, wine, pots, and cloth, and bakeries had piles of
10   bread. By late morning, the center of the city was crowded. Women filled the marketplace, buying food or clothes for their families. Some men sat in the cafés, having drinks or snacks. Others sat in the bath houses, talking with friends. Some of the most important men of the city were in a meeting at the city hall.

Suddenly, the ground began to shake and the buildings all moved. People
15   looked around, and they looked at each other. Was this another earthquake? Earthquakes were common in the area. Then there was a loud noise—boom! The top of Mt. Vesuvius exploded. Fire came shooting out of the mountain, and a huge black cloud of ash and smoke rose into the sky.

The ground shook again, and people went running outside. They saw the
20   mountain and were afraid. In a short time, the sun was hidden by the black cloud. It was as dark as night in Pompeii. Men shouted for their wives, and women screamed for their children. Rich people ran to get their jewelry and gold. Religious people called to the gods for help. In the marketplace, bakers forgot about the bread, and farmers left their vegetables.
25   As the people ran, hot ash and rocks fell on them. The ash got into their mouths and eyes, and it covered their clothes. Some of the rocks were very small, but some were the size of tennis balls. People tied cushions to their heads to protect themselves. The ash and rocks soon filled the streets and piled up on top of the houses. The town was soon covered with gray ash.

B. ***Write your finishing time.***
    Then turn the page and answer the questions.

C. Circle the best answers. Don't look back at the passage.

1. This passage is about
    a. how Pompeii was covered with ash.
    b. what happens during a volcano.
    c. Pompeii before and during the volcano.
    d. life in Pompeii in Roman times.

2. Which of these sentences is NOT true?
    a. People in Pompeii were poor.
    b. Pompeii had a marketplace.
    c. There were farms near Pompeii.
    d. People used boats for trading.

3. When did the volcano explode?
    a. late at night
    b. early in the morning
    c. in the evening
    d. late in the morning

4. What was the first sign of the volcano eruption?
    a. The weather was hot.
    b. The ground shook.
    c. There were big waves.
    d. Ash fell from the sky.

5. When the volcano exploded, people
    a. hid in their houses.
    b. stopped and watched.
    c. talked to their friends.
    d. ran and shouted.

6. Soon after the volcano exploded,
    a. ash and rocks began to fall.
    b. the city began to burn.
    c. people went home.
    d. it began to rain.

D. Check your answers with your teacher. Write your comprehension score (the number of correct answers): _____ . Then read the passage again and look for the answers to the questions.

E. Write your reading time.   Finishing time – Starting time = _____

F. Find your reading rate on page 229. Write your comprehension score and reading rate on the progress chart on page 230.

A. *Write your starting time. Preview the passage. (See the guidelines on page 224.) Then read the passage to the end.*

Starting time: _____

Pompeii

Some people ran to the seaside and tried to escape in boats. There were huge waves, and many boats were overturned, but some families got away. Other people ran into the country, away from the mountain. In the end, most of the people escaped from Pompeii in time. But about 2,000 people didn't get away. They died under the ashes. In fact, the city was covered with about 15–20 feet (4.5–6 meters) of ashes. When it rained later, the ashes became as hard as rock.

Not far from Pompeii was another small city. The people who lived there could see the volcano, and they talked to the people who escaped. A boy named Pliny watched and listened to everything. When he grew up, he wrote about Pompeii, but his writings were lost.

After many years, people built a new town over Pompeii. The old Roman city was forgotten. Then, in the 19th century, people found some of Pliny's writings. They read his story about Pompeii and wondered where it was. One day near Vesuvius, some workers were making a hole in the ground, and they found pieces of an old wall. A few years later, more walls and buildings were found. There was also a stone with the name of the city—*Pompeii.*

In 1860, the King of Italy told scientists to uncover Pompeii. They took away a lot of rock and dirt, and found the city just as it was before the volcano. In one café there was still money on a table. In a house, there were pots and pans in a fireplace and a bowl of eggs on a table. The ash kept all these things the same for two thousand years.

At first, the scientists wondered why they found few human bones. But then, they understood what had happened. The bodies and bones were gone, but in their place, there were holes in the rocks. These holes still had the shape of the people they had covered. The scientists learned what people were doing when they died. Some people were holding onto each other. Other people were holding onto their jewels. There was even a dog trying to get free from his chain.

Today, Pompeii is an open-air museum. People come from all over the world to see it. Scientists continue to study the Roman city. From it, they have learned a lot about the way people lived in those days.

B. *Write your finishing time.*   Finishing time: _____
        Then turn the page and answer the questions.

C. Circle the best answers. Don't look back at the passage.

1. This passage is about
   a. the history of Pompeii.
   b. Pompeii after the volcano exploded.
   c. the open-air museum of Pompeii.
   d. Pompeii's people and buildings.

2. Most of the people who lived in Pompeii
   a. died under the ashes.
   b. built a new town.
   c. stayed in the city.
   d. left the city.

3. Who was Pliny?
   a. a man that was digging a hole
   b. a boy who lived in a nearby city
   c. a person who escaped from Pompeii
   d. a scientist who studied Pompeii

4. Which sentence is NOT true about people before the 19th century?
   a. They didn't know where Pompeii was.
   b. They were interested in Roman cities.
   c. They didn't know where the volcano was.
   d. They knew all about Pompeii.

5. When scientists uncovered Pompeii, they found
   a. lots of human bones.
   b. Pliny's writings about the city.
   c. everything just as it was.
   d. only the walls of houses.

6. What did scientists learn from the holes in the rocks?
   a. when the volcano erupted
   b. why some people stayed in Pompeii
   c. the names of the people who died
   d. what people were doing when they died

D. Check your answers with your teacher. Write your comprehension score (the number of correct answers): _____ . Then read the passage again and look for the answers to the questions.

E. Write your reading time.   Finishing time – Starting time = _____

F. Find your reading rate on page 229. Write your comprehension score and reading rate on the progress chart on page 230.

Reading Rate Table

Find the reading time that is closest to your time. Then look across at the reading rate. (For example, if your reading time is 2:38, the closest time is 2:45. Your reading rate is 145.)

Reading Time (minutes)	Reading Rate (words per minute)
:30	800
:45	533
1:00	400
1:15	320
1:30	267
1:45	229
2:00	200
2:15	178
2:30	160
2:45	145
3:00	133
3:15	123
3:30	114
3:45	107
4:00	100
4:15	94
4:30	89
4:45	84
5:00	80
5:15	76
5:30	73
5:45	70
6:00	67
6:15	64
6:30	62
6:45	59
7:00	57

Faster Reading Progress Chart

Under the exercise number, write your comprehension score (number of correct answers). Then check (✓) your reading rate. Write the date at the bottom.

Introduction and Unit 1 Progress Chart

Exercise	Introduction 1	Introduction 2	1	2	3	4	5	6	7	8	9	10
Comprehension Score →												
800												
533												
400												
320												
267												
229												
200												
178												
160												
145												
133												
123												
114												
107												
100												
94												
89												
84												
80												
76												
73												
70												
67												
64												
62												
59												
57												
Date												

Reading Rate

Unit 2 Progress Chart

Reading Rate

Exercise	1	2	3	4	5	6	7	8	9	10
Comprehension Score →										
800										
533										
400										
320										
267										
229										
200										
178										
160										
145										
133										
123										
114										
107										
100										
94										
89										
84										
80										
76										
73										
70										
67										
64										
62										
59										
57										
Date										

Unit 3 Progress Chart

Exercise	1	2	3	4	5	6	7	8	9	10
Comprehension Score →										
800										
533										
400										
320										
267										
229										
200										
178										
160										
145										
133										
123										
114										
107										
100										
94										
89										
84										
80										
76										
73										
70										
67										
64										
62										
59										
57										
Date										

Reading Rate

UNIT 1

The White Woman of the Genesee

A. Write your starting time.
Then preview and read the passage.

Starting time: _____

Mary Jemison Is Born

The Genesee River is in the northwest part of New York State. It flows over a waterfall and through a wide and beautiful valley. In the 1700s, this valley was home to a large group of Seneca Indians.

It was also home to "The White Woman of the Genesee." That was how
5 many people knew her in the valley. She was well respected by Indians and whites. To the Indians, she was known as Dehgewanus, "Two Falling Voices." She lived and dressed in the Indian way, she was married to an Indian, and her children grew up as Indians. But she had blond hair and blue eyes, and she spoke English. When she was born, she was called Mary Jemison.

10 Her parents were Thomas and Jane Jemison from Ireland. In the 1740s, they still lived in Ireland, but they were not happy there. People were not free to practice any religion they wanted. There was a lot of suffering and fighting over religion.

In 1743, Thomas and Jane made a big decision. By then, they had three children (John, Thomas, and Betsey), and Jane was expecting another child. They
15 wanted their children to have more freedom and a better life. They decided to leave Ireland and go to Pennsylvania, in America.

Mary was born on the ship on the way to America. She and her family arrived safely in Philadelphia, but they didn't stay there for long. Thomas bought some land in western Pennsylvania, and soon the family moved there to start a farm.

20 At that time, western Pennsylvania was very wild. There were a few other farms started by other European families. But most of the land was covered by forest. When Mary's father started his farm, he had to cut down trees and clear the land. Then he planted corn, potatoes, wheat, rye, barley, and fruit trees. For the first few years, he worked alone. Then the boys began to help him.

25 Mary's mother also didn't have an easy life in Pennsylvania. She had to carry water from a stream. She had to make all the food and clothes. And she had to take care of the children. After Mary, two more baby boys were born. Betsey was soon helping her mother in the house. Mary, too, began to help at an early age.

B. Write your finishing time.
Then turn the page and answer the questions.

Finishing time: _____

C. *Circle the best answers. Don't look back at the passage.*

1. This passage is about
   a. Mary Jemison's parents in Ireland.
   b. how people left Ireland and went to America.
   c. Mary Jemison's birth and arrival in Pennsylvania.
   d. Mary Jemison's farm in Pennsylvania.

2. Which sentence is NOT true about The White Woman of the Genesee?
   a. She had an Indian name.
   b. She lived like an Indian.
   c. She had blond hair and blue eyes.
   d. Her husband was English.

3. Why did Mary's parents leave Ireland?
   a. They wanted more religious freedom.
   b. They were in trouble in Ireland.
   c. They wanted to make more money.
   d. They had a fight with their family.

4. Where was Mary born?
   a. in Ireland
   b. on the ship
   c. in Pennsylvania
   d. in New York state

5. When Mary's father arrived in western Pennsylvania, he
   a. bought an old farm.
   b. found many open fields.
   c. had to cut down many trees.
   d. worked for another farmer.

6. Which sentence is NOT true about Mary's mother?
   a. She carried water to the house.
   b. She had two more babies.
   c. She made all their clothes.
   d. She had an easy life.

D. *Check your answers with your teacher. Write your comprehension score (the number of correct answers): _____. Then read the passage again and look for the answers to the questions.*

E. *Write your reading time.*　　　　Finishing time − Starting time = _____

F. *Find your reading rate on page 229. Write your reading rate and comprehension score on the progress chart on page 230.*

A. *Write your starting time.*
Then preview and read the passage.   Starting time: _____

War in Western Pennsylvania

Mary never saw a town when she was growing up. The nearest one was many miles away. At their home in the woods, the family was very much alone. They sometimes saw neighboring farmers or their families. A few travelers went by on their way east or west. They always stopped to talk and eat something and
5   often stayed for the night. But there were no stores nearby, no newspapers, mail, doctors, or police.

For some years, the Jemisons lived happily on their farm. The children were healthy and growing. Thomas Jemison added land to the farm, and got more animals—horses, cows, and some chickens. He built a
10 bigger house and a barn for the animals.

Then, in 1754, war broke out between the French and the English. Both countries wanted control over a large area of eastern North America. The French were trying to push south from Canada. The English were trying to push
15 west from the Atlantic coast. Most of the fighting was in the wild areas of western New England, New York, and Pennsylvania. Both the French and the English wanted the Indians on their side. The Indians knew how to get around the woods very well. They could travel quickly and attack
20 suddenly.

The Indians held a big meeting about the war. The Frenchmen they knew were mostly traders. They bought furs and animal skins from the Indians and then returned north to Canada. The English people, however, were settlers. They were living on land where Indians had always lived,
25 and this made the Indians very angry. They decided to fight with the French.

In Pennsylvania, the English formed an army to protect the settlers. This army lost a battle against the French and the Indians, and had to move east. After that, the French and the Indians began to attack settlers. They killed whole families, took food and horses, and burned the houses to the ground.

30 In the spring of 1755, the Jemisons and their neighbors heard terrible stories about these attacks. Some neighbors decided to move back east with their families for a while. But so far, there were no attacks close by. The Jemisons hadn't heard guns or seen the smoke of houses burning. Thomas Jemison didn't believe that there was any danger right away. He also didn't want to leave his farm after so
35 many years of work. It was springtime, time for planting.

B. *Write your finishing time.*   Finishing time: _____
Then turn the page and answer the questions.

C. Circle the best answers. Don't look back at the passage.

1. This passage is about
   a. the Jemisons and the war.
   b. the Indians in Pennsylvania.
   c. the British army in the war.
   d. the Jemison's life on their farm.

2. Which sentence is NOT true about the Jemisons?
   a. They often went to town.
   b. They saw a few travelers.
   c. They saw neighboring families.
   d. They never saw a doctor.

3. Thomas Jemison's farm
   a. had a lot of problems.
   b. had no animals.
   c. was very poor.
   d. was doing well.

4. Both the English and the French wanted the Indians on their side
   a. because there were a lot of Indians.
   b. because the Indians could fight well in the woods.
   c. because the Indians had a lot of furs and animal skins.
   d. because they had a lot of guns.

5. The Indians were angry because the English
   a. didn't pay for the Indian furs.
   b. hunted in the Indians' woods.
   c. took land from the Indians.
   d. didn't let the Indians hunt.

6. Which sentence is NOT true?
   a. The Jemisons decided to go east.
   b. There were no attacks near the Jemisons.
   c. Some farmers went east with their families.
   d. Thomas Jemison wanted to start planting.

D. Check your answers with your teacher. Write your comprehension score (the number of correct answers): _____. Then read the passage again and look for the answers to the questions.

E. Write your reading time.   Finishing time – Starting time = _____

F. Find your reading rate on page 229. Write your reading rate and comprehension score on the progress chart on page 230.

A. *Write your starting time.*
Then preview and read the passage.

Starting time: _____

The Attack

In April 1755, Mary was 12 years old. Though she was small for her age, she was quick and strong. She never went to school, but she learned to read and write from her mother. She also learned to make cloth, sew clothes, and make bread and corn cakes. Unlike her sister Betsey, Mary was never very good at these jobs. She

5   liked best to be outside, helping her father. She loved the farm, especially in spring with the flowering peach and apple trees.

Sometimes, Mary's father sent her through the woods with a message for their neighbors.

10   Her mother didn't like this, but no one else could go. The older boys were working on the farm and Betsey was busy in the house. Mary's father always said that

15   Mary would be safe. No one would touch her pretty blond head.

One evening, he sent her to the Johnson's house about a mile away. It was almost dark when she came near their house. Then she heard a noise in the woods. Was it an animal? Indians? She ran fast to the Johnson's. When she arrived, she wanted to go home again. She was afraid something bad had

20   happened at home. But it was dark by then and the Johnsons kept her there. Later, she was sure she had heard Indians in the woods.

Very early the next morning, she ran back home. Nothing had happened. Another family was there, too—the Smiths. They were on their way east and had stopped for the night. Mary's mother was preparing breakfast, with help from

25   Mrs. Smith and Betsey. They were making corn cakes and cooking them over the fire. Mary's father was outside, cutting wood beside the house. Her brothers were in the barn, feeding the animals. Mr. Smith was out hunting for meat in the forest.

Suddenly, they heard shooting. Everyone in the house stopped what they were

30   doing. Mary's mother opened the door. There on the ground was Mr. Smith, dead. Behind him was a group of Indians and Frenchmen. They were already holding Mary's father. Some of them ran into the house and brought out the women and children. Others began looking through the house and the barn. They killed the animals and took all the food they could carry. Fortunately, Mary's brothers

31   escaped into the woods when they heard the shooting.

B. *Write your finishing time.*
Then turn the page and answer the questions.

Finishing time: _____

C. *Circle the best answers. Don't look back at the passage.*

1. This passage is about
   a. Indians attacking white people.
   b. Mary's family and their farm.
   c. the Indian attack at the farm.
   d. Mary's life and the Indian attack.

2. Which sentence is NOT true about Mary?
   a. She could read and write.
   b. She could make bread.
   c. She liked working outside.
   d. She liked working in the house.

3. Mary's father sometimes asked her to
   a. write a letter to relatives.
   b. take a message to the neighbors.
   c. pick peaches and apples.
   d. make bread and corn cakes.

4. What happened when Mary went to the Johnson's?
   a. The Indians attacked her family.
   b. Someone attacked her in the woods.
   c. She heard something in the woods.
   d. She saw a large animal in the woods.

5. Which sentence is NOT true about the morning Mary returned?
   a. The Indians were already at the farm.
   b. Her mother was preparing breakfast.
   c. Her father was cutting wood.
   d. Another family was there.

6. Mary's family was attacked by
   a. Indians on horses.
   b. Indians and Frenchmen.
   c. English soldiers.
   d. Frenchmen with guns.

D. *Check your answers with your teacher. Write your comprehension score (the number of correct answers): _____. Then read the passage again and look for the answers to the questions.*

E. *Write your reading time.*   Finishing time – Starting time = _____

F. *Find your reading rate on page 229. Write your reading rate and comprehension score on the progress chart on page 230.*

A. *Write your starting time.*
Then preview and read the passage.

Starting time: _____

The Long March

As quickly as possible, the Indians tied up Mary's father and led the two families into the woods. They didn't burn down the house and barn. Perhaps they were afraid someone might see the smoke.

Then they started walking to the west. Two Indians
5   led the way through the forest. The Frenchmen and the families followed. An Indian with a stick walked behind and hit anyone who went too slowly. An older Indian followed everyone and carefully covered up any signs of the group.

10   All day Mary and the others marched through the woods. They couldn't stop for food or water. Mary and her mother and sister carried the little children. Hour after hour, they walked like this. Mary's arms, feet, and legs hurt badly.

15   Finally, when it was dark, they stopped. There was no fire and no food for them. Mary's mother held the children close and sang to them quietly until they slept. Her father sat silently all night, his hands still tied. Before daylight, they were up and marching again. They got hardly any food or rest for another long day.

20   In the evening, they stopped in a cold, dark, lonely place. The Indians offered them food, but no one wanted to eat. They were afraid now. The Indians and Frenchmen were talking and arguing. Something was going to happen. Then the older Indian sat beside Mary. He took off her shoes and socks and put on a pair of Indian shoes—moccasins. He did the same with Davy, a boy from the other
25   family.

Mary's mother understood what this meant. The Indians were going to keep the two children. All the others would probably die. Mary cried and held on to her mother, but her mother told her to go with the Indians. "Don't try to escape," she said. "You could never get away. Be strong and good. Whatever happens, make
30   the best of things and be happy." All her life, Mary remembered these words.

Then the older Indian led Mary and Davy away from the group. He made a bed on some soft grass, and looked at them with kind eyes. "Go sleep," he said in English. The children held each other close and fell asleep.

Mary never saw her family again. She later learned that her parents, her sister
35   and brothers, and the other family were all killed that night.

B. *Write your finishing time.*
Then turn the page and answer the questions.

Finishing time: _____

C. *Circle the best answers. Don't look back at the passage.*

1. This passage is about
   a. how Mary's family was killed.
   b. the first two days after the attack.
   c. Indians and Frenchmen in the war.
   d. the two children who were saved.

2. Why did the older Indian follow the group?
   a. so he could cover up the signs
   b. so he could go hunting for meat
   c. so he could watch them carefully
   d. so he could walk more slowly

3. Which sentence is NOT true about the long march?
   a. They got very little food or drink.
   b. They had to walk quickly.
   c. They had to carry the little children.
   d. They often stopped for rest.

4. The Indians decided to keep
   a. all of the children.
   b. only Mary's family.
   c. only two children.
   d. all of the white people.

5. Mary's mother told her she must
   a. try to escape soon.
   b. not try to run away.
   c. try to kill the Indians.
   d. not speak to the Indians.

6. After the older Indian took Mary and Davy away,
   a. the children went home.
   b. the children were badly hurt.
   c. their families were killed.
   d. their families were sent home.

D. *Check your answers with your teacher. Write your comprehension score (the number of correct answers): _____. Then read the passage again and look for the answers to the questions.*

E. *Write your reading time.*   Finishing time − Starting time = _____

F. *Find your reading rate on page 229. Write your reading rate and comprehension score on the progress chart on page 230.*

A. **_Write your starting time._**
Then preview and read the passage.

Starting time: _____

An Uncertain Time

The next few days were very hard for Mary. She and Davy had to walk far and fast through the cold and rain. Mary was so unhappy that there were moments when she wanted to die. But Davy was there with her, and he needed her help.

One evening, they were joined by another group of Indians. They had a
5　prisoner, too, a young Englishman. Mary hoped they might escape together. But he was very tired and very sad. In the end, Mary had to help him, too. She told him what her mother had said. She made him eat what the Indians gave him.

Then they arrived at a French camp, Fort
10　Duquesne, on the Ohio River. Before they entered the fort, the Indians painted the faces of their three prisoners. Mary was afraid again. What did this mean? The Indians led the prisoners into a room in the fort and left them there for the night. That was a
15　terrible night. The three young people didn't know if they were going to live or die the next day.

In the morning, the Indians gave Davy and the young man to some French soldiers. Mary never saw them again and never learned what happened to
20　them.

Mary was now alone. Before long, two Indian women came in. They looked at her closely, talking quietly to each other. A few minutes later, they returned, and Mary understood that now she belonged to them. She left the fort with them and traveled down the river in their canoe to a Seneca village.

25　The women didn't bring Mary into the village right away. First, they took off her clothes and threw them in the river. Then they washed Mary and dressed her in new Indian clothes. Mary watched her old clothes go down the river. They were now dirty and torn, but her mother had made them.

But there was no time for tears. The women brought Mary to their house in
30　the village. It soon filled with Indians who were crying and singing. At first, Mary was terrified. What were they going to do to her? But slowly the Indians became quieter. They turned to her, smiling and happy. They lightly touched her blond hair. When she couldn't keep her eyes open, they put her in a soft bed of animal skins, and she slept deeply.

B. **_Write your finishing time._**
Then turn the page and answer the questions.

Finishing time: _____

C. *Circle the best answers. Don't look back at the passage.*

1. This passage is about
   a. two Indian women from an Indian village.
   b. how Mary went to an Indian village.
   c. three prisoners of the Indians.
   d. how Mary wanted to go home.

2. Which sentence is NOT true about the young Englishman?
   a. He was tired and sad.
   b. He didn't want to eat.
   c. He wanted to escape.
   d. He needed help.

3. At the fort, the three prisoners
   a. didn't know what was going to happen.
   b. thought they were going to return home.
   c. met some friendly Frenchmen.
   d. believed their friends would save them.

4. Mary left the fort with
   a. her friends and family.
   b. a group of Indians.
   c. some French soldiers.
   d. two Indian women.

5. What did the women do before they took Mary to the Indian village?
   a. They dressed themselves in clean clothes.
   b. They painted her face with Indian colors.
   c. They dressed her in Indian clothes.
   d. They threw her into the river.

6. When the Indians came into the house, they were
   a. crying and singing.
   b. angry and shouting.
   c. afraid and uncertain.
   d. sleepy and tired.

D. *Check your answers with your teacher. Write your comprehension score (the number of correct answers): _____. Then read the passage again and look for the answers to the questions.*

E. *Write your reading time.*   Finishing time − Starting time = _____

F. *Find your reading rate on page 229. Write your reading rate and comprehension score on the progress chart on page 230.*

A. ***Write your starting time.***
Then preview and read the passage.

Starting time: _____

A New Life

Mary woke up the next morning in a Seneca longhouse. These houses were long halls made of wood and animal skins. There were beds along the side walls. Curtains of blankets hid the beds and divided the house
5 among several families. In the middle of each part, there was an open fireplace. A hole above the fireplace allowed smoke to go out. Large pots held food and water. Corn, pumpkins, and baskets were hanging from the walls.

The two women were cooking something over a fire.
10 Other women and children were eating around their fires. Mary was very hungry, so she got out of bed. The sisters smiled at her and gave her a corn cake. Mary ate a little bit. This corn cake was cooked in water without any salt. It wasn't like the wonderful cakes her mother made. The thought of her
15 mother made Mary unhappy and angry. She threw the cake in the fire.

Everyone in the house fell silent. Then, a tall Indian came forward. Mary hadn't noticed him before. He was very strong and good-looking. Mary was surprised that an Indian could look so wise and so kind. He didn't say anything, but his dark eyes met Mary's eyes. She knew she had done something wrong.

20 She picked up another corn cake and ate it. One of the sisters gave her a bowl of soup, and she drank it, even though it tasted terrible to her. Then once again, she felt very sad and alone, without her mother, her father, her family. She ran to the bed, hid under a blanket and cried. One of the women touched her lightly. They waited for a while, and then quietly left her.

25 When Mary could cry no longer, she got up and went outside. The women were working with other Indian women. They were all pounding whole corn into corn flour.

Mary was happy to see something familiar. "My mother does that too!" she said.

30 The two sisters jumped up. They made it clear to her that she must not speak English. She must speak only the Seneca language. And they began teaching her. One of the first things they taught her was the word for *corn*. And they taught her that Indians always show respect for corn. It was an important part of their lives, so they never burnt it or threw it away.

B. ***Write your finishing time.***
Then turn the page and answer the questions.

Finishing time: _____

C. Circle the best answers. Don't look back at the passage.

1. This passage is about
   a. life in a Seneca longhouse.
   b. how Mary learned the Seneca language.
   c. Mary's first morning with the Indians.
   d. some Seneca Indian families.

2. When Mary woke up, the two women were
   a. taking care of the children.
   b. talking with other women.
   c. sewing clothes for Mary.
   d. cooking over the fire.

3. Which sentence is NOT true?
   a. Mary didn't like the corn cake.
   b. Mary was angry with the Indians.
   c. Mary was very hungry.
   d. Mary liked the Indian food.

4. What surprised Mary about the tall Indian?
   a. He spoke very loudly.
   b. He was very good-looking.
   c. He was very young.
   d. He spoke to her in English.

5. Mary knew she had done something wrong
   a. from the way the tall Indian looked at her.
   b. from the shouts of the Indian women.
   c. because the Indian women told her.
   d. because the tall Indian told her.

6. The two Indian women
   a. didn't let her eat any corn cakes.
   b. didn't let her go back to bed.
   c. told her not to speak English.
   d. told her not to use Seneca words.

D. Check your answers with your teacher. Write your comprehension score (the number of correct answers): _____ . Then read the passage again and look for the answers to the questions.

E. Write your reading time.   **Finishing time – Starting time = _____**

F. Find your reading rate on page 229. Write your reading rate and comprehension score on the progress chart on page 230.

A. *Write your starting time.*
Then preview and read the passage.

Starting time: _____

Learning Indian Ways

From the first day, Mary joined the Seneca children in their everyday jobs. They gathered wood in the forest for the cooking fires. They carried water up from the river, and they helped the women with their work. But

5   they also had time for games in the forest, and for teaching her Seneca words. Soon she could understand the Seneca language quite well, and before long, she was speaking it.

She understood now what had happened on the

10 night of her arrival. The Indians had been crying and singing about a young man, the brother of the two women. He had died in the war. The two women had taken Mary into the family in his place. She was a sister to them now.

As part of the family, Mary helped care for the little children. At first, Mary

15 wondered at the Indian ways. Their babies were tied tightly in a basket. They couldn't move their arms or legs. They could only open their mouths. But Mary noticed that they didn't cry very often. They learned early to be quiet and patient, and not to show pain or sadness.

Mary couldn't always hide her own sadness. Sometimes she went into the

20 forest alone to cry. Then she often spoke to herself in English so she wouldn't forget her language. She said the names of all her family. She sang the songs her mother had taught her. She knew that her parents were probably dead, but still, she hoped one day to return to the farm.

Meanwhile, she learned about farming the Indian way. The women planted

25 corn, squash, and beans in a field. Mary helped to clear away the weeds and grass around the little plants. When the corn grew tall, she helped keep away the crows. She shouted and waved at them. But when she picked up a stone, the Indians stopped her. They said she must never kill an animal if it wasn't necessary. Crows took the Indians' corn, but they were not really bad. The Indians believed that

30 many years ago, crows had brought them corn from the southwest.

At the end of August, she helped gather the corn. Then all the Indians in the town had a great corn festival—four days of eating, games, dancing, and giving thanks for the corn. In the evenings, Mary sat with the other children and listened to their songs and stories.

B. *Write your finishing time.*
Then turn the page and answer the questions.

Finishing time: _____

C. *Circle the best answers. Don't look back at the passage.*

1. This passage is about
   a. how Mary learned the Indian way of life.
   b. how the Seneca Indians planted corn.
   c. how Indian children learned to be quiet.
   d. how Mary learned the Seneca language.

2. Which sentence is NOT true about the Indian children?
   a. They played games in the forest.
   b. They had jobs to do for the village.
   c. They taught Mary Seneca words.
   d. They stayed away from Mary.

3. Indian babies learned early to
   a. move their arms and legs.
   b. be quiet and patient.
   c. cry for their mothers.
   d. get out of their baskets.

4. Which sentence is NOT true about Mary?
   a. She went into the forest to cry.
   b. She didn't want to forget English.
   c. She still hoped to return home.
   d. She often spoke English with the Indians.

5. What did the Indians tell Mary?
   a. to kill all the crows she saw near the corn
   b. not to make noise near the corn field
   c. not to kill animals if it wasn't necessary
   d. to eat only certain animals in the forest

6. The Indians had a festival
   a. for the end of the war.
   b. to give thanks for the corn.
   c. for the end of the summer.
   d. to get ready for hunting.

D. *Check your answers with your teacher. Write your comprehension score (the number of correct answers): _____ . Then read the passage again and look for the answers to the questions.*

E. *Write your reading time.*   Finishing time − Starting time = _____

F. *Find your reading rate on page 229. Write your reading rate and comprehension score on the Progress Chart on page 230.*

A. *Write your starting time.*
Then preview and read the passage.

Starting time: _____

A Visit to the Fort

   In September, the Indians moved for the winter. They went to live further south on the Ohio River where there was good hunting. That winter, Mary learned many things. She learned how to prepare meat the Indian way. She learned how to clean and dry animal skins and furs, how to make pots and
5 baskets, and how to sew Indian clothes.

   Most of all, she learned to work quietly and well. Her Indian sisters were always kind and patient with her. The other children treated her like one of them. She began to love her Indian family, and she thought less about her old life.

   In spring, they all moved back to their summer village. Once again, Mary
10 helped the women plant their fields, and she watched the corn grow. Then one day, her sisters told her they were going to the fort with their husbands to trade furs—and they were taking Mary. It was now called Fort Pitt, and it belonged to the English. Mary's heart jumped at the thought of seeing English people. Suddenly, she
15 wanted terribly to return to her old life.

   They arrived by canoe in the evening and camped across the river. In the morning, they took their furs to the fort. The Indians told Mary to wait
20 outside while they talked with the trader. Some English soldiers went in and out, but they didn't seem to see her. Then another soldier came out and he noticed Mary right away. He seemed surprised to see an Indian girl with blond hair.

25 "Who are you?" he said, "Where are you from?" At first, Mary looked down. She was afraid to say anything. But once she started speaking in English, the words came pouring out of her. She began to tell him how the Indians had taken her.

   But then her Indian sisters saw her. They guessed what was happening and they pulled her away. Down to the camp they ran with Mary. As fast as they could, they
30 gathered their things and left in the canoe, without waiting for the men. Mary was a sister to them now, and they didn't want the white people to take her.

   But Mary felt lost and alone a second time. Again, she wanted her old life and her family. Again, she practiced her English and was unhappy. But as before, with the passing of time, her sadness slowly went away.

B. *Write your finishing time.*
Then turn the page and answer the questions.

Finishing time: _____

C. *Circle the best answers. Don't look back at the passage.*

1. This passage is about
   a. the Englishman at Fort Pitt.
   b. Mary's Indian family.
   c. how the fort became English.
   d. how Mary went to the fort.

2. The most important thing that Mary learned was to
   a. speak English to herself.
   b. work quietly and well.
   c. go hunting in the woods.
   d. play with the Indian children.

3. Which sentence is NOT true about Mary's life?
   a. She was not happy with her Indian family.
   b. Her Indian sisters were kind to her.
   c. She learned how to do things the Indian way.
   d. The Indian children treated her like one of them.

4. When her sisters told her about the trip to Fort Pitt, Mary
   a. was not interested.
   b. was very excited.
   c. didn't want to go.
   d. was very afraid.

5. Which sentence is NOT true about the English soldier?
   a. He was surprised to see a blond Indian.
   b. He wanted to know about Mary.
   c. He asked her questions about her life.
   d. He spoke to her in the Seneca language.

6. The Indian women returned quickly to the village
   a. because they had finished trading furs.
   b. because they didn't speak English.
   c. because they were afraid of losing Mary.
   d. because they couldn't wait for the men.

D. *Check your answers with your teacher. Write your comprehension score (the number of correct answers): _____. Then read the passage again and look for the answers to the questions.*

E. *Write your reading time.*   Finishing time – Starting time = _____

F. *Find your reading rate on page 229. Write your reading rate and comprehension score on the progress chart on page 230.*

A. *Write your starting time.*
Then preview and read the passage.

Starting time: _____

An Indian Husband

The summer passed, and another winter. Then two more summers and winters. Mary's life followed the seasons. There was always work to do, but it was never terribly hard work. And it was the kind of work Mary enjoyed. She liked being outside, gathering wood or working in the corn field. She liked listening to
5 the birds or the wind in the trees.

Then, when Mary was 16, her Indian sisters said it was time for her to get married. The man they chose for her was called Sheninjee. He was tall and good-looking, but Mary didn't know him very well.
10 She didn't want to get married, and she didn't want to marry an Indian. But she couldn't say no.

So one day, she was married to Sheninjee and went to live with him. Soon she was glad to be married to him. Her husband was not just good-
15 looking. He was also gentle, kind, and good, and he always treated Mary with great respect.

As a married woman, she had her own part of the longhouse. But she still worked together with the other married women and helped them with their children. Then, a year later, she was expecting a baby
20 herself.

The baby was born early, while her husband was away. It was a girl, but it only lived for two days. Mary was terribly sad to lose her little daughter. She was also very ill. For two weeks, she was too ill to move. Her husband returned and did everything he could for her comfort. Still, she was sure that she would die. Little
25 by little, though, she got better and she went back to her usual life.

The next year, she had another baby. He was a strong, healthy boy and she had no trouble when he was born. She named him Thomas, after her father. Like the other women in the village, she carried her son everywhere. When she was walking, she carried him on her back. When she worked in the fields, his basket
30 hung from a tree.

When Thomas was a few months old, Mary went with her husband on another trip to Fort Pitt. This time it was different. She had her baby with her, and she didn't want to answer questions. While the Indians talked with the traders, she stayed in the camp by the river. She no longer wanted to return to the
35 white people.

B. *Write your finishing time.*
Then turn the page and answer the questions.

Finishing time: _____

C. *Circle the best answers. Don't look back at the passage.*

1. This passage is about
   a. how Mary didn't want to marry an Indian.
   b. how Mary got married and had children.
   c. how the Seneca Indian families lived.
   d. how Mary's son, Thomas, was born.

2. Which sentence is NOT true about Mary's husband?
   a. He didn't want to marry her.
   b. He was tall and good-looking.
   c. He was chosen by her Indian family.
   d. He was an Indian.

3. Mary's husband, Sheninjee,
   a. was not a good man.
   b. stayed away from her.
   c. treated her very badly.
   d. treated her with respect.

4. Which sentence is NOT true?
   a. Mary's first baby was a girl.
   b. Mary's first baby died after two days.
   c. Mary didn't want to have a baby.
   d. Mary was very ill when the baby was born.

5. During the day, the Indian women usually
   a. left their babies at home.
   b. carried their babies everywhere.
   c. gave their babies to older women.
   d. stayed home with their babies.

6. Why didn't Mary go to the fort?
   a. She didn't want to talk with English people.
   b. She was afraid of French soldiers.
   c. She had work to do in the camp.
   d. She didn't want anyone to see her son.

D. *Check your answers with your teacher. Write your comprehension score (the number of correct answers): _____. Then read the passage again and look for the answers to the questions.*

E. *Write your reading time.*   Finishing time – Starting time = _____

F. *Find your reading rate on page 229. Write your reading rate and comprehension score on the progress chart on page 230.*

A. *Write your starting time.*
Then preview and read the passage.

Starting time: _____

Seneca on the Genesee

When Thomas was nine months old, Mary and her family moved to Genesee, in northern New York State. The trip was long and difficult. Mary walked for more than 500 miles with Thomas on her back or in her arms.

That winter, Mary's husband was away hunting. Mary was comfortable in
5 Genesee with her Indian family, but she missed her husband. In the spring, he didn't come back and Mary became fearful. The corn was growing high, and still he didn't come.

Then bad news arrived. He had become sick and died in the winter. Her fine and gentle husband was gone. Once
10 again, Mary was sad. But her Indian family stayed close to her. They comforted her as best they could. They gave her everything she needed. Slowly, she forgot her sadness.

Meanwhile, the King of England decided that he wanted to get English prisoners back from the Indians. He promised
15 money to anyone who brought them in. A Dutchman who lived near Mary wanted some of this money. He started watching Mary. One day, he ran up to her when she was alone in a corn field. But when she saw him, she ran away even faster.

For three days she hid in the woods. Then she went at night to talk with her
20 Indian brother. She told him she didn't want to return to the English. She wanted to stay with the Indians. He spoke to the Seneca leader. The next day, the Indians sent the Dutchman away.

For the rest of Mary's life, she stayed in Genesee. She married again, to an older Indian named Hiokatoo. They had four daughters and two sons. All of them
25 were named for her English relatives. Hiokatoo lived long, always a kind and loving husband. Mary, too, lived to a great old age. She was known in the valley for her hard work and her kindness. When people were in trouble—white people or Indians—they often went to her for help.

At the end of her life, only three of her children still lived, three daughters.
30 The fourth daughter died young of illness. All three of her sons died violent deaths. They weren't killed in war. Like many other Indian men, they began to drink the white man's "fire water" (alcohol). They died in senseless fighting among themselves.

This was Mary's last great sadness. The white men with their alcohol were
35 destroying the Indian way of life.

B. *Write your finishing time.*
Then turn the page and answer the questions.

Finishing time: _____

C. Circle the best answers. Don't look back at the passage.

1. This passage is about
   a. Mary's Indian family.
   b. The death of Mary's husband.
   c. Mary's life in Genesee.
   d. how Indian life was destroyed.

2. Mary's first husband died
   a. in the war.
   b. of illness.
   c. in an accident.
   d. violently.

3. Why did the Dutchman run up to Mary?
   a. He wanted to bring her to the English.
   b. He wanted to marry her.
   c. He wanted to tell her something.
   d. He wanted to help her work.

4. Mary told her Indian brother that she
   a. didn't want to stay in the valley.
   b. didn't know what to do.
   c. wanted to return to the English.
   d. wanted to stay with the Indians.

5. Which sentence is NOT true about Mary?
   a. She married a second time.
   b. She had six more children.
   c. She was known for her kindness.
   d. She died young of illness.

6. For Mary, the Indian way of life was being destroyed by
   a. illness and bad food.
   b. the English soldiers.
   c. white men and alcohol.
   d. the war against the English.

   Comprehension score: _____

D. Check your answers with your teacher. Write your comprehension score (the number of correct answers): _____ **. Then read the passage again and look for the answers to the questions.**

E. Write your reading time.   **Finishing time – Starting time =** _____

F. Find your reading rate on page 229. Write your reading rate and comprehension score on the progress chart on page 230.

UNIT 2

Two Popular Authors

A. *Write your starting time.*
Then preview and read the passage.

Starting time: _____

J.K. Rowling: Early Years

Harry Potter and the Philosopher's Stone is a best-selling book in 55 languages. So are the six other *Harry Potter* books. They've also been made into very successful movies. Millions of people around the world know Harry's story. They know about his magical powers, his friends, and his enemies.

5   Harry Potter was the invention of a writer named J.K. Rowling. Who is she, and where did she get the idea for her famous books?

    Her full name is Joanne Kathleen Rowling. She was born in 1966 in Chipping Sodbury, near Bristol, England. Chipping Sodbury is a strange name for a town, but Rowling likes that name. She likes places and people with strange names. She

10 writes the names down and uses them again in her books.

    When Rowling was growing up, books were always important to her. There were lots of books in her family's house. Her mother loved reading, and so did her father. They often read books aloud to her. Then she learned to read by herself. When she was only six, she even wrote a book. It was called *Rabbit.* She wanted

15 to publish it. From then on, that was her dream. She wanted to be a writer.

    Rowling and her younger sister started school in Bristol. She was very happy at the elementary school there. But, when she was nine, her mother and father decided to move to the country. So they moved to the village of Tutshill, near Chepstow in South Wales. The village was in the Forest of Dean, not far from the

20 River Wye. The family's house was next to the church and the cemetery. Rowling's friends were afraid of the cemetery, but she and her sister liked it. She liked reading the names of all the dead people. She says she still likes cemeteries and still goes to them to look at the names.

    There were many interesting and unusual places to visit near Tutshill. Not

25 far away, there was an old castle on a hill. There was also the river and lots of big rocks to climb on. Rowling and her sister loved to play outdoors. They didn't have computers or video games, and they didn't watch much television. Instead they invented games and adventures for themselves.

B. *Write your finishing time.*
Then turn the page and answer the questions.

Finishing time: _____

C. *Circle the best answers. Don't look back at the passage.*

1. This passage is about
   a. the *Harry Potter* books.
   b. a writer of children's books.
   c. the early life of J.K. Rowling.
   d. J.K. Rowling's hometown.

2. What does Rowling like about the town where she was born?
   a. the strange name
   b. the people there
   c. the other children
   d. the library

3. Rowling's parents
   a. never read books.
   b. published many books.
   c. had strange names.
   d. loved reading.

4. When Rowling was six, she
   a. went to Bristol.
   b. read a book.
   c. wrote a book.
   d. got a rabbit.

5. Which sentence is NOT true about Rowling's new home in Tutshill?
   a. It was in a forest.
   b. It was near a cemetery.
   c. It was near a river.
   d. It was near the city.

6. When she was young, Rowling enjoyed
   a. watching television.
   b. playing outdoors.
   c. going to church.
   d. playing video games.

D. *Check your answers with your teacher. Write your comprehension score (the number of correct answers): _____ . Then read the passage again and look for the answers to the questions.*

E. *Write your reading time.*   Finishing time – Starting time = _____

F. *Find your reading rate on page 229. Write your reading rate and comprehension score on the progress chart on page 231.*

A. *Write your starting time.*   Starting time: _____
Then preview and read the passage.

School Years

When Rowling's family moved to Tutshill, she went to a new school. Her new teacher was not warm and friendly like her teachers in Bristol. This teacher gave math tests every day. The children who could answer all the questions sat on one side of the room. The "stupid" children sat on the other side of the room.

5   On her first day at school, the teacher asked Rowling a math question. Rowling was so afraid of this teacher, she couldn't think. She gave the wrong answer, so the teacher put her with the "stupid" children.

When Rowling started writing the *Harry Potter* books, she remembered this experience She remembered how she feared and hated this teacher. These

10   memories helped her invent the character of Snape, the teacher that Harry hates the most.

Later, in high school, Rowling liked her teachers and her school better. She had an English teacher who was very important to her. Miss Shepherd was not an easy teacher, but she cared about her students. Rowling learned a lot from her about

15   books and about writing. When Rowling's first book was published, Miss Shepherd wrote to her to say she liked the book. This letter made Rowling very happy.

English was Rowling's favorite subject in school, but she was good at other subjects, too. She always wanted to have all the answers in class. She wanted to be the best student. In fact, she was probably a little like Hermione in the *Harry*

20   *Potter* books. Hermione is one of Harry's closest friends. But she sometimes makes Harry angry because she is always good in all her subjects.

Rowling wasn't good at everything. At her school, all the children had to learn metalworking and woodworking. Rowling hated these subjects. She was not good at making things with her hands. A teaspoon she made was completely flat

25   and useless. A picture frame she made was mostly glue. She was also not good at sports, and she hated the gym.

In her teenage years, she was not very happy with herself and her body. She thought she was too short and fat and not as pretty as her sister. She wished she could play sports better. That may be why she invented the sport called

30   "quidditch," and she made Harry a champion quidditch player. He does what his author always wished she could do.

B. *Write your finishing time.*   Finishing time: _____
Then turn the page and answer the questions.

C. *Circle the best answers. Don't look back at the passage.*

1. This passage is about
    a. Rowling's years in school.
    b. Rowling's favorite subjects.
    c. the schools in England.
    d. the teachers in Rowling's high school.

2. Which sentence is NOT true about Rowling's new teacher?
    a. She made some children afraid.
    b. She became a character in Rowling's books.
    c. She thought Rowling was stupid.
    d. She was warm and friendly to all the children.

3. Who was important to Rowling in high school?
    a. a teacher named Snape
    b. her English teacher
    c. her math teacher
    d. a friend named Hermione

4. In high school, Rowling
    a. didn't do very well.
    b. was good only in English.
    c. never spoke in class.
    d. was a very good student.

5. Rowling was not good at
    a. working with her hands.
    b. answering the teacher's questions.
    c. studying for her classes.
    d. writing papers for English.

6. As a teenager, Rowling
    a. wasn't happy about her writing.
    b. liked the way she looked.
    c. knew she was very pretty.
    d. wasn't happy with herself.

D. *Check your answers with your teacher. Write your comprehension score (the number of correct answers): _____ . Then read the passage again and look for the answers to the questions.*

E. *Write your reading time.*　　　**Finishing time – Starting time = _____**

F. *Find your reading rate on page 229. Write your reading rate and comprehension score on the progress chart on page 231.*

A. *Write your starting time.* Starting time: _____
      Then preview and read the passage.

From High School to University and Work

   While Rowling was in high school, her mother became very ill. This had a
strong effect on Rowling. She was not a relaxed person in any case, and as a girl,
she was always worrying about what might happen. Now something terrible really
was happening. Her mother was slowly dying.

5   In these difficult years, Rowling depended very much on her friends. She
needed to have someone to talk to about her feelings. Fortunately, she had good
friends who could listen to her and help her. In her last year at school, she made
friends with Sean Harris. He became her best friend in Tutshill, and he remained
a friend for life. He was important to her also because he had a car. He would

10 take her on long drives, far from her unhappy home and far from the quiet, boring
village of Tutshill.

   Much later, when Rowling began to write about Harry Potter, she took some
important ideas from this part of her life. She made Harry an orphan, and she
wrote with great feeling about the loss of his parents. She also created several close

15 friends for Harry. They give him love and support and helped him survive his
adventures. In fact, Rowling says that Harry's closest friend, Ron Weasley, is a lot
like her friend Sean.

   After graduating from high school, Rowling went to Exeter University. She
knew she wanted to be a writer, but she didn't study English or writing. She

20 was afraid she might not find a job as an English major. Instead, she studied
languages. For one year of her university studies, she lived in Paris. That year, she
also had a job teaching English to French students.

   Her next step after the university was to take a secretarial course in London.
In her own opinion, she was a terrible secretary. But she did learn how to type

25 quickly, and this was very useful later. After the course, she got a job with
Amnesty International, an international human rights organization.

   Rowling's job was very interesting, but the most important thing for her was
her writing. She was already working on a book. Every day at lunchtime, she went
to a café alone so she could write. She also went out to write in a pub or café on

30 the weekends. She didn't yet want her friends or family to know what she was
doing.

B. *Write your finishing time.* Finishing time: _____
      Then turn the page and answer the questions.

C. *Circle the best answers. Don't look back at the passage.*

1. This passage is about
   a. Rowling's studies at Exeter University.
   b. the problems in Rowling's family.
   c. the importance of friends and family in a teenager's life.
   d. Rowling's life from high school until after university.

2. When she was young, Rowling
   a. worried a lot.
   b. was a happy girl.
   c. was very relaxed.
   d. never worried.

3. Which sentence about Sean Harris is NOT true?
   a. He had a car.
   b. He lived in the village.
   c. He was very ill.
   d. He was Rowling's closest friend.

4. Rowling included many things from her life in her books. What did she NOT include?
   a. her feelings about her mother's death
   b. her job as a secretary
   c. a boy like her friend Sean
   d. the importance of friendship

5. When she went to Exeter University, what did Rowling want to be?
   a. a secretary
   b. an English major
   c. a writer
   d. a French teacher

6. Why did Rowling work on a book in a café?
   a. She didn't have room in her apartment.
   b. She often met friends at the café.
   c. She liked to drink coffee when she was writing.
   d. She didn't want anyone to know about her writing.

D. *Check your answers with your teacher. Write your comprehension score (the number of correct answers): _____. Then read the passage again and look for the answers to the questions.*

E. *Write your reading time.*   Finishing time − Starting time = _____

F. *Find your reading rate on page 229. Write your reading rate and comprehension score on the progress chart on page 231.*

A. *Write your starting time.*
Then preview and read the passage.

Starting time: _____

Harry Potter

The idea for the *Harry Potter* books came to Rowling on a train. She was traveling from Manchester to London when she began thinking about a boy with magical powers. From the first moment, she knew his name, and
5   she knew she had a good idea. She was very excited.

She thought about the book for the rest of the trip. By the time she arrived in London, many things were clear to her. She knew the names of Harry's friends and his school. She knew what was going to happen to him
10   in the book. She even knew that she was going to write seven books and she had a plan for all the books. Rowling stopped working on her earlier novel and started writing about Harry Potter.

Soon after that, she moved to Manchester, England, to live with a friend. She
15   only stayed there a short while. That year, after many years of illness, her mother died. Rowling was very unhappy. She decided that she needed to leave England for a while, so she went to Oporto, Portugal, and taught English in a language school. After six months, she met a Portuguese journalist, Jorge Arantes. They got married, and the next year their daughter, Jessica, was born. This was a very happy
20   moment in Rowling's life. However, the happy times didn't last. After only a few months, Rowling realized that her marriage wasn't working. She also needed a better job, so she decided to return to England. She and Jessica went to live near Rowling's sister in Edinburgh, Scotland.

All this time, Rowling was working on the first *Harry Potter* book. In
25   Edinburgh, it was hard for her to find time for writing. She was taking courses to become a teacher in English schools, and she had to take care of little Jessica. Rowling often took Jessica for long walks until the child fell asleep. Then she went to a café, ordered a cup of coffee, and started writing.

When the book was finally finished, Rowling began to look for a publisher.
30   Many publishers told her they were not interested. But at last, she got a letter of acceptance from a small publisher. Rowling says that this was one of the best moments of her life. When *Harry Potter and the Philosopher's Stone* was published in July 1997, Rowling says she walked around all day with a copy under her arm.

B. *Write your finishing time.*
Then turn the page and answer the questions.

Finishing time: _____

C. *Circle the best answers. Don't look back at the passage.*

1. This passage is about
   a. how to write books and publish them.
   b. how Rowling wrote the first *Harry Potter* book.
   c. how Rowling thought of Harry Potter on a train.
   d. how a publisher accepted *Harry Potter*.

2. Which sentence is NOT true about Rowling and the idea of Harry Potter?
   a. She knew it was a good idea.
   b. She knew Harry Potter's name.
   c. She knew what was going to happen to him.
   d. She knew the book was going to be a success.

3. After her mother died, Rowling
   a. started teaching Portuguese.
   b. went to live in London.
   c. got the idea for Harry Potter.
   d. wanted to leave England.

4. Which sentence is NOT true about Rowling in Portugal?
   a. She taught in a language school.
   b. She married a Portuguese journalist.
   c. She didn't like the country.
   d. She had a daughter.

5. In Edinburgh, it was hard for Rowling to find
   a. a good job.
   b. a place to live.
   c. time to write.
   d. good coffee.

6. Which sentence IS true?
   a. It was not easy to find a publisher for *Harry Potter*.
   b. Rowling found a publisher very quickly.
   c. Many publishers were interested in *Harry Potter*.
   d. The publisher wanted her to change *Harry Potter*.

D. *Check your answers with your teacher. Write your comprehension score (the number of correct answers): _____. Then read the passage again and look for the answers to the questions.*

E. *Write your reading time.*　　　　Finishing time − Starting time = _____

F. *Find your reading rate on page 229. Write your reading rate and comprehension score on the progress chart on page 231.*

A. *Write your starting time.*   Starting time: _____
Then preview and read the passage.

Success

At first, not many of the *Harry Potter* books were sold. Rowling was an unknown writer, and the publishing company was small. But children who read the book liked it a lot. They told their friends about it, and it soon became popular in England. Then an American company decided to publish it in the United States and paid Rowling a lot of money. People began talking about the book and about Rowling.

At this time, she was working part-time as a teacher and trying to write the second book, *Harry Potter and the Chamber of Secrets*. She needed more time for writing, but she was afraid to give up her job. Finally, she decided to stop teaching for two years to finish the book.

Rowling never went back to teaching. The second book was quite long for a children's book—341 pages. But when it was published, it was a bestseller immediately. The next books were even longer, but children still lined up to buy them.

In 2007, the seventh and last book was published. Harry Potter was grown up, and his story was finished. Rowling said that finishing the books made her both happy and sad. She is still busy with writing relating to Harry Potter. For example, she is writing a dictionary of words used in the books, and she is helping to write the movies based on the books.

Rowling is very glad, of course, that millions of children are reading the *Harry Potter* books. But she doesn't always like being a famous author. In the early years, she enjoyed reading aloud from her books at bookstores. However, she had to stop when thousands of people began coming to hear her. She also stopped doing some things for her publishers and the movie people. She doesn't often go on television, for example, and she doesn't allow journalists to take pictures of her or her family.

Rowling's private life is very important to her, and she tries very hard to keep it normal. Fortunately, people usually don't recognize her on the streets in Edinburgh. Rowling is now married to a doctor, Neil Murray, and she has two more children.

The big question that everyone asks about Rowling is this: What will she do next? As one of the richest people in England, she certainly doesn't need to write more books. But she says that she wants to continue writing. It's what she likes to do best.

B. *Write your finishing time.*   Finishing time: _____
Then turn the page and answer the questions.

C. *Circle the best answers. Don't look back at the passage.*

1. This passage is about
   a. what Rowling will write next.
   b. why children like Rowling's books.
   c. how Rowling became successful.
   d. successful children's books.

2. The first book became popular because
   a. children told their friends about it.
   b. the publisher spent a lot of money on it.
   c. there was a movie about it.
   d. Rowling was a famous writer.

3. Why did Rowling stop working as a teacher?
   a. The publisher told her to stop.
   b. Her daughter wanted her to stay home.
   c. She didn't like teaching children.
   d. She needed more time for writing.

4. Compared with most other children's books, the *Harry Potter* books are
   a. shorter.
   b. longer.
   c. easier.
   d. funnier.

5. Which sentence is NOT true about Rowling?
   a. She doesn't want her family in the news.
   b. She doesn't read from her books at bookstores.
   c. She wants to keep her life private.
   d. She is often on television shows.

6. Rowling says she wants to continue writing because
   a. she likes writing books.
   b. she needs more money.
   c. the publisher wants more books.
   d. she doesn't want to work in an office.

D. *Check your answers with your teacher. Write your comprehension score (the number of correct answers): _____ . Then read the passage again and look for the answers to the questions.*

E. *Write your reading time.*   Finishing time – Starting time = _____

F. *Find your reading rate on page 229. Write your reading rate and comprehension score on the progress chart on page 231.*

A. *Write your starting time.*
Then preview and read the passage.

Starting time: _____

Stephen King: First Experiences

People love a good horror story. That's why *Frankenstein* and the stories of Edgar Allen Poe are still favorites. And that's why Stephen King has so many readers. He knows how to scare us and tell a good story at the same time. He has done that in more than 30 books, many of them bestsellers.

Stephen King was born in Portland, Maine, in 1947. When he was only two, his father left the family. After that, Stephen and his older brother, David, lived with their mother. She never got any money from Stephen's father to help bring up the boys. Her parents couldn't help her, so she always had to work. At different times, she worked in a bakery, at a laundromat, and at a home for sick or old people. She moved the family several times, looking for a better situation—to Wisconsin, Indiana, and Connecticut. Then she moved back to Maine to be near her parents.

Because their mother had to work, the boys spent a lot of time with babysitters. Some of the babysitters didn't take very good care of them. When Stephen was only four years old, one babysitter made him eat seven fried eggs. He got very sick, and she never came back. Another babysitter was not very interested in the boys. One day while she was there, she didn't notice when six-year-old David climbed out the bathroom window and onto the roof. Stephen stood at the window and watched him. He wondered if his brother was going to fall. Finally, a neighbor called the police. That babysitter lost her job, too.

When Stephen was in first grade, he got quite sick. He had problems with his throat and his ears. He missed most of the school year. During those long months at home, he read many books, especially adventure books.

Then he began to write stories. The first ones were taken from comic books. He showed one to his mother, and she told him to write a story himself. So he did. He wrote a four-page story about magical animals that rode around in an old car and helped little children. When his mother read it, she said it was good enough to be in a book. That made him extremely happy. He wrote four more stories about the magical animals, and his mother paid him 25 cents for each one—his first money from writing.

B. *Write your finishing time.*
Then turn the page and answer the questions.

Finishing time: _____

C. *Circle the best answers. Don't look back at the passage.*

1. This passage is about
   a. the life of a famous writer.
   b. the books by Stephen King.
   c. Stephen King's early years.
   d. Stephen King's mother.

2. Which sentence is NOT true about Stephen's mother?
   a. Stephen's father didn't help her.
   b. She didn't get any money from her parents.
   c. She always had to have a job.
   d. She worked as a writer.

3. Stephen and his brother
   a. always had the same babysitter.
   b. never stayed with a babysitter.
   c. liked their babysitter.
   d. had many babysitters.

4. Which sentence is NOT true?
   a. A babysitter made Stephen eat seven fried eggs.
   b. Another babysitter let his brother climb onto the roof.
   c. Some babysitters didn't take good care of the boys.
   d. The neighbors often took care of the boys.

5. Stephen read a lot when he was six
   a. because his mother wanted him to read.
   b. because he was sick for a long time.
   c. because he didn't like television.
   d. because he couldn't hear anything.

6. Stephen's first stories were about
   a. magical animals.
   b. his mother.
   c. little cars.
   d. his babysitters.

D. *Check your answers with your teacher. Write your comprehension score (the number of correct answers):* _____. *Then read the passage again and look for the answers to the questions.*

E. *Write your reading time.*   Finishing time – Starting time = _____

F. *Find your reading rate on page 229. Write your reading rate and comprehension score on the progress chart on page 231.*

A. *Write your starting time.*
Then preview and read the passage.

Starting time: _____

From *Dave's Rag* to "Poe-Pictures"

When Stephen was young, his family didn't have a television. They got one when he was about 11 years old. He loved television and everything about it, even the advertisements. But he didn't stop reading and writing stories.

When he was 11, his mother gave him a typewriter for Christmas. In 1960,
5   at the age of 13, he sent one of his stories to a magazine. The magazine didn't publish the story, but that didn't stop Stephen. He continued to write short stories and send them to magazines. He also helped his brother Dave with a monthly newsletter, called *Dave's Rag*. They printed the newsletter at home and sold it to family and friends. Soon they were selling 50 copies every month. Stephen wrote
10   jokes, news about people in their town, and a continuing story.

But *Dave's Rag* was his brother's idea. Stephen was not really interested in journalism. What he really loved at this time in his life was movies. His family was now living in Durham, Maine. Every weekend, he went to the movies in Lewiston. Sometimes he went with a friend and sometimes he went alone. Many
15   times he couldn't get a ride, so he had to walk many miles to get home. But unless he was sick, he always went. Already the young "King of Horror" knew what he liked. He definitely did not like musicals or children's movies. In his opinion, they were stupid and boring. He liked mysteries, science fiction, crime stories, and especially horror stories.

20   In middle school, his favorite horror movies had titles from the stories of Edgar Allen Poe. He called them "Poe-Pictures." They were very, very scary. After seeing one of them, Stephen had an idea. He could write a story like the one in the movie and sell it to his friends! For two days, he worked hard. He wrote eight pages and printed 40 copies. He brought them to school, and began selling
25   them at 25 cents each. By lunch time, he had nine dollars in his pocket. His first bestseller!

But at the end of the day, the school principal stopped him. She was very angry. She told him to give back the money and stop writing horror stories. Stephen gave back all the money, but he refused to stop writing. He wasn't sure if
30   his stories were any good. But now he knew that people wanted to read them.

B. *Write your finishing time.*
Then turn the page and answer the questions.

Finishing time: _____

C. *Circle the best answers. Don't look back at the passage.*

1. This passage is about
   a. what Stephen wrote for *Dave's Rag*.
   b. how Stephen started to write horror stories.
   c. why Stephen loved horror movies.
   d. why people liked Stephen's horror stories.

2. Which sentence is NOT true about Stephen when he was 11?
   a. He published many stories.
   b. He wrote stories.
   c. He got a typewriter.
   d. His family got a television.

3. What did Stephen love most when he was in middle school?
   a. sports
   b. journalism
   c. movies
   d. jokes

4. Stephen's favorite movies were
   a. war stories.
   b. children's movies.
   c. musicals.
   d. horror stories.

5. Stephen's first "bestseller" was
   a. a horror story.
   b. about people in town.
   c. a newsletter.
   d. about Edgar Allen Poe.

6. In middle school, Stephen realized that
   a. he didn't want to write anymore.
   b. people wanted to read his stories.
   c. his stories were not any good.
   d. no one wants to read horror stories.

D. *Check your answers with your teacher. Write your comprehension score (the number of correct answers): _____ . Then read the passage again and look for the answers to the questions.*

E. *Write your reading time.*   **Finishing time – Starting time = _____**

F. *Find your reading rate on page 229. Write your reading rate and comprehension score on the progress chart on page 231.*

A. ***Write your starting time.***
Then preview and read the passage.

Starting time: _____

Writing in High School

Stephen continued to write, and he continued to send stories to magazines. Finally, a story called, *In a Half-World of Terror* was accepted in a horror magazine. This helped him continue. He was still only a teenager, but he already knew he wanted to be a writer, and he knew just what he wanted to write.

5   In high school, he had to do some different writing. His teachers learned about his work on *Dave's Rag.* They made him editor of the school newspaper, *The Drum.* As the editor, he had to write class reports and sports news. He didn't enjoy this kind of writing at all. One night, he was so bored that he decided he had to do something different. He wrote a newsletter of his own and called it

10   *The Village Vomit.* This newsletter made fun of the school. It gave funny names to the teachers and told about strange things that happened to them.

Stephen brought it to school to show his friends, and they loved it. Then a teacher decided to find out what they were laughing about. She found the newsletter and saw Stephen's name on it.

15   Once again, Stephen was in trouble because of his writing. He was afraid he might be sent away from the school. Instead, he had to stay in the detention hall for two weeks. That meant that he spent every school day in a special room for bad students. Stephen didn't mind this much. In the detention hall, the students told jokes and made paper airplanes.

20   But that wasn't the only result of *The Village Vomit.* The high school principal thought Stephen should use his writing skills. In a nearby town, the *Weekly Enterprise* newspaper needed a sports reporter. The principal sent Stephen to talk to the editor about the job. Stephen didn't like writing for newspapers, and he wasn't interested in sports. But he did need a job.

25   In the end, Stephen learned a lot about writing from the editor of the *Weekly Enterprise.* In fact, he learned much more at the *Enterprise* than in all the writing courses he took in college. The main thing he learned was how to tell a story—any kind of story. Then, just as importantly, he learned how to rewrite a story, taking out all the things that were not necessary. This was a lesson he never forgot.

B. ***Write your finishing time.***
Then turn the page and answer the questions.

Finishing time: _____

C. Circle the best answers. Don't look back at the passage.

1. This passage is about
   a. the sports Stephen played in high school.
   b. the writing Stephen did in high school.
   c. the jobs Stephen had in high school.
   d. the courses Stephen took in high school.

2. When he was a teenager, what did Stephen want to be?
   a. a newspaper editor
   b. a newspaper reporter
   c. a writer of horror stories
   d. an actor in horror movies

3. Why did Stephen become editor of the high school newspaper?
   a. He wrote good stories in class.
   b. He liked writing for newspapers.
   c. His brother was the editor before him.
   d. His teachers heard about *Dave's Rag*.

4. Which sentence is NOT true about Stephen's newsletter?
   a. The teachers thought it was funny.
   b. It made fun of the school.
   c. It made fun of the teachers.
   d. His friends thought it was funny.

5. When Stephen got in trouble, he
   a. was sent away from the school.
   b. didn't have to do anything special.
   c. had to talk to all the teachers.
   d. had to stay in a special room for two weeks.

6. How did Stephen feel about his job at the *Weekly Enterprise*?
   a. He thought it was very boring.
   b. He learned some important things about writing.
   c. He didn't learn as much as he did in college.
   d. He learned a lot about writing horror stories.

D. Check your answers with your teacher. Write your comprehension score (the number of correct answers): _____. Then read the passage again and look for the answers to the questions.

E. Write your reading time.   Finishing time − Starting time = _____

F. Find your reading rate on page 229. Write your reading rate and comprehension score on the progress chart on page 231.

A. *Write your starting time.*
Then preview and read the passage.

Starting time: _____

Becoming a Successful Writer

In 1966, Stephen became a student at the University of Maine. To pay for his college expenses, he had to work. At different times, he worked in the university library, in a factory, and in a high school as a cleaner. He studied English, but he also took education courses so he could become a teacher. This was his mother's
5   idea. She thought he could make a good living as a teacher.

He wasn't making much money as a writer at that time. He continued to write stories, and he continued to send them to magazines. Several of Stephen's stories were published, but he wasn't paid much for them. Finally, in 1969, a magazine paid him $200 for a story. He felt rich, but only for a short time.

10   1969 was an important year for Stephen in another way. That year, he met a young student named Tabitha Spruce in a poetry course, and soon they fell in love. The next year, Stephen graduated from university. In January 1971, he and Tabitha got married.

15   Before long, Stephen and Tabitha had their first child, a baby girl. Stephen couldn't find work as a teacher, so he took a job in a laundromat. He sold a few more stories to magazines, but he and Tabitha never had enough money. They had a car, but it often broke down. When their daughter got sick, they
20   didn't have money for medicine.

Then Stephen got a job as a teacher. He earned more money, but sometimes he was too tired to write. At that time, he was working on a novel about a high school girl. One day, he decided he didn't like the story or the girls in his novel. He felt he didn't know
25   enough about girls in general. He threw all the pages he had written into the wastebasket. But the next day, Tabitha found them and read them. She told him it was a very good story and he had to finish it. She could tell him all about high school girls.

She did help him, and he finished the book. That novel was *Carrie*, his first
30   real success. Stephen didn't get paid much money at first. But a few months later, the publisher got a lot of money for the paperback edition and Stephen was paid $200,000. He and Tabitha didn't have to worry about money anymore. Stephen was a successful writer.

B. *Write your finishing time.*
Then turn the page and answer the questions.

Finishing time: _____

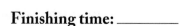

C. *Circle the best answers. Don't look back at the passage.*

1. This passage is about
   a. Stephen's jobs after high school.
   b. Stephen's life as a college student.
   c. how Stephen got married to Tabitha.
   d. how Stephen became successful.

2. Stephen took education courses because
   a. he really wanted to be a teacher.
   b. Tabitha thought it was a good idea.
   c. his mother thought it was a good idea.
   d. he was interested in education.

3. Which sentence is NOT true about Stephen in 1969?
   a. His first child was born.
   b. He met Tabitha.
   c. He sold a story for $200.
   d. He took a poetry course.

4. When his first child was born, Stephen
   a. had lots of money.
   b. got money from his mother.
   c. had very little money.
   d. lived comfortably.

5. Stephen threw away the pages of his book
   a. because Tabitha said it was no good.
   b. because he didn't think it was good.
   c. because his students didn't like it.
   d. because the publisher didn't want it.

6. Stephen finished *Carrie*
   a. with Tabitha's help.
   b. with his mother's help.
   c. without any help.
   d. with the editor's help.

D. *Check your answers with your teacher. Write your comprehension score (the number of correct answers): _____ . Then read the passage again and look for the answers to the questions.*

E. *Write your reading time.*   Finishing time − Starting time = _____

F. *Find your reading rate on page 229. Write your reading rate and comprehension score on the progress chart on page 231.*

A. *Write your starting time.
Then preview and read the passage.*

Starting time: _____

Life After Success

After the success of *Carrie*, Stephen stopped teaching so he could write full time. His next books were *Salem's Lot* and *The Shining*. Both of these were very popular. Meanwhile, the family was growing. He and Tabitha had two more children. They bought a house near a lake in western Maine. They also bought
5   a house in the city of Bangor, Maine. They lived in Bangor in the winter and in western Maine in the summer.

Stephen's life seemed perfect. He was famous, he was rich, and he had a lovely wife and children. However, one thing was not perfect: He was drinking a lot. Many famous writers drank a lot, so he thought his drinking was normal.
10   One evening, when he took out the garbage, he looked at all the empty beer and whiskey bottles. He realized that he was drinking too much. But he was afraid that he wouldn't be able to write without drinking.

For five more years, he continued this way. He also started using drugs. He hardly remembered the last book he wrote at that time. Then Tabitha decided she
15   had to try to stop him. She told him he had to change. If he didn't, she and the children would leave him. He was killing himself, and she didn't want to watch him.

Stephen didn't want to lose his family. He finally realized that he had to change. He stopped drinking and taking drugs, and he found that he didn't need them to write. His stories were as good as before. In the next 12 years, he wrote
20   many more bestsellers. When he was working on a book, he wrote all day every day, even on holidays.

Then he was nearly killed in a terrible accident. One day in 1999, as he was walking by the road, he was hit by a van. He had to have many operations to save his life and to save his leg. But by August, he was back at his desk. He was still in
25   pain, but he couldn't imagine a life without writing.

Since then, Stephen has continued to have health problems because of the accident. But he has also continued to write books, including another bestseller, *Lisey's Story*. He and Tabitha bought a house in Sarasota, Florida, where they go in the winter. His children have grown up, and he now has three grandchildren.

30

B. *Write your finishing time.
Then turn the page and answer the questions.*

Finishing time: _____

C. Circle the best answers. Don't look back at the passage.

1. This passage is about
   a. success and problems in Stephen's life.
   b. a terrible accident on the road.
   c. Stephen's marriage and his family.
   d. the importance of writing.

2. After *Carrie* was published, Stephen
   a. never had problems with money.
   b. spent more money than he was paid.
   c. still didn't have enough money.
   d. bought lots of big cars.

3. One night, Stephen realized that he
   a. worked too much.
   b. drank too much.
   c. couldn't write anymore.
   d. wanted to take drugs.

4. Which sentence is NOT true about Tabitha?
   a. She thought Stephen was killing himself.
   b. She wanted Stephen to stop drinking.
   c. She left Stephen and the children.
   d. She didn't want to see Stephen drinking.

5. What made Stephen finally decide to stop drinking?
   a. Other famous writers told him to stop.
   b. He thought the alcohol was bad for his writing.
   c. The doctor told him to stop.
   d. He didn't want to lose his family.

6. After Stephen's accident, he
   a. started writing as soon as possible.
   b. went back to drinking.
   c. lost his leg.
   d. never wanted to write again.

D. Check your answers with your teacher. Write your comprehension score (the number of correct answers): _____. Then read the passage again and look for the answers to the questions.

E. Write your reading time.   Finishing time – Starting time = _____

F. Find your reading rate on page 229. Write your reading rate and comprehension score on the progress hart on page 231.

A. *Write your starting time.*
Then preview and read the passage.

Starting time: _____

An Apple a Day

We hear a lot of good things about fruits and vegetables: Carrots make your eyesight better. Spinach makes you stronger. Oranges keep away colds. "An apple a day keeps the doctor away." But is there any truth in these sayings?

Doctors all agree that fruits and vegetables in general are good for you. First
5 of all, they help you stay thinner. People who eat a lot of fruits and vegetables lose weight more easily. And thinner people are less likely to have health problems. Another reason for eating fruits and vegetables is that they have many vitamins and minerals. These are important for your health in different ways. They help you have good teeth, clear skin, nice hair, and strong bones. They also help prevent
10 many kinds of disease.

But what about the special powers of some fruits and vegetables. Is it true, for example, that eating carrots will help you see better? The answer is no, for most people. It's true that carrots have a lot of Vitamin A, and that Vitamin A is necessary for your eyes. But most people get enough Vitamin A already. Eating
15 carrots only makes a difference if you are not getting enough Vitamin A.

There is also some truth in the saying about spinach. It does have lots of vitamins, as well as some iron. In fact, iron is important for your blood. If you aren't getting enough iron, you will feel weak and tired. In this case, eating spinach is a good idea. But you have to eat a lot of it to get much iron. If you need iron,
20 you should also eat other iron-rich foods, such as meat, eggs, and beans.

As for oranges, they will not keep away colds. This has been shown by many studies. But the Vitamin C in oranges does help people with colds get better more quickly. So keep eating oranges and other foods with Vitamin C, such as lemons, kiwis, tomatoes, spinach, and broccoli.
25 And finally, do apples really "keep the doctor away"? This time, the answer is yes, apples do help prevent cancer and heart disease. Studies have shown that people who eat several apples a day are less likely to get these diseases. This is because apples have natural chemicals that protect the body.

B. *Write your finishing time.*
Then turn the page and answer the questions.

Finishing time: _____

C. *Circle the best answers. Don't look back at the passage.*

1. This passage is about
   a. what fruits you should eat.
   b. how to cook fruits and vegetables.
   c. why you should eat fruits and vegetables.
   d. how to lose weight.

2. Which sentence is NOT true about fruits and vegetables?
   a. They help you hear better.
   b. They help you lose weight.
   c. They have vitamins and minerals.
   d. They help prevent many diseases.

3. For most people, eating lots of carrots
   a. can improve their eyesight.
   b. makes no difference.
   c. will cause health problems.
   d. is good for their eyes.

4. What does spinach have in it?
   a. nothing healthy
   b. special chemicals
   c. many vitamins and iron
   d. lots of iron

5. Which sentence is NOT true about Vitamin C?
   a. It is in oranges.
   b. It is in some vegetables.
   c. It helps you get over colds.
   d. It prevents colds.

6. Apples help prevent disease because they have
   a. natural chemicals.
   b. lots of minerals.
   c. Vitamin A.
   d. a good taste.

D. *Check your answers with your teacher. Write your comprehension score (the number of correct answers): _____. Then read the passage again and look for the answers to the questions.*

E. *Write your reading time.*   Finishing time – Starting time = _____

F. *Find your reading rate on page 229. Write your reading rate and comprehension score on the progress chart on page 232.*

A. *Write your starting time.*   Starting time: _____
      Then preview and read the passage.

Time to Dance

Are you the kind of person who likes to move with the music? It's a natural thing to do. Even little children start moving when they hear music. In fact, dancing is part of the human experience, like music and storytelling. These three arts were probably invented together. After all, dancing is a way to tell a story to music.

5   Scientists say that animals dance, too, but their dancing is different. The "dances" of animals have a purpose. They send messages to other animals about important physical needs such as hunger, danger, or desire. But when people dance, they express many different feelings—love, joy, anger, sadness. They also tell stories about people, places, life, or death. By dancing these feelings or stories,

10 people can share them with others.

Dancing is also an important part of a country's history and culture. In the past, each country had its own dances. These days, the situation is very different. In the past 200 years, many people have moved from one country to another. When they moved, they brought along their music and their dances. This means

15 that in many places today, it's possible to see and learn different kinds of dances. In the United States, for example, you can learn American square dancing, or Greek, Scottish, or Egyptian dances. You can learn the Viennese waltz or the Argentine tango.

All of these dances are good for you. For one thing, they're good for you

20 physically. Dancing is good exercise. It makes you use your arms and legs, and it makes your heart work. It's an enjoyable way to keep healthy or to lose weight.

Another important point about dancing is that it makes you feel better about yourself. It gives you a chance to express your feelings. If you are angry or upset about something, dancing helps those feelings go away. You may feel very tired

25 afterwards, but you'll probably also be relaxed and happy. And if you are a quiet or fearful kind of person, dancing can help you be more open. When you are dancing, you can forget yourself and your fears.

And finally, there's another important point about dancing. It's a social activity. Some dances are for two people, and some are for groups. But all kinds of dances

30 give you a chance to meet new people or to do something enjoyable with friends.

B. *Write your finishing time.*   Finishing time: _____
      Then turn the page and answer the questions.

C. Circle the best answers. Don't look back at the passage.

1. This passage is about
   a. different kinds of dances.
   b. the importance of dance.
   c. how animals dance.
   d. dancing for exercise.

2. Animals dance
   a. because they have experiences.
   b. for the same reasons as humans.
   c. to express their feelings.
   d. to send messages to other animals.

3. Which sentence is NOT true?
   a. Each country had its own dances in the past.
   b. When people moved, they brought their dances with them.
   c. Many countries didn't have any special dances.
   d. In the United States, you can learn many kinds of dances.

4. Dancing is good for you physically
   a. because it makes you move.
   b. because you can learn the tango.
   c. because it's very enjoyable.
   d. because you don't have to move much.

5. Which sentence is NOT true about dancing?
   a. It makes you feel better about yourself.
   b. It makes you feel more angry or upset.
   c. It helps you open up.
   d. It helps you forget bad feelings.

6. What is one important point about dancing?
   a. You can become famous.
   b. You do it with other people.
   c. You usually do it alone.
   d. You don't have to pay much.

D. Check your answers with your teacher. Write your comprehension score (the number of correct answers): _____. Then read the passage again and look for the answers to the questions.

E. Write your reading time.   Finishing time – Starting time = _____

F. Find your reading rate on page 229. Write your reading rate and comprehension score on the progress chart on page 232.

A. *Write your starting time.*   Starting time: _____
       Then preview and read the passage.

Taking Control of the Dining Room

In the United States, many people are overweight and want to be thinner. They often try eating different kinds of foods, and they try exercising more. But there's one thing they probably haven't tried: changing the conditions in their dining room. What's happening around them when they're eating? And how is
5   the food served?

Many restaurant owners know, for example, that lighting and music change the way people eat. Bright lighting and fast music generally make people eat faster and more. Surprisingly, very low lighting and slow music also make people eat more. In this case, they eat slowly, but they continue eating for much longer.

10 When you go to a restaurant, you can't change the conditions of the dining room. But you can make changes at home. So if you want to eat less, think about the lighting and music. The lighting shouldn't be too low or too bright, and the music shouldn't be too fast or too slow.

At home, there are other things to think about. One of these is the television.
15 Many people watch the news or other programs during meals. This is not a good idea. First, the music on television is often loud and fast, and that makes you eat more. Second, when you watch television, you think about what's on television. You don't think about what you are eating and you don't know how much you have eaten.

20 It's also important to think about the way food is served. The amount you eat depends a lot on portion size. A portion is the amount of food served to one person. Today, in restaurants and at home, portions are much bigger than they used to be. Doctors think this is one reason why many people are overweight. In fact, studies show that most people eat everything on their plate, even if they
25 aren't hungry. If the food is in front of them, they eat it. This means that people are generally eating more these days.

What can you do about this? In a restaurant that gives large portions, you can share a meal with someone. Or you can eat only half the meal and take home the rest. At home, where you are in control, you can make the portions smaller. It's
30 also a good idea to serve them on smaller plates, so they seem bigger. This is a very simple but effective way to lose weight.

B. *Write your finishing time.*   Finishing time: _____
       Then turn the page and answer the questions.

C. *Circle the best answers. Don't look back at the passage.*

1. This passage is about
   a. losing weight by eating different kinds of foods.
   b. reasons why people sometimes eat fast.
   c. the right dining room conditions for losing weight.
   d. eating in restaurants and gaining weight.

2. What do many restaurant owners know about music?
   a. Very fast or slow music makes you eat more.
   b. Music makes no difference in your eating.
   c. Slow music makes you eat less.
   d. Music is not a good idea in a restaurant.

3. Which sentence is NOT true?
   a. Television often has loud and fast music.
   b. When you watch television, you don't think about your meal.
   c. You eat more when you watch television at meals.
   d. If you watch television, you'll eat less at meals.

4. Doctors think that people are fatter because
   a. people go to restaurants more often.
   b. portions are larger than in the past.
   c. food tastes better than in the past.
   d. everyone has bright lights now.

5. People usually
   a. don't like to share meals.
   b. eat less at restaurants.
   c. finish the food on their plates.
   d. prefer smaller portions.

6. What is one simple way to eat less?
   a. Put your food on small plates.
   b. Use big dinner plates.
   c. Eat your meal very slowly.
   d. Eat in restaurants often.

D. *Check your answers with your teacher. Write your comprehension score (the number of correct answers): _____. Then read the passage again and look for the answers to the questions.*

E. *Write your reading time.*   Finishing time – Starting time = _____

F. *Find your reading rate on page 229. Write your reading rate and comprehension score on the progress chart on page 232.*

A. *Write your starting time.*
Then preview and read the passage.

Starting time: _____

A Good Night's Sleep

Many people have trouble getting to sleep at night. Others wake up often during the night, and still others wake up very early and can't get back to sleep again. These people all have *insomnia*. That is, they don't sleep well.

Insomnia can cause many different problems. When people are not sleeping
5   well, they often become unhappy and anxious. They may also become very tired and sleepy. This may have negative effects on their family life or their work. It can even lead to accidents. A tired bus driver, for example, could fall asleep while driving.

There are two types of insomnia. The first is caused by worrying. You have
10 probably been in this situation at some time in your life. When you have a family problem or a difficult exam, you keep thinking about it. At night in bed, your brain won't turn off. This kind of insomnia usually doesn't last long. When the problem is solved or the exam is over, you can sleep through the night again. The second type of insomnia has other kinds of causes. For example, it is often
15 the result of drinking too much coffee or tea. The caffeine in these drinks can keep you awake. You may also be eating too much at your evening meal. Or you may be drinking too much alcohol in the evening. A lot of food or alcohol may help you fall asleep at first. But you may not sleep well later.

Insomnia can also be caused by other unhealthy habits. One bad habit is
20 cigarette smoking. The nicotine in cigarettes has an exciting effect on many people. Another bad habit is lack of exercise. If you don't get exercise in any way, you are more likely to have trouble sleeping. And finally, you shouldn't go to bed at a different time every day. It's important to have a regular bedtime. It's easier for your body to fall asleep at about the same time every night.

25 Other causes of insomnia may be found in your bedroom. First of all, you should check your bed. Is it really comfortable for you? It shouldn't be too hard or too soft. The temperature of the room is also important. A cool room is better for sleeping than a warm room. Finally, there shouldn't be too much light or noise. A few people can sleep in the middle of a brightly lit, noisy room. But most people
30 sleep better in a dark, quiet place.

B. *Write your finishing time.*
Then turn the page and answer the questions.

Finishing time: _____

C. *Circle the best answers. Don't look back at the passage.*

1. This passage is about
   a. how to fall asleep quickly.
   b. the causes of insomnia.
   c. why sleep is important.
   d. the problem of insomnia.

2. Insomnia often makes you
   a. hungry at night.
   b. sleepy during the day.
   c. sleepy at night.
   d. happy during the day.

3. What happens when you worry a lot about something?
   a. You may get very sleepy.
   b. You may not be able to sleep.
   c. You feel tired during the day.
   d. You dream about your problems.

4. What should you NOT do in the evening?
   a. study for an exam
   b. have a snack
   c. watch television
   d. eat a large meal

5. What will help you sleep better?
   a. going to bed early in the evening
   b. drinking alcohol before bedtime
   c. not exercising very much
   d. going to bed at the same time

6. Which sentence is NOT true?
   a. You will sleep better in a large bedroom.
   b. You will sleep better in a cool bedroom.
   c. You will sleep better in a quiet bedroom.
   d. You will sleep better in a dark bedroom.

D. *Check your answers with your teacher. Write your comprehension score (the number of correct answers): _____ . Then read the passage again and look for the answers to the questions.*

E. *Write your reading time.*   Finishing time − Starting time = _____

F. *Find your reading rate on page 229. Write your reading rate and comprehension score on the progress chart on page 232.*

A. *Write your starting time.*
Then preview and read the passage.

Starting time: _____

The Art and Science of Meditation

Why do people meditate? The answer is simple: Meditation makes you a happier and healthier person.

Meditation is not difficult to do. You don't need any special equipment or place. You just sit with your eyes closed and think about only one thing. That one
5   thing can be your own breathing, or it can be a certain word. If it's a word, you repeat it again and again. You don't move or think about anything else for ten to forty minutes. You don't think about plans for the day, friends, family, or money problems. You stop thinking about the past or the future, and think only about the present. This way, you become more peaceful.

10 People have known about the effects of meditation for a long time. In 3,000– 2,000 B.C.E., people in India wrote about meditation. It was an important part of the Hindu and Buddhist religions. But they weren't the only ones. There were also Jewish, Christian, and Muslim people who practiced meditation. They all believed that it brought them closer to God.

15 In more recent times, some religious people in the United States and Europe became interested in Eastern religions, and they began to practice meditation. For other people in these countries, however, meditation seemed strange and foreign. But then, in the 1960s, popular music stars such as the Beatles became interested. Other people followed them, and soon there were many courses and books about
20 meditation.

Today, meditation is no longer just for religious people, and it no longer seems strange. It has become very popular among Americans, for example. Over ten million Americans practice it at least once a week. Among those ten million people are students, football players, lawyers, doctors, businesspeople, and actors.

25 All these people find that meditation helps them lead better lives. In fact, scientists have discovered that it can change the way people think. People who often meditate are more positive. They think less about the problems and negative things in their lives. Instead, they think about the good things. In general, they feel happier with themselves and their lives.

30 This is also good for their health. In fact, doctors say that meditation is a good way to reduce stress. They also have learned that it lowers blood pressure, so it can help prevent heart trouble. And in some important ways, meditation is better than any medicine: It's free and it has no bad side effects.

B. *Write your finishing time.*
Then turn the page and answer the questions.

Finishing time: _____

C. Circle the best answers. Don't look back at the passage.

1. This passage is about
   a. religion and meditation.
   b. how to meditate.
   c. the effects of meditation.
   d. the history of meditation.

2. When you meditate, you think about
   a. only one thing.
   b. lots of things.
   c. your problems.
   d. the past.

3. In the past, meditation was for
   a. football players.
   b. businesspeople.
   c. sick people.
   d. religious people.

4. In the United States today,
   a. only music and sports stars meditate.
   b. many different kinds of people meditate.
   c. people meditate for religious reasons.
   d. mostly foreign people meditate.

5. Which sentence is NOT true about people who meditate?
   a. Their brain changes.
   b. Their way of thinking changes.
   c. They feel happier about themselves.
   d. They think more about their problems.

6. Which sentence is NOT true about meditation?
   a. It reduces stress.
   b. It lowers blood pressure.
   c. It has some bad side effects.
   d. It's good for people's health.

D. Check your answers with your teacher. Write your comprehension score (the number of correct answers): _____ . Then read the passage again and look for the answers to the questions.

E. Write your reading time.   Finishing time – Starting time = _____

F. Find your reading rate on page 229. Write your reading rate and comprehension score on the progress chart on page 232.

A. *Write your starting time.*
Then preview and read the passage.

Starting time: _____

How to Improve Your Memory

Language students often think they have memory problems. They worry because they can't remember words. In fact, the problem usually isn't with their memory. The problem is with the way they study.

To remember words better, you need to understand how memory works. There
5 are two kinds of memory: short-term and long-term. When you see, hear, or read something, it goes first into short-term memory. But short-term memory lasts for only a few seconds. You will only remember something longer if it goes into long-term memory.

Why is it that some things go into your long-term memory and some things
10 don't? One reason you remember something is because it's important to you. If you love soccer, for example, you probably remember the names of many soccer players. If you are an engineer, you remember engineering words. People who don't care about soccer or engineering will likely forget those names or words.

Another way that you remember something is if you think about it a lot. Many
15 students study vocabulary by repeating the words. This may work for a short time, but after a day or a week, the words are gone. In fact, just repeating a new word isn't enough. It doesn't connect the word to anything else in your memory.

Your long-term memory is like a very big library with many, many books. And like a library, it's organized. When you put away a book—or a memory—you can't
20 just leave it anywhere. You have to choose a place that makes sense to you. You have to make space there for the new information. And you need some way to find the word again.

How can you do this with vocabulary? The key is to work with the word and think about it in new ways. You can do this by writing new sentences that include
25 it. Even better, you can invent a little story about the word, with people or places that you know. Another way is to make a picture in your mind with the word. For example, if the word is *height*, you can think of the tallest person you know and try to guess his or her height.

All of these activities are ways to think about words. They make the meaning
30 of words stronger in your long-term memory. And they give you a way to find a word when you need it.

B. *Write your finishing time.*
Then turn the page and answer the questions.

Finishing time: _____

C. *Circle the best answers. Don't look back at the passage.*

1. This passage is about
   a. how to improve your memory.
   b. how to study vocabulary.
   c. how to repeat words.
   d. how to remember important events.

2. Where does information go first?
   a. into a picture in your mind
   b. into a big library
   c. into long-term memory
   d. into short-term memory

3. You are more likely to remember
   a. things that are important to you.
   b. the names of people.
   c. words in English.
   d. names of sports players.

4. The passage says that your memory is like a
   a. computer.
   b. library.
   c. store.
   d. picture.

5. What should you do to remember a word longer?
   a. Put it in short-term memory.
   b. Write it down on a list.
   c. Think about it in new ways.
   d. Repeat it a few times.

6. Which is NOT a good way to study words?
   a. Write sentences with the words.
   b. Make stories with the words.
   c. Repeat the words a few times.
   d. Think of a picture with the word.

D. *Check your answers with your teacher. Write your comprehension score (the number of correct answers): _____ . Then read the passage again and look for the answers to the questions.*

E. *Write your reading time.*   **Finishing time − Starting time = _____**

F. *Find your reading rate on page 229. Write your reading rate and comprehension score on the progress chart on page 232.*

A. Write your starting time.
Then preview and read the passage.

Fear of Flying

Are you afraid of flying on an airplane? If you are, you're not alone. About one in four people is afraid of flying. Every time there is a plane crash on the news, more people become afraid.

For most of them, the fear goes away with time. When they have to fly, they try not to think about the danger. To feel better, they may have a few drinks, or they may take some medicine. If there are no problems during the flight, they're fine. But with the smallest problem they become very anxious. Other people, however, become very anxious just thinking about planes. If they get on a plane, they can become ill from fear. They may become so ill that they have to get off the plane before it leaves.

In reality, there are very few plane accidents. The United States National Safety Council says that flying in a plane is much less dangerous than riding in a car. Airline companies check their planes carefully before every flight. If the pilot thinks there is any problem with the plane, he doesn't take off. This means that accidents are very unlikely. But these facts don't matter to the people who are afraid.

These people can be divided into two groups. In the first group are the people who are afraid of falling out of the sky. Since the terrorist attacks of September 11, 2001, more people suffer from this fear. They think about all the bad things that could possibly happen. And there are lots of bad things that could happen to a plane high in the sky.

In the second group, there are people who are afraid of closed places. People with this fear never want to be in small, closed places—like elevators or planes. The plane feels terribly small to them. If anything happens on a plane, they won't be able to get out.

Some fearful travelers decide not to travel by plane at all. They use only transportation that stays on the ground or water—cars, buses, trains, or boats. Other people, however, need to travel by air for work. In this case, they must find a way to get over their fear. Doctors and scientists say it's not easy, but it is possible. There are special courses for people who suffer from fear of flying. These courses are offered by some airline companies, and by many psychologists and hospitals.

B. Write your finishing time.
Then turn the page and answer the questions.

C. *Circle the best answers. Don't look back at the passage.*

1. This passage is about
    a. the things people are afraid of.
    b. the dangers of flying on planes.
    c. courses for people with fear of flying.
    d. people who are afraid of flying.

2. People who are very afraid of flying can
    a. watch the news.
    b. become ill.
    c. feel better.
    d. learn to drive.

3. Which sentence is NOT true?
    a. Flying is more dangerous than riding in a car.
    b. There are very few plane accidents.
    c. Airline companies check their planes carefully.
    d. Pilots don't take off if there's a problem.

4. Why are some people more afraid of flying since September 11, 2001?
    a. They're afraid of planes hitting tall buildings.
    b. They think there will be a big war.
    c. They're afraid of falling out of the sky.
    d. They think the plane might not take off.

5. Other people are afraid
    a. the plane will go to the wrong place.
    b. they won't be able to get out of the plane.
    c. the pilot won't know how to fly the plane.
    d. they won't be able to sleep on the plane.

6. How can you get over fear of flying?
    a. by taking a course
    b. by taking medicine
    c. by driving a car
    d. by flying on small planes

D. *Check your answers with your teacher. Write your comprehension score (the number of correct answers): _____ . Then read the passage again and look for the answers to the questions.*

E. *Write your reading time.*　　　　Finishing time – Starting time = _____

F. *Find your reading rate on page 229. Write your reading rate and comprehension score on the progress chart on page 232.*

A. Write your starting time.
Then preview and read the passage.

Starting time: _____

How Children Learn Language

All human beings can learn a language. And all human babies learn language the same way. It doesn't matter what language they are learning. In fact, babies can learn any language, but they learn the language they hear around them.

All babies make only one kind of sound at first: crying. In little babies, crying
5   has a purpose. It calls the parents and tells them about a problem. The baby is hungry, afraid, or hurt. That's the first kind of conversation babies have with their parents. Soon babies begin making other, happier sounds. These sounds make parents want to stay close and talk to them more. This is how babies begin to learn language—by listening to their parents.

10 By the time they are two months old, babies can tell the difference between human voices and other sounds. They can also recognize their mother's voice. In the next few months, their listening skills improve some more. They begin to recognize different spoken sounds. For example, they can hear the difference between "pa" and "ba."

15 When they are about six months old, babies begin "babbling." This means that they make sounds like "mamama" or "bababa." The babies aren't trying to communicate with these sounds. They're just trying out sounds and learning how to use their mouths. In fact, babies often babble when they are alone. These babbling sounds are the same for all babies in the beginning. But soon babies
20 begin to practice mostly the sounds they hear around them.

Children start using words when they are about one year old. At first, they use just one word at a time. They often say the word and do something at the same time to explain their meaning better. For example, a child might say, "Up!" and hold out her hands. The parent understands that she wants to be picked up.

25 When they are about 18 to 24 months old, children begin using two-word sentences, such as "Train coming" or "New shoes." These sentences become longer in the next few years, but they may not be complete. There may also be some grammatical errors.

By the time they are five or six, most children know a lot of words and can
30 speak in complete sentences. They may still make some mistakes, but now they are ready for the next big step in language learning: reading and writing.

B. Write your finishing time.
Then turn the page and answer the questions.

Finishing time: _____

C. Circle the best answers. Don't look back at the passage.

1. This passage is about
   a. how parents speak with children.
   b. how children learn language.
   c. why children learn to speak.
   d. ways to learn language.

2. How do babies begin to learn language?
   a. by listening to their parents
   b. by crying for their parents
   c. by saying lots of words
   d. by listening to other babies

3. Which sentence is NOT true about two-month-old babies?
   a. They know their mother's voice.
   b. They can recognize different languages.
   c. They can recognize a human voice.
   d. They can make happy sounds.

4. Babies babble so they can
   a. learn new words.
   b. talk to their parents.
   c. get more food.
   d. practice sounds.

5. Which sentence is NOT true about one-year-old children?
   a. They use one word at a time.
   b. They often do something as they speak.
   c. They use complete sentences.
   d. They start using words.

6. When children are five or six, they
   a. are ready to learn to read.
   b. never make grammatical mistakes.
   c. often use two-word sentences.
   d. don't know very many words.

D. Check your answers with your teacher. Write your comprehension score (the number of correct answers): _____ . Then read the passage again and look for the answers to the questions.

E. Write your reading time. Finishing time – Starting time = _____

F. Find your reading rate on page 229. Write your reading rate and comprehension score on the progress chart on page 232.

A. ***Write your starting time.***
Then preview and read the passage.

Starting time: _____

Parks for Better Health

How can you improve your health and live longer? Doctors have many different answers to this question. They tell you to eat the right foods, to get exercise, or to reduce stress. Your friends may tell you to do meditation or dance. You may want to try all of these suggestions. But you also might want to move to
5   a greener area.

A new study shows that you are more likely to stay well and live longer in an area with lots of greenery—trees, flowers, and plants. If you live in the country, you're already in a good situation. But if you live in the city, do you live near any parks? The study showed that people who live in areas with parks are much
10   healthier and live longer than people who live in areas without parks. According to the scientists, it doesn't matter if the people are rich or poor. Parks are good for everyone.

There are several reasons for this, according to the scientists. The main reason is that people who live near parks get more exercise. There are many
15   ways that getting exercise is good for your health. It helps you lose weight and build a stronger heart. It even helps your brain stay healthier. All these health improvements also make it possible to live longer.

It's not surprising that people who live near parks get more exercise. They don't have to go to a gym or find a sports center. They can just step outside. When
20   exercising is so easy—and free—people do it more often. The kind of exercise doesn't really matter. Active people might go running or play soccer, but you don't have to run or play sports. You can be healthier just by going for a walk several times a week.

However, a walk under trees is better for you than a walk along city streets.
25   Scientists say this is another reason why parks help people become healthier. It's good for you to be in a place with trees and green plants. The greenery helps reduce stress, it lowers blood pressure, and it helps people get better after illness.

The message of the study is important for governments. Now many countries spend a lot of money advertising and telling people about health. It might be
30   better to spend the money differently: planting trees and making more green spaces in the cities.

B. ***Write your finishing time.***
Then turn the page and answer the questions.

Finishing time: _____

C. Circle the best answers. Don't look back at the passage.

1. This passage is about
   a. what kind of people live near parks.
   b. how people should get lots of exercise.
   c. why people who live near parks are healthier.
   d. what governments should do for our health.

2. What did the new study look at?
   a. people who are rich and people who are poor
   b. people who exercise and people who don't exercise
   c. people who like to walk and people who don't like to walk
   d. people who live near parks and people who don't live near parks

3. People who live near parks
   a. exercise more.
   b. eat more.
   c. are younger.
   d. are richer.

4. Which sentence is NOT true about people who live near parks?
   a. It's easier for them to exercise.
   b. They don't have to pay to exercise.
   c. They are more likely to exercise.
   d. It's easier for them to stay home.

5. Which sentence is NOT true about green places?
   a. The greenery helps people feel better.
   b. The greenery reduces stress.
   c. The greenery lowers blood pressure.
   d. The greenery causes heart problems.

6. What does the study say about governments?
   a. They should make more city parks.
   b. They should move people to the country.
   c. They should tell people to get exercise.
   d. They should study heath problems.

D. Check your answers with your teacher. Write your comprehension score (the number of correct answers): _____. Then read the passage again and look for the answers to the questions.

E. Write your reading time.   Finishing time – Starting time = _____

F. Find your reading rate on page 229. Write your reading rate and comprehension score on the progress chart on page 232.

EXERCISE 10

A. **Write your starting time.**
Then preview and read the passage.

Starting time: _____

The Magic Pill

Sometimes the best medicine is no medicine. It's what doctors call a *placebo*. When the problem isn't serious, they may give it to patients instead of real medicine. A placebo doesn't have any real medical effect. It may be just a sugar pill. But when a doctor gives a patient a placebo, it often helps.

5   How does the placebo work? Scientists say it only works if you believe that it's real medicine. Then, because you expect to feel better, you really do feel better—even if the pill just has sugar in it. However, if you find out that it's only sugar, it won't work for you anymore.

    The effect of a placebo is both psychological and physical. In fact, beliefs
10 and feelings can have physical effects on your body. Scientists saw this in an experiment about pain. The people in the experiment had a painful shot in their face. Then they were given a placebo. But they weren't told it was a placebo; they were told it was a painkiller. Soon the people felt less pain. How was this possible? Their brains began making a natural painkilling chemical.

15   Sometimes it's hard to understand how a placebo works. A lot depends on the doctor and the way he or she talks to you. If the doctor seems very certain and uses a serious voice, the placebo is more likely to help.

    Doctors may give a patient a placebo for many kinds of problems that have no clear cause. For example, they are sometimes given for skin problems, for
20 headaches, or for allergies. Studies have shown that placebos can really help in these cases. Doctors also sometimes give a placebo to people who are anxious or depressed. There may be as much improvement after a placebo as after real medicine. And there are two big advantages to a placebo. It has no side effects, and it is inexpensive.

25   There are many reasons for doctors to use placebos. However, some doctors have doubts about how well a placebo really works. These doctors prefer to give real medicine, just in case. Other doctors have a different reason for not giving placebos. They don't want to tell lies to their patients. In fact, the placebo effect only works if the doctor tells a lie. If the patient finds out the truth, how can he or
30 she trust the doctor in the future?

B. **Write your finishing time.**
Then turn the page and answer the questions.

Finishing time: _____

C. *Circle the best answers. Don't look back at the passage.*

1. This passage is about
   a. how the placebo effect works.
   b. the beliefs about placebos.
   c. experiments with placebos.
   d. when doctors give medicines.

2. A placebo only works if
   a. you know it's a placebo.
   b. your doctor has tried it.
   c. you believe it will work.
   d. you like sugar pills.

3. How can a placebo help treat pain?
   a. It makes you think about something else.
   b. Your doctor also gives you a painkiller.
   c. It causes your brain to make a natural painkiller.
   d. It really has a painkiller in it.

4. Which sentence is NOT true about placebos?
   a. They may work for itchy skin.
   b. They may work for headaches.
   c. They don't work for painful conditions.
   d. They work if the doctor sounds certain.

5. Which is NOT a reason for a doctor to give a placebo?
   a. It has no side effects.
   b. The patient may not believe the doctor.
   c. It is inexpensive.
   d. It may work as well as real medicine.

6. Some doctors don't give placebos because they don't
   a. want to lie to their patients.
   b. want to tell the truth to their patients.
   c. know what to say to their patients.
   d. know what medicine to give to their patients.

D. *Check your answers with your teacher. Write your comprehension score (the number of correct answers): _____. Then read the passage again and look for the answers to the questions.*

E. *Write your reading time.*   Finishing time – Starting time = _____

F. *Find your reading rate on page 229. Write your reading rate and comprehension score on the progress chart on page 232.*

able	arm	box	color	detail	enough
about	army	boy	come	determine	enter
above	around	branch	command	develop	equal
accept	arrive	bread	committee	die	escape
accord	art	break	common	difference	even
account	article	bridge	company	difficult	evening
accountable	as	bright	complete	direct	event
across	ask	bring	concern	discover	ever
act	associate	broad	condition	distance	every
active	at	brother	consider	distinguish	example
actor	attack	build	contain	district	except
actress	attempt	burn	content	divide	exchange
actual	average	business	continue	do	exercise
add	away	but	control	doctor	exist
address	back	buy	corn	dog	expect
admit	bad	by	cost	dollar	expense
adopt	ball	call	cotton	door	experience
advance	bank	can	could	doubt	experiment
advantage	bar	capital	council	down	explain
adventure	base	captain	count	draw	express
affair	battle	car	country	dream	extend
after	be	care	course	dress	eye
again	bear	carry	court	drink	face
against	beauty	case	cover	drive	fact
age	because	castle	cross	drop	factory
agent	become	catch	crowd	dry	fail
ago	bed	cause	crown	due	fair
agree	before	center	cry	duty	faith
air	begin	certain	current	each	fall
all	behind	chance	cut	eat	familiar
allow	believe	change	danger	early	family
almost	belong	character	dark	earth	famous
alone	below	charge	date	east	far
along	beneath	chief	daughter	easy	farm
already	beside	child	day	eat	fast
also	best	choose	dead	effect	father
although	between	church	deal	efficient	favor
always	beyond	circle	dear	effort	fear
among	big	city	decide	egg	feel
amount	bill	claim	declare	eight	fellow
ancient	bird	class	deep	either	few
and	black	clear	defeat	elect	field
animal	blood	close	degree	eleven	fight
another	blow	cloud	demand	else	figure
answer	blue	coal	department	empire	fill
any	board	coast	depend	employ	find
appear	boat	coin	describe	end	fine
apply	body	cold	desert	enemy	finish
appoint	book	college	desire	English	fire
arise	both	colony	destroy	enjoy	first

*Adapted from Michael West. *A General Service List of English Words*. London: Longman. 1936/1953.
Available at http://www.lextutor.ca.

fish	happy	kind	marry	new	past
fit	hard	king	mass	news	pay
five	hardly	know	master	newspaper	peace
fix	have	lack	material	next	people
floor	he	lady	matter	night	per
flow	head	lake	maybe	nine	perhaps
flower	hear	land	mean	no	permit
fly	heart	language	measure	noble	person
follow	heat	large	meet	none	picture
food	heaven	last	member	nor	piece
for	heavy	late	memory	north	place
force	help	latter	mention	not	plain
foreign	here	laugh	mere	note	plan
forest	high	laughter	metal	notice	plant
forget	hill	law	middle	now	play
form	history	lay	might	number	please
former	hold	lead	mile	numerical	point
forth	home	learn	milk	numerous	political
fortune	honor	leave	million	object	poor
four	hope	left	mind	observe	popular
free	horse	length	miner	occasion	population
fresh	hot	less	minister	of	position
Friday	hour	let	minute	off	possess
friend	house	letter	miss	offer	possible
from	how	level	mister	office	post
front	however	library	modern	official	pound
full	human	lie	moment	often	poverty
furnish	hundred	life	Monday	oh	power
future	husband	lift	money	oil	prepare
gain	idea	light	month	old	present
game	if	like	moon	on	president
garden	ill	likely	moral	once	press
gas	important	limit	more	one	pressure
gate	in	line	moreover	only	pretty
gather	inch	lip	morning	open	prevent
general	include	listen	most	operate	price
gentle	increase	literature	mother	opinion	private
get	indeed	little	motor	opportunity	problem
gift	independent	live	mountain	or	produce
girl	industry	local	mouth	order	product
give	influence	long	move	ordinary	profit
glad	instead	look	Mrs.	organize	progress
glass	interest	lord	much	other	promise
go	into	lose	music	otherwise	proof
god	introduce	loss	must	ought	proper
gold	iron	love	name	out	property
good	it	low	nature	over	propose
great	join	machine	native	owe	protect
green	joint	main	nature	own	prove
ground	jointed	make	near	page	provide
group	joy	man	necessary	paint	provision
grow	judge	manner	necessity	paper	public
half	just	manufacture	need	part	pull
hand	justice	many	neighbor	particular	purpose
hang	keep	mark	neither	party	put
happen	kill	market	never	pass	quality

quantity	run	single	strong	today	wave
quarter	safe	sir	struggle	together	way
queen	sail	sister	student	ton	we
question	sale	sit	study	too	wealth
quite	salt	situation	subject	top	wear
race	same	six	substance	total	Wednesday
raise	Saturday	size	succeed	touch	week
rank	save	sky	such	toward	welcome
rate	say	sleep	suffer	town	well
rather	scarce	small	suggest	trade	west
reach	scene	smile	summer	train	western
read	school	snow	sun	travel	what
ready	science	so	Sunday	tree	when
real	sea	social	supply	trouble	where
realize	season	society	support	true	whether
reality	seat	soft	suppose	trust	which
reason	second	soldier	sure	try	while
receipt	secret	some	surface	Tuesday	white
receive	secretary	son	surprise	turn	who
recent	see	soon	surround	twelve	whole
recognize	seem	sort	sweet	twenty	why
record	sell	soul	sword	two	wide
red	send	sound	system	type	wife
reduce	sense	south	table	under	wild
refuse	sensitive	space	take	understand	will
regard	separate	speak	talk	union	win
relation	serious	special	tax	unite	wind
relative	serve	speed	teach	university	window
religion	service	spend	tear	unless	winter
remain	set	spirit	tell	until	wise
remark	settle	spite	temple	up	wish
remember	seven	spot	ten	upon	with
reply	several	spread	term	use	within
report	shadow	spring	test	usual	without
represent	shake	stage	then	valley	woman
republic	shall	stand	the	value	wonder
reserve	shape	standard	then	variety	wood
respect	share	star	there	various	word
rest	she	start	therefore	very	work
result	shine	state	they	vessel	world
return	ship	station	thing	victory	worth
rich	shoot	stay	think	view	would
ride	shore	steel	thirteen	village	wound
right	short	step	thirty	virtue	write
ring	should	still	this	visit	wrong
rise	shoulder	stock	through	voice	year
river	show	stone	thousand	vote	yes
road	side	stop	three	wages	yesterday
rock	sight	store	through	wait	yet
roll	sign	story	throw	walk	yield
room	silence	strange	Thursday	wall	you
rough	silver	stream	thus	want	young
round	simple	street	till	war	youth
royal	since	strength	time	watch	
rule	sing	strike	to	water	

Credits

Text Credits: Page 9 Reprinted with the permission of Scribner, a Division of Simon & Schuster, Inc., from *WINNER TAKE NOTHING* by Ernest Hemingway. Copyright © 1933 by Charles Scribner's Sons. Copyright renewed © 1961 by Mary Hemingway. A Day's Wait from *Winner Take Nothing in the First 49 Stories* by Ernest Hemingway. Published by Jonathan Cape. Reprinted by permission of The Random House Group Ltd. **Page 17** excerpt from *Anne of Green Gables* from Penguin Readers/Active Reading. www.penguinreaders.com. Published by Pearson Longman. Reprinted with permission. **Page 129** Adapted from the *International Herald Tribune*, September 14, 2007. Originally from *The New York Times*, 9/13/2007, © 2007. *The New York Times*. All rights reserved. Used by permission and protected by the Copyright Laws of the United States. The printing, copying, redistribution, or retransmission of the Material without express written permission is prohibited. **Page 130** Reprinted by permission of *The Associated Press*, Sept. 8, 2008. **Page 141** excerpt from *Anne of Green Gables* from Penguin Readers/Active Reading. www.penguinreaders.com. Published by Pearson Longman. Reprinted with permission. **Page 142** *Sarah, Plain and Tall*. Copyright © 1985 by PATRICIA MACLACHLAN. Used by Permission of HarperCollins Publishers. **Pages 143-144** *Gentlehands*. Copyright © 1978 by M.E. KERR. Used by permission of HarperCollins Publishers. **Page 200** from *The New York Times*, 8/6/2006, © 2006. *The New York Times*. All rights reserved. Used by permission and protected by the Copyright Laws of the United States. The printing, copying, redistribution, or retransmission of the Material without express written permission is prohibited.

Photo Credits: Cover (left to right) © iStockphoto.com, © Jeffrey Coolidge/Corbis, © Shutterstock, © Shutterstock; **Part One Opener** © iStockphoto.com; **Page 3** © Jupiter Images; **Part Two Opener** © Jeffrey Coolidge/Corbis; **Page 79** © Shutterstock.com; **Page 83** © Getty Images; **Part Three Opener** © Shutterstock.com; **Page 100** © Corbis Premium RF/Alamy; **Page 123** © V&A Images/Alamy; **Page 125** © Shutterstock.com; **Page 129** © Getty Images; **Page 130** © AFP/Getty Images; **Part Four Opener** © Shutterstock.com; **Page 259** © WireImage; **Page 263** © Pictorial Press Ltd/Alamy